My BRITISH INVASION

My BRITISH INVASION

HAROLD BRONSON

Publisher's Cataloging-in-Publication data
Names: Bronson, Harold, author.
Title: My British invasion / Harold Bronson.
Description: Includes index. | First Trade Paperback Original Edition | A Genuine Vireo Book | New York, NY; Los Angeles, CA: Rare Bird Books, 2017.
Identifiers: ISBN 9781945572098
Subjects: LCSH Bronson, Harold. | Rhino Records—History. | Sound recording executives and producers—United States. | Sound recording industry—United States—History. | Rock music—Great Britain—History and criticism. | Rock music—United States—History and criticism. | BISAC MUSIC / History & Criticism | MUSIC / Genres & Styles / Rock
Classification: LCC ML3792.R55 B76 2017 | DDC 384—dc23

CONTENTS

PREFACE

RIOR TO THE BEATLES, Britain was like a backwater country with little to offer me culturally. There were its authors: H. G. Wells, Sir Arthur Conan Doyle, and George Orwell were my favorites. And its films: James Bond, Alfred Hitchcock, and Peter Sellers. The British song I was most familiar with was the theme from TV's *The Adventures of Robin Hood*, sung by Dick James, later The Beatles' publisher. The Beatles' music was different. It was an immediate tour de force of electricity and harmony that, because of the way it was recorded (especially the dominance of the electric guitar), seemed more powerful and exuberant than anything I had ever heard. Records such as "She Loves You," "I Saw Her Standing There," and "Twist and Shout," were exciting, exuding an abandon not heard since the early days of rock 'n' roll. As a teenager in the 1960s, The Beatles and other artists of the British Invasion sparked my interest in rock music. (Although most pop music fans associate *the British Invasion* with the large number of British artists who broke through in America during the mid-sixties, the term surfaced in the media five months before The Beatles set foot in America, referring to the numerous Broadway plays that originated in London's West End.)

It's acknowledged by those in the know that this mid-sixties period, among both Brits and Americans, produced the best music in the history of the rock era. In a 2003 poll of 271 music industry insiders, myself included, published as "*Rolling Stone*'s 500 Greatest Albums of All Time," seven of the Top 10 albums were from the sixties.

What do you do when you're too young to hang out in clubs and you aren't living in London? You play records. In the early 1970s, as a UCLA student, I wrote about popular music for the campus newspaper, the *Daily Bruin,* and then for *Rolling Stone* and other rock magazines. Prior to *Rolling Stone* and a few other magazines that formed in the late-sixties, pop music writers rarely plumbed for depth. The teen magazines, which appealed primarily to girls, were concerned with finding out a musician's likes and dislikes, what kind of girls he favored, and asked questions along the lines of "do you wish you were more screamed at?" (An actual question.) At the expense of my wallet, my preference was to interview members of bands I liked from the sixties over popular, contemporary acts. I wasn't interested in talking to members of Santana, Yes, The Allman Brothers, Lynyrd Skynyrd, or Chicago, even though their stories would have been more saleable. I preferred Herman's Hermits, The Hollies, The Bee Gees, The Yardbirds, Procol Harum, and others. When I visited London, I tracked down performers who rarely came to Los Angeles.

Producer and Beatles expert Martin Lewis opened my eyes to the concept that oral histories have to be questioned. We were discussing the ten-hour *Beatles Anthology* TV documentary that aired on ABC (in the US) and ITV (in the UK) in November 1995. Martin pointed out that many of The Beatles' recollections weren't accurate accounts of what occurred, but merely retellings of how they had related the stories through the decades.

The interviews I conducted were closer to the events that transpired than ones done by others decades later, and are probably more accurate given the natural decline in memory with age. I feel I've told my subjects' stories with more veracity, insight, and context than others have.

In film classes at UCLA, I learned that many of the recommended books on the history and criticism of American film came from British and French authors. Similarly, as an American fan, I feel I have a perspective different from those who were participants in an ongoing and vibrant scene. I've taken an American viewpoint. The whole British pop scene was thrust on America in a manner that was totally counter to the more leisurely absorption available to the British. This resulted initially in a more intense experience.

The sixties even influenced me in business. The Beatles' Apple Records inspired the formation of Rhino Records, the label I cofounded with Richard Foos. Launched in August 1968 with high ideals, Apple reflected the quality that fans had come to expect from Beatles' records: from the graphics and press materials to the initial slate of artists signed—Mary Hopkin, Badfinger, and James Taylor among them. The Beatles press officer Derek Taylor established a distinct writing style in the artist bios and advertising. Unfortunately, the essence of Apple was short lived. Because of the times, the drugs, and their insular environment, The Beatles initiated the large number of naïve, absurd, hubristic, and delusional projects recounted in Richard DiLello's outstanding book *The Longest Cocktail Party*. Richard Foos and I did a lot of crazy things at our label, but we always tried to keep our heads on straight.

We couldn't hope to measure up to Apple: we didn't have The Beatles' money, taste, or charisma. Still, there were things we could learn. That Apple wasn't limited to being a record company, but included films, electronics, and a clothes boutique encouraged us to expand into other areas. In growing our company, we embraced the sixties ethos that anything was possible, but we were also realistic. Although we would have loved to have produced hit records, we discerned early on that it was beyond our expertise. Atypical of record companies, we produced films and published books. We had a few meetings in Las Vegas about a Rhino-themed restaurant, but the project was unrealized. Interestingly enough, ten years after I had interviewed The Monkees, The Turtles, The Zombies, The Spencer Davis Group, and other artists of the sixties as a student, I was reissuing their records at Rhino. Major labels allocated the least amount of money possible to maximize profits from these old masters. We approached reissuing the great music of the past as a reflection of how important the music was to us growing up. Our goal was to provide an excellent package—well-written liner notes and rare photos—and a superior-sounding album, even if it may have cost us more money.

This is my story: the story of a passionate music fan who explored the British music scene and met many of the performers whose music he loved, and in some cases got to know as a journalist, music executive, or even friend. I've always been interested in history, and that fueled my desire to learn more about the history of the artists and the music they created. There are chapters on my immersion in London's rock scene in the early seventies and chapters on significant music-makers from the sixties and seventies, structured somewhat lineally. Although the reader would benefit from reading them in order, as information is introduced, one can also skip around, as each chapter holds up on its own. Rock on!

INTRODUCTION

AGE IS AN IMPORTANT factor in providing any cultural movement with added personal significance. Whether it's a teenage girl cooing over Frank Sinatra in the 1940s or a haggard hippie immersing himself in the political philosophy of Phil Ochs before joining a protest march in the 1960s, one is most impressionable in their teenage years. Or maybe not. One is impressionable as a preteen, too, but soon thereafter one recognizes that many prepubescent fascinations lack the proper intellectual reasoning for a significant, personal choice. Imagine: "Those were the days… *The Partridge Family* were the best, it was all downhill from there."

For Americans, life in the Eisenhower years was very safe, which perhaps made it possible for American teenage culture to become more aware of itself and its needs, and of its moral and political feelings. In previous eras, it was broken down to adults and children—there was no separate teenage culture. But World War II brought America out of the Great Depression, and these newly emerged teenagers had money to burn, money to support a commercial market that was aimed directly at them. It was still a conservative, insular world, with domestic life coping with the flux of the family, rock 'n' roll, and the newfound influence of television.

Everyone knows the story of how, as the 1950s became the 1960s, most of America's potent rockers had disappeared, whether through plane or car crashes, social ostracism, or lifestyle transitions like Elvis going into the Army. By 1963, Little Richard, Jerry Lee Lewis, Gene

Vincent, and Fats Domino had disappeared from the Top 30, but that didn't mean that there wasn't good music. It was just *different* music. Male and female vocal groups, folk groups, and the rise of the female singer defined the pre-Beatles years.

Over in Britain, there was a flux of another kind. Britain's bundle of wartime babies was the first generation to be interested in what was going on in America. World War II had a lot to do with that. In Britain there were bombed-out buildings and rubble, but America was untarnished. The visiting, affable GIs planted the seeds of interest, and soon American culture was fervently embraced. The English marveled at the flashy cars, the Western and gangster films, modern appliances, Coca-Cola, and Marilyn Monroe. The mystique was irresistible.

There were reports that when Bill Haley belted "Rock Around the Clock" over the opening credits of the *Blackboard Jungle* movie, the normal, sedate British kids tore up the theater seats. For the first time they were able to betray their rigid schoolkid uniforms and feel outright liberation! This is what rock 'n' roll triggered. With young America manipulated to favor the pop singers who appeared on *American Bandstand*, many of whom lived in Philadelphia where the show was produced, America's eminent rockers, now considered passé, set their sights on more receptive audiences in Europe, England particularly.

Finally, with an opportunity to see the real thing compared to the pretenders who populated their turf, the English responded enthusiastically, both as fans and as imitators. What an odd phenomenon—scrawny English schoolboys casting themselves as second-generation bearers of rock 'n' roll and the blues. What could possibly have moved so many timid, pale classroom nebbishes to cast themselves as anguished blues belters in the manner of Ray Charles, or drugged-out cool jazz musicians? Perhaps it was a search to develop a new identity and get as far away as possible from class consciousness, English manners, or just tea and crumpets.

Many, like The Beatles, were inspired by Elvis Presley, Eddie Cochran, Gene Vincent, and The Everly Brothers to form rock 'n' roll combos to further experience the exhilaration. The hippest English music fans responded to genuine rock 'n' roll figures, like Little Richard, Jerry Lee Lewis, Fats Domino, Chuck Berry, and Buddy Holly, over the less substantial Fabian, Freddy Cannon, and Frankie Avalon. We might note that England's equivalents—Lonnie Donegan (King of Skiffle), Marty Wilde, Billy Fury, Vince Eager, Duffy Power— were "safe" enough to offer a homebred rock 'n' roll that was at least acceptable to BBC's conservative radio.

All the same, Americans couldn't have cared less about England's pop stars. Among the handful of Brits who had American hits, there were pop singers Anthony Newley and Frank Ifield; folk singer Lonnie Donegan; folk-pop trio The Springfields; and one instrumental band, The Tornados. Their token chart appearances reflected a lack of interest in sounds from the UK. Even Cliff Richard, the British equivalent of Elvis Presley, at that time invincible in his own land, failed to dent America's Top 20 until 1976. One thing was evident: as the 1950s spilled into the 1960s, rock 'n' roll was in desperate need of a shot in the arm.

Prior to the British Invasion, American teenage culture was conventional. Our role models were sports stars, baseball players like Mickey Mantle and Willie Mays. Closer to home, it was he-man, physical stuff embodied by the high school football hero whose girlfriend was invariably a cheerleader. Even Jan and Dean and Brian Wilson, leaders of California's pre-Beatles surf music craze, had played for their high school teams.

Similarly, regular ads in comic books for Charles Atlas pitched an exercise program with illustrations of a muscular bully kicking sand in the face of an undernourished kid. The program promised "the 'Greek god' type of physique that women rave about at the beach." Cars also fascinated teenagers, especially hot rods, dragsters, and so-called muscle cars. In contrast, I found the cultural stimulation and intelligence offered by The Beatles and their ilk much more appealing than what had passed for American teenage culture. And it didn't matter that they were skinny, like the kid bullied in the Charles Atlas ad, girls went crazy for them. It also planted the seed that less-than-burly American teenagers could form Beatle-like combos and arouse a similar appeal.

When The Beatles stormed the American shores in February 1964, they opened the doors for an onslaught of similarly attired Englishmen who sang and played guitars and drums and who came to dominate the American pop music scene. But The Beatles and the other groups might not have happened if it hadn't been for the revision of the National Service Act, similar to the US draft that required young adults to serve in the armed forces. Brits born after September 1939 were no longer called for service, freeing them to follow their rock 'n' roll passions.

Although the sound of the bands that made up the British Invasion was different, the influences were invariably American. The more discerning English fans embraced American blues and rhythm and blues artists whose honest and emotive approach many found more appealing.

Imagine these Englishmen able to see past America's early-sixties stars to get to the real thing: bloodshot, bourbon-drinking, sinister-looking Negroes who played a simple, sexual rock 'n' roll—a music too threatening for the mass American audience. Young British musicians were attracted to their authenticity and poetic imagery. They made efforts to find records by bluesmen such as John Lee Hooker, Slim Harpo, Bo Diddley, Muddy Waters, and Jimmy Reed. When The Rolling Stones and The Animals toured America, teenagers received their first dose of American blues in this second-hand manner.

One can use Slim Harpo as an example. The sleepy-eyed Louisianan was almost unknown among white Americans. But this didn't stop the English from embracing him, with the result that most of the songs on his first album were covered by top English groups: The Rolling Stones, The Kinks, The Who, Them, The Pretty Things, and The Moody Blues, who even took their name from one of his songs. The lyrics were often deeper than cutesy boy-girl relationships. Sexual innuendo and references to voodoo were commonplace. Many times it was life and death on the line; Slim Harpo sang of having one foot in the grave in "This Music's Hot." The musicianship, especially the blues guitar, was adventurous by pop music standards, and, again, proved an instrumental inspiration.

These smitten English rockers were on a mission. They played the music because they were enamored of it, and wanted to spread "the gospel," as it were, not because they ever thought they could be successful. No one performing this music had ever broken through before. If one wanted to be successful, he had to mold himself into a Cliff Richard or Tommy Steele and be a solo singer.

When the music of sinister-looking American Negroes proved saleable, it gave rise to the concept of the anti-star, the ones who broke all the rules and didn't look like well-groomed pop stars with slicked back hair, shiny smiles, and polished shoes. The Rolling Stones were the trend's poster boys. Here's a particularly unkind assessment by Bill Whitworth in the *New York Herald Tribune*: "One of them looks like a chimpanzee. Two look like very ugly Radcliffe girls. One resembles the encyclopedia drawings of pithecanthropus erectus. The fifth is a double for Ray Bolger in the role of *Charley's Aunt.*"

While American kids were reeling under the metal weight of orthodontic braces, along came the British, who not only made it acceptable to sport less-than-perfect movie star smiles, but whose crooked teeth lent an aura of distinctive character to their faces. George Harrison's timid personality was enhanced when his smile revealed vampire-sized canines. Peter Asher's cute overlapping incisors and unhip, black plastic-framed glasses inspired Austin

Powers' look decades later. A Rolling Stones' fan could keep score as Keith Richards kept losing teeth. (Do you think I'm kidding? Bob Kirsch was interviewing Keith for *Billboard* when one of his teeth came out. Keith unceremoniously dropped it in an ashtray, not breaking stride with the interview.) New standards were set. No longer did one have to look like Troy Donohue to be a star. (Donohue, an uncommonly handsome film and TV star of the fifties and sixties, provided the inspiration for *The Simpsons* character Troy McClure, and is mentioned in a song from *Grease*.) It didn't matter if one wore glasses, had a misshapen face, or sticks for legs.

There were a number of factors that shaped the unique sounds of the British Invasion. The British bands records weren't as intense as those of the American masters, but they were more spirited than what was passing for American rock 'n' roll at the time. Many of the American rock acts were trios of singers who worked with impermanent backing bands, whereas the English were mostly self-contained units, four or five musicians who also sang. As part of paying their dues, many of the bands were required to play uncommonly long sets (as had The Beatles, who endured eight-hour work days in Hamburg), resulting in a vibrant sound characterized by a certain amount of sloppiness and bashing.

Bev Bevan, best known as the drummer in the Electric Light Orchestra and The Move, performed in Germany in 1965 with Carl Wayne & The Vikings: "When we arrived, the accommodation was ankle-deep in rubbish, and infested with rats. There were blood and semen stains on the bed. We spent what little spare time we had cleaning it all up. We started playing each night at 7:00 p.m. and did seven forty-five-minute spots, with fifteen-minute breaks, until two o'clock in the morning. Each weekend there were three-hour matinees, too. Any last hopeful beliefs I might have had that pop could earn me easy money were swept away in those weeks in Germany."

Members of almost every English rock band of that time—The Beatles, The Rolling Stones, The Who, The Kinks, The Zombies, The Animals, The Yardbirds—had gone to art school. The Yardbirds and The Who even described their music as "pop art." This exposure inspired progressive and creative concepts and helped to magnify and color the resulting sound. For instance, when The Who debuted their second single, "Anyway Anyhow Anywhere," many were confused by the purposeful inclusion of feedback. Pete Townshend had attended Ealing Art College, as had Freddie Mercury, Ronnie Wood, and Thunderclap Newman's John Keene. In interviews Pete kept referring to Gustav Metzger and his auto-destructive art as an influence. Other effects were more nuanced. At Hornsey College of Art and Crafts, Ray Davies watched people in train stations and sketched them. This helped shape his writing, where many of his songs, like "Waterloo Sunset," placed him in the role of the detached observer.

As unlikely a form as music hall found its way into the charts. A vaudeville equivalent that flourished earlier in the century, music hall was rich in melody and humor. Herman's Hermits scored big with three music hall-styled songs: "Mrs. Brown, You've Got a Lovely Daughter" and "I'm Henry VIII, I Am" in 1965, and then a year later with George Formby's "Leaning on the Lamp Post." Ian Whitcomb classified The Kinks' "Sunny Afternoon"—newly composed by Ray Davies—as a music hall-styled song: "a chug-a-long satire in the style of Formby's great 'Fanlight Fanny, the Frousy Night Club Queen.'" Peter Asher identified his (Peter and Gordon's) hit "Knight In Rusty Armour" as part of the genre. Small Faces had their second biggest UK hit—at number two—with "Lazy Sunday," which they considered part of the music hall tradition.

With The Beatles opening the door, record moguls realized that America offered a much larger and more profitable market, and encouraged displaying British characteristics: The early Kinks sported frilly shirts and red hunting jackets; Ian Whitcomb, on the back cover of his debut album, was decked out like Sherlock Holmes in a deerstalker hat and herringbone suit; The Beatles and Herman's Hermits were dressed for photo sessions as English businessmen in suits, bowler hats and umbrellas. American kids were so mad for anything British that a few artists coming over, like Chad & Jeremy and Ian Whitcomb, had Top 10 hits without ever making the chart in their homeland. While on tour in the US, Herman's Hermits' Peter Noone ran into an unfamiliar group whose gimmick was their bleached blond hair. "We're The Hullaballoos," they said. "We're from Hull." It was new, it was exciting, and America lapped it up.

The Beatles' sense of humor added to their appeal. Inspired by *The Goon Show*, they came across as hip: from their quips during the press conference when they landed in America, to their films, to their songs. When Brits were interviewed on radio and TV, in many cases their accents promised sophistication. They came across as polite, cultural, and intelligent. John Lennon assumed the status of an intellectual by cranking out two imaginative books characterized by wordplay and humorous illustrations. America's stars seemed dull by comparison.

In any event, it all meshed into a gigantic wallop that left America with its trousers around its ankles. It mattered little that America's teen idols were invariably handsome, suave, and of Italian lineage: Bobby Darin, Bobby Rydell, Joey Dee, James Darren, Lou Christie, Fabian, and Dion, among others. Britain's milky-white, pencil-neck geeks created their own appeal with an affable, quirky, fun image.

The look was different, too. Most apparent was the hairstyle. To me The Beatles' long hair was more comedic (recalling Moe of The Three Stooges) than threatening. All of the other bands that followed had to have long hair like The Beatles. If not, it was as if they aligned themselves to a previous era, or were simply too insecure to take the step into the post-1963 world. When one later saw photos of the early Beatles with drummer Pete Best, you just knew he was doomed to be axed from the group. His hair was slicked-back 1950s style—theirs was combed forward. Consequently, groups with more conservative hairstyles, like Billy J. Kramer with the Dakotas, The Searchers, and Freddie and The Dreamers, were only as good as their last hit record (as compared to, say, a serious long-hair group like The Pretty Things, who had no hits in America, but prolonged a critically acclaimed career well into the 1970s).

As innocuous as it all was, it was so threatening to America's post-teen population that vast amounts of offense and anger were generated by a mere few inches of hair. The Yardbirds' Chris Dreja told me that, on tour in America, not only did they get dirty looks, but at times they were spat upon.

The Beatles' manager Brian Epstein understood this, and that the group had to be made "more acceptable" in order to make it big. He kicked away the group's earlier leathers, jeans, and T-shirts in favor of custom-made suits. Most of the British rockers who followed adopted suits and ties, although with less stylishness than The Beatles. Somehow these strange invaders neutralized the threat of their long hair by compromising their dress and by smiling a lot.

Obviously there had to be an antithesis. The Rolling Stones had a sullen, sleepless appearance. It looked like their wardrobe came from a thrift-store, and their longer, unkempt hair seemed consistent with a reputation for boorish behavior. Even when liberal American parents consented to let their sons grow their hair long, it was usually, "Okay, you can wear it like The Beatles, but if I ever see you looking like The Rolling Stones, I'll throw you out of the house!" Author Tom Wolfe put it this way: "The Beatles want to hold your hand, but The Stones want to burn your town."

The Stone's casualness mirrored their raw, chaotic, not-quite musical records, ones like "It's All Over Now," "I Wanna Be Your Man," and "Not Fade Away." Americans were slow to respond to this more serious approach, but it's one that's sustained a career that's lasted over fifty years. The irony here is that the Stones persona was similar to that of The Beatles before they were smartened up. Cavern-going audiences, unlike those years-later US fans, knew that the early Beatles were a motley, sloppy bunch who sprinkled their song intros with lascivious and bawdy barbs. In Hamburg, John Lennon appeared on stage with a toilet seat around his neck. Imagine how far they would've gotten on America's squeaky-clean *Ed Sullivan Show* with that!

Those musicians who had attended art school embraced fashion as it became outrageous. The Beatles' collarless jackets and Cuban-heeled boots were just the start. New fashions were sold by a handful of boutiques that sprang up on Carnaby Street, located in a backstreet of London's more formal Oxford Street shopping district. The tailors and designers catered to the more flamboyant tastes of homosexuals and thespians. When mods stumbled upon the area and noticed that there were more than various shades of black and grey in which to be suited, the area exploded.

Clothes consciousness extended past the mod period. The Troggs wore loud, candy-striped suits. The Who were splendidly shocking in their colorful jackets—one fashioned from a Union Jack flag and another covered in sequins. Stripped down, singer Roger Daltrey was the image of masculinity. That didn't stop him from teasing his hair into a bouffant and dying it bright orange, and wearing a shawl, lace, and ladies' slingback shoes. Others *en masse* adopted frilly shirts, Indian Nehru jackets, kaftans, and madras shirts, and military-inspired dress. Jimi Hendrix's antique, military breast-plated jacket was purchased at I Was Lord Kitchener's Valet (actually the name of the boutique). It was all new, colorful, and exciting, and there was too much to grasp.

After the initial hits had been registered, all manner of new television shows sprang up to showcase this talent, and it was from these that American baby boomers derived their most indelible images of the period. ABC's *Shindig!* was filmed in Hollywood in black and white. Some segments were produced in England. It was a fine showcase indeed, if a little too weighted by the (old wave) cast of regulars: The Blossoms, The Shindogs, The Wellingtons, Bobby Sherman, and Billy Preston. There rarely seemed to be enough of the people we wanted to see, but it was here, primarily, that the various personalities (if any) behind the hits were on display. And the audience was as enthusiastic at a TV taping as in a concert hall. As Ian Whitcomb recollected, "The kid audience screamed at every shake of my long hair. Beatles stardust had fallen like dandruff onto my shoulders."

NBC's *Hullabaloo* had a more mainstream appeal, and was in color! It mattered little that the newer rock stars shared the stage with those more trusted by the establishment—Peter Noone and Vikki Carr were paired for a vocal duet—there was more than enough meat. Unfortunately, neither show lasted long. Mostly, Americans had no other choice but to wade through little Italian puppets, dancing Hungarian folk companies, trapeze artists, and rotating Jewish comedians in order to see the week's rock artist—only one per week—on *The Ed Sullivan Show*. It was always professionally done, but never quite enough. Other shows, those hosted by Red Skelton, Dean Martin, and later The Smothers Brothers (who offered the most sensitive and best framework for these artists), and even Mike Douglas, whose afternoon show appealed mostly to housewives, had their weekly token rock group.

When The Beatles and others made it, it was with their own sound, not an already accepted one that fit into preexisting formats. Their adventurousness led them to altering these proven formulas to create newer and more far-out approaches. This may not have appeared to be good business, but it sustained a long career. Every time one turned around, the recordings had progressed, the clothes and hair had changed, and so had one's perspective on the world. The "hippie" subculture evolved, and with it new political, social, and cultural stances. Imagine a hundred years of contemporary history crammed into five. That's how it felt.

Peter Noone's perspective is that the British Invasion was even bigger than most people realized: "Before the British Invasion, England was this quaint little country. It wasn't considered a haven of brilliant musicians and songwriters. Can you imagine what it's done for the British economy? Britain became a new place."

What's astonishing is how much the sixties live on in our culture, and I'm not talking about *Mad Men*. As my tastes developed, I came to appreciate nonmusical aspects: pop art, modern furniture, photography, fashion. The last few years have seen an uptick in sixties-inspired designs from Paul Smith, Ted Baker, Robert Graham, Valentino, Liberty of London, and Moods of Norway. There is also a wellspring of boutique designers, such as Madcap England, Pretty Green, Friday On My Mind, and David Watts. In 2014, John Varvatos refashioned Hendrix's military jacket into a linen blazer that sold in clothing stores for $2,000. In the September 2015 issue of *C Magazine*, a fashion spread showcasing numerous designers proclaimed, "This fall, sixties Mod—replete with shortened hemlines, bold colors and statement coats—makes a welcome return." In a retrospective on sixties designer Mr. Fish in the March 2016 *New York Times Style Magazine*, a photo caption reads: "Fish's influence on the spring runways, at, from left, Gucci, J. W. Anderson, Dolce & Gabbana, Dunhill, and Ann Demeulemeester." *GQ*'s spring 2016 style issue included an eight-page feature on Jimi Hendrix subtitled "The Man Who Inspired This Season's Look," as well as sixties photos of Mick Jagger and Keith Richards illustrating contemporary fashion trends.

Sixties hits used in commercials are nothing new. The Kinks' "All Day and All of the Night" provided the soundtrack for a recent Yoplait commercial, as did The Spencer Davis Group's "Gimme Some Lovin'" for Activia, and The Zombies' "She's Not There" for Coco Chanel. But obscure songs have been cropping up with more frequency throughout the media: The Kinks' "I'm Not Like Everybody Else" in an Acura commercial; The Yardbirds' "Glimpses" in Amazon's *Transparent*, The Zombies' "Can't Nobody Love You" in HBO's *Girls* and "This Will Be Our Year" in *Mad Men*; and The Creation's "Making Time" (revived in Wes Anderson's *Rushmore*) in commercials for Depends and Best Buy. The less obscure Cream's "I Feel Free" was featured over the opening scenes of *Joy* and The Animals' "Boom Boom" over the closing credits of HBO's *The Brink*. It's all fine by me.

MY SENIOR YEAR

1971–1972 TIME CAPSULE

SEPTEMBER

I'VE GOT A FEELING *twenty-one is going to be a good year,* The Who sang on *Tommy.* In the rock opera they referred to the year 1921, but I took it as a theme for my twenty-first year. It wasn't just that I could now vote or drink legally. I was transitioning into adulthood. Although I had a year left before graduating from UCLA, I was champing at the bit to make my way in the world.

On September 10 with the new school year weeks away, I was, unexpectedly, seated in a fourth-row box at the Hollywood Bowl on a beautiful summer's evening eating a fried chicken dinner. I couldn't believe how good I felt. Paul Rappaport had invited me to join him and his boss, Bill Shaler, for the evening's concert by jazz-rock band Chicago. I didn't own any of their three albums, but close up, Chicago's musicianship and repertoire won me over.

I had met Paul at the *Daily Bruin* office the previous year when he stopped by to introduce himself as the college rep promoting Columbia Records product. Sporting an Afro hairstyle, Paul could have passed for the fourth member of The Jimi Hendrix Experience. He thought of himself as a blues guitarist, but he wised up in time to realize that a full-time gig working for Columbia wouldn't be such a bad thing.

We became friendly, and toward the end of the spring quarter I asked Paul if I could succeed him. As he was graduating, he had already promised the job to someone else. I should have asked him earlier. When his friend changed his mind, though, Paul called and I accepted.

Writing about rock music, I got a glimpse of the people who worked at record companies and came to realize that I wanted to work at a record company after I graduated. Being a college rep was a good stepping-stone, and I looked forward to the year.

September was a big month for me as a writer. In addition to a handful of record reviews, I had two major magazine pieces. My second article published in *Rolling Stone* was a feature on singer Howard Kaylan, who transitioned from The Turtles to The Mothers of Invention. Howard was funny, opinionated, and scintillating. I even received a congratulatory comment from *Rolling Stone* publisher Jann Wenner on my pay stub. *Coast Magazine* ran my comprehensive feature on The Monkees.

The Conception Corporation was a four-man comedy group. Two were alumni of Second City in Chicago. I interviewed them for a feature I wrote titled "The New Comedy" for *Rock Magazine*. (I had also interviewed George Carlin and Cheech and Chong for the article.) The Conception Corporation's first album, *A Pause in the Disaster*, had been released on Atlantic Records' subsidiary Cotillion, but hadn't sold much. I loved it, especially the tracks "Black for a Day" (a take off on the radio/TV show *Queen for a Day*) and the soap opera spoof "The Love of Grass," which concluded with a drug bust in a leather shop. The album was funny, imaginative, and well produced. I visited them at Wally Heider Recording in Hollywood as they worked on their second album.

Fellow *Bruin* writer Heather Harris and I went to a screening in Beverly Hills of the new Frank Zappa movie *200 Motels*. As a fan of Zappa's, I was looking forward to it, and to seeing the current Mothers of Invention/ex-Turtles Howard Kaylan and Mark Volman in their acting debuts. There was a clear theme that "touring can make you crazy," but little that held it together: it lacked dramatic structure, an ending, and had too many self-indulgent scenes. Ringo Starr, as Larry the Dwarf, portrayed Zappa; Keith Moon, in drag, played a nun; and original Mothers drummer Jimmy Carl Black sang a song that provided one of the few high points.

On the fourteenth, I saw Bill Withers on a bill with Cheech and Chong at the Troubadour. Withers' current single, "Ain't No Sunshine," was a big hit. At thirty-three he was older than most up-and-coming performers, and had recently quit his job installing seats in airplanes. He assumed the role of a guitar-strumming, urban folk singer. He was a confident, engaging storyteller, and his voice had a rich tone. Cheech and Chong, whose debut album had just been released, billed themselves as countercultural comedians. Their act was far from polished, but funny. Among the few comedians who embraced the new drug culture, their Latino and musical references added to their uniqueness. When I interviewed them they gave me ceramic roach clips with their images on the handles. Given their flaunting of the drug culture, I was amused to learn that Cheech's (Richard Marin) father was a policeman for the LAPD.

The following week at the Troubadour I saw Fairport Convention, the best of the rock bands that forged their sounds on traditional English folk songs. Others in the genre included Steeleye Span, Lindisfarne and Pentangle. The music wasn't totally unfamiliar to American fans of folk music. Jerry Garcia used to play "Matty Groves," a staple of Fairport's, in his pre-Dead days. Four of Fairport's albums had made the Top 20 in the UK, with the most recent, *Angel Delight*, in the Top 10, but they were largely unknown in America. I liked the group but they lacked a strong singer. At the Troubadour, new member Dave Swarbrick excelled on the fiddle.

Peter and Gordon, a guitar-playing duo who fashioned themselves after The Everly Brothers, were an important part of the 1960s British Invasion. Buddy Holly was also a big influence. The duo had a hit with Holly's "True Love Ways," and Peter Asher even wore glasses like Buddy's. After the hits dried up, from which Peter revealed he received little money, he transitioned into a record producer, and then head of A&R (artists and repertoire) for The Beatles' new Apple Records. His stay was short, as he soon departed to manage and produce James Taylor, whom he had signed to Apple. As I realized the limitations of my vocals in fronting a rock group, I wanted to learn more about the production side. By interviewing Peter, not only could I bone up on my history of Peter and Gordon, but also get insight into the tasks of a producer.

I met Peter at the offices of Gibson and Stromberg, the premier rock public relations firm. Bob Gibson had a beard and gut, was a sloppy dresser, and didn't seem to care about his appearance. He looked more like an aging Greenwich Village folkie than a hotshot Hollywood press agent. Despite his unattractive presence, he projected confidence and intelligence. His partner, Gary Stromberg, also came across as smart, but hipper, with straight, long hair and a beard. Their offices were on the second floor of a building catty-corner from Tower Records on the Sunset Strip. Rather than conducting business from individual offices with desks, they shared a large living room area with a comfortable black leather sectional sofa. The phones were on the large coffee table. It was relaxing, and it seemed like a natural way to conduct business. I always felt welcome. I liked their clients, and covered more of their acts than anybody else's.

Peter was shy, but congenial and forthcoming. He became friends with Paul McCartney when Paul began dating his sister, Jane. When Paul was in London, the Ashers invited him to stay in the garret of their eighteenth-century, five-story townhouse, in a small servant's room next to Peter's larger one. Through the wall, Peter heard Paul working on a song that he liked. Paul didn't know what to do with it. Billy J. Kramer, whose first three hits were composed by Lennon and McCartney, had rejected it. The Beatles were never going to record it; John Lennon made fun of the opening line, *Please lock me away*. Peter had Paul write a bridge and "A World Without Love" became Peter and Gordon's first, and biggest hit—number one on both sides of the Atlantic. McCartney wrote the duo's next two hits, as well as 1966's "Woman" under a pseudonym. Peter and Gordon hit the Top 10 with another reject, Del Shannon's "I Go to Pieces," after The Searchers turned it down.

I naively asked Peter if orchestra sessions were ever prerecorded. What I meant was that for rock sessions, which were usually low budget, or for times when an orchestra was heard for a short duration on the record, whether it was sourced from a stock or library tape. I was thinking of the vast expense of hiring twenty-plus musicians. He chuckled and clarified that orchestral accompaniment was always newly recorded.

On Saturday, September 25, a group of *Bruin* writers trekked thirty-two miles to the Long Beach Arena to see Black Sabbath in concert. Seeing the young teen crowd I felt old, even though I was only twenty-one. Black Sabbath's music was simple but solid. What struck me most was how singer Ozzy Osbourne's good-natured demeanor seemed at odds with the seriousness of the group's music. They performed songs titled "Wicked World," "Children of the Grave," "War Pigs," and "Paranoid," and here's Ozzy, his shirt off, grinning and waving his arms. His hands were configured into V-sign peace symbols, just like President Nixon. They closed their set with "Fairies Wear Boots."

A couple of nights later, Sherman Cohen got tickets from the radio station where he worked to see Ike & Tina Turner at the Greek

Theater. I had been a friend of Sherman's since Cub Scouts. We'd reconnected in our senior year in high school. Sherman was into girls, dancing, the Top 40, and, atypically, bodybuilding. Although we shared a love of music, we disagreed on the criteria of quality. Sherman felt that if a record wasn't a hit, it wasn't any good, failing to consider that many mediocre records became hits because radio DJs and programmers were (illegally) paid to play them. The Turners' set was almost identical to the one I saw when they opened for The Rolling Stones two years previously. Seeing them again reminded me of how much Mick Jagger had copied Tina's moves.

A full-page in *Rolling Stone* advertised the new Beach Boys' album in the creative manner that readers had come to expect from Warner Brothers: "For a Dollar and an Old Surfin' Safari LP, We'll Send You a Dry New Reprise LP by (Believe It) 1971's Beach Boys— Surf's Up." By the mid-sixties, Warner Brothers—and its sister label Reprise—was largely a MOR company. The inner sleeve of its first significant rock signing, The Kinks, featured photos of Bing Crosby, Frank Sinatra, Sammy Davis Jr., Duke Ellington, Rosemary Clooney, and Lou Monte. Creative services head Stan Cornyn responded to the company's A&R overhaul later in the decade by concocting imaginative ads such as: "How we lost $35,509.50 on 'The Album of the Year'" (Van Dyke Parks' *Song Cycle*); "Pigpen look-alike contest" (promoting the first two Grateful Dead LPs); "Win a Fug Dream Date Competition" (The Fugs' *It Crawled Into My Hand, Honest*). They ran mostly in *Rolling Stone* and contributed to elevating the label's status to the hippest of the seventies.

I spent part of Tuesday afternoon, September 28—the day after the fall quarter started—with The Moody Blues, as I had been assigned to write a feature article on them for *Rock Magazine*. I was a fan of the group's music, and had all of their albums. Along with Bob Dylan, the lyrics of The Moody Blues and Procol Harum sparked my interest in poetry. I wrote poetry, incorporated elements into my song lyrics, and even took an introductory class at UCLA. The Moody Blues staged a press conference at the Bel-Air Hotel during which they were presented with a gold album for sales of five hundred thousand for *Every Good Boy Deserves Favour*. These natives of Birmingham, England, chose American Indian actor Jay Silverheels—best known for portraying Tonto in the 1950s TV series *The Lone Ranger*—to make the presentation because they saw him as an early representation of American culture. Typically, Jay wore a fringed buckskin jacket. Atypically, he wore hip striped trousers.

I interviewed them afterward, but it was difficult for them to focus. Mostly they would drift in and out of the seating area to give a few perfunctory answers. Justin Hayward, the exception, sincerely responded to my questions. Talkative, but shy, he was the most accomplished member of the group. He sang most of the lead vocals, played lead guitar, and contributed the best songs: "Nights in White Satin," "Tuesday Afternoon," and "Question," among them. I got what I needed for the article by incorporating quotes from the other members from the press conference.

I found the story of the group's breakthrough album, *Days of Future Passed*, most interesting. Justin Hayward: "Before that LP we weren't selling any records and were seriously considering breaking up when the record company wanted us to record a stereo demonstration record. Their idea was to make something along the lines of Dvorak's *New World Symphony*. I'd written a song called 'Nights in White Satin,' Mike had written 'Dawn Is a Feeling,' and John had written a song called 'Peak Hour.' It occurred to us that they were all three parts of a day. What a great theme of an album to just build it around a day!"

This was not an ambitious, high-minded project. Decca Records wanted a budget-priced album to further interest in the growing stereo format. The Moody Blues agreed, in part, because Decca offered to erase their debt to the company. During the summer of 1967, the group recorded their parts in little more than a week, with the London Festival Orchestra added later. The album—now regularly priced—became a fluke hit. Interest built slowly. It took six months for the album to make the *Billboard* album chart. Eventually it rose to number three and was among the Top 200 selling LPs for over two years.

That night I took Tom Matye, a friend since junior high school and a Moody Blues' fan, to The Forum to see the group in concert. The public relations firm provided a pair of complimentary tickets, as was customary, but they were positioned on the highest row behind the stage. It was hardly the consideration I would have expected for someone writing a cover story on the band.

On the turntable (where I list my favorite albums, not previously mentioned, from the month's new releases): The Beach Boys' *Surf's Up*, The Bee Gees' *Trafalger*, John Lennon's *Imagine*, The Firesign Theatre's *I Think We're All Bozos On This Bus*, Kris Kristofferson's *Me and Bobby McGee, Who's Next, New Riders of the Purple Sage, Judee Sill, Live Yardbirds: featuring Jimmy Page.*

OCTOBER

As a COLLEGE REP for CBS Records, whose main labels were Columbia and Epic, my primary duties were to promote our new releases to the four Westwood Village record stores—Vogue, Discount, and the two Wherehouses—and to get our records added to campus radio station KLA, which was accessible only to students living in the dorms, which meant it had few listeners. Even though I received a paltry salary of $17.50 a week, I looked for ways to expand the job.

On making my rounds of the Westwood record stores, I noticed a stack of albums by String Cheese at the Wherehouse store on Galey Avenue. I had never heard of them, and couldn't understand why a store would stock so many copies of an unknown act. The manager explained that it was a way for a new artist to get noticed, and said that the record company, in this case RCA—the album was on Wooden Nickel, a distributed label—provided extra advertising as an incentive.

On October 6, in the first meeting of my Principles of Cultural Anthropology class, I noticed a young woman who was more attractive than the typical hippie coed. I followed her to a food machine and engaged her in conversation about the class, which she was dropping. Thinking I might not see her again, I boldly invited Terri Roese (pronounced "rose") to go to the Whisky a Go-Go that night.

Edgar Winter and White Trash headlined, and were musically impressive. Edgar's brother, Johnny, had received a lot of attention as a hotshot blues guitarist. I hoped he would sit in, but the slot was filled by Rick Derringer, who had played in Johnny's band, and had been a member of The McCoys—who'd had a hit with "Hang on Sloopy." Edgar was an adept musician who excelled on sax and keyboards. I enjoyed the music, but I was more excited by Terri, who had dressed for the evening in a lavender hot pants jumpsuit.

I liked Terri, and she seemed to like me. She suggested we meet on campus and have lunch together. I chose a bench in the Murphy Sculpture Garden, my favorite place at the university. She packed a lunch for each of us from her dorm cafeteria, a sandwich and an orange. It was the first time I'd seen someone peel an orange using her fingers.

One afternoon I recognized Ed Ames slowly cruising by on his bicycle. He'd had a Top 10 hit with "My Cup Runneth Over" in 1967, but was best known for portraying Mingo on the *Daniel Boone* TV series. As he was in his forties, I wondered what he was doing on campus.

Terri was soft spoken, smart, and easy to talk to. I wish I could have been as open with her. She gave me a small red plastic box that she'd purchased from the campus art store. It wasn't much, but it was the first gift I ever received from a girl.

The Conception Corporation invited me to see their video satire of network TV, *Void Where Prohibited By Law*, so on Thursday night I picked Terri up from her dorm. She was dressed in a suit. She said that she'd had lunch with her mother, a businesswoman, and wanted to dress to her mother's expectation. I got the impression that her mother didn't have a warm personality. Beforehand, we dined at Café Figaro on Melrose Avenue, an upscale hippie restaurant with old newspapers passing for wallpaper and where one could order an organic salad or veggie burger. Terri talked of her artistic aspirations, about wanting to design textiles.

We then drove to a store space on La Brea Avenue, the New Vacuum Theater, which touted The Cushion Room, "the world's largest waterbed." (Waterbed mattresses were water-filled vinyl shells.) Four video monitors provided the screens, pillows and waterbeds the seats. It was cozy for Terri and me, until I took a bathroom break and ended up with soggy socks owing to a massive leak from "the world's largest waterbed."

Friday, October 29, was Terri's twenty-first birthday. I took her out to dinner at an upscale Westwood Village hippie restaurant. Serving omelets for dinner was a new trend, so I thought I'd take a chance and ordered one with spinach, but it came with the unwanted bonus of eggshells. We went to the Long Beach Arena to see the Jeff Beck Group in concert. I loved Beck's guitar playing. He'd been a member of The Yardbirds, and then had led his own Jeff Beck Group, which included Rod Stewart and Ronnie Wood. His latest band was too jazzy for my taste, too colored by pianist Max Middleton's playing. I also found singer Bob Tench's vocals grating. Still, it was the first time I had seen Beck play. His band performed "New Ways/Train Train," the song I liked best on the new *Rough and Ready* album, and a cover of Don Nix's "Goin' Down." He experienced sound problems at the beginning, and his set never fully recovered. Much more entertaining was the 1950s revival group Flash Cadillac and the Continental Kids. Wet Willie, a Southern rock band I didn't care for, opened the show. I drove Terri to her parent's apartment in Downey. We made out in the car.

The next night a number of us *Daily Bruin* writers trekked to the Anaheim Convention Center to see a sold-out show headlined by Traffic. Steve Winwood was in fine vocal form, but the set overall seemed unfocused: poor stage presence, too much jamming, unexciting new material—especially compared to the group's first four LPs. A highpoint was a cover of "Gimme Some Lovin'" from their new live album, which had been getting a lot of airplay. More notable was Fairport Convention who turned in a fun, energetic set of reels and jigs.

Paul encouraged me to order any LPs I wanted from the CBS catalogue. I had first been introduced to Bob Dylan while playing Risk at Harvey Portz's house. His brother Chuck—the bassist in The Crossfires, soon to be The Turtles—had his early albums. I thought Dylan had an unappealing, whiney voice, and I wasn't interested. Years later—with a small budget for purchasing records—I spent time in the UCLA listening lab trying to understand what Dylan's lyrics meant, as well as enjoying his wordplay. I ordered Dylan's albums, the first three Firesign Theatre releases, and *Having a Rave Up With The Yardbirds*.

On the turntable: Cat Stevens' *The Teaser and the Firecat*, John Entwistle's *Smash Your Head Against the Wall*, Dan Hicks and His Hot Licks' *Where's the Money?*, The Move's *Message From the Country*, Wishful Thinking's *Hiroshima*, Lenny Bruce's *What I Was Arrested For*.

NOVEMBER

ON NOVEMBER 3, FLASH Cadillac and the Continental Kids played a free noon concert at UCLA's Ackerman Grand Ballroom. Sha Na Na's appearance at the Woodstock festival, and in the subsequent film, had fueled a revival of interest in 1950s rock 'n' roll. Flash Cadillac, too, recreated the era well, and were imaginative in their staging, character mugging, and humor. I had a good relationship with their manager, Peter Rachtman, and had booked them to appear. It was an excellent show, one unlike anyone had ever seen at the university. They had students dancing on stage in a twist competition with a hubcap for the prize. The campus media, and the cultural commissioner, said it was the "best received contest in the history of UCLA."

The next day the *Daily Bruin* finally published my interview with Emitt Rhodes. He had been a member of one of LA's popular bands, The Merry-Go-Round. When Paul McCartney signaled the breakup of The Beatles by releasing his first solo album, *McCartney*, in May 1970, the album impressed the music community because it was the first by a major artist who played all of the instruments himself. Six months later, *Emitt Rhodes* was released, and it was even better. The Beatles heavily influenced Emitt, so his style was similar, and, like Paul, he played all the instruments himself.

Emitt lived in Hawthorne, but while performing at the Troubadour in February had stayed at a house in Studio City, on Laurel Canyon Boulevard, which is where I interviewed him. I had conducted more than a handful of interviews and all had gone well, but was stymied by a disinterested Rhodes. I did get usable quotes out of him, but I was at a loss on how to get better responses. He did clarify how his album differed from McCartney's: "His concept is a happiness thing with his chick, and I wasn't there when I was doing mine." Emitt's theme on the album was loneliness, with thoughts of death lurking in the background.

I salvaged a decent article, and submitted it to *Rolling Stone*. Paul Scanlon, the managing editor, liked it and said he wanted to publish it. He kept telling me, "We'll use it in an issue or two." After eight months, I gave it to the *Daily Bruin*.

I finally got a copy of *Brian Jones Presents the Pipes of Pan at Joujouka* (on Rolling Stones Records). Although Brian had shown that he was an extremely talented musician as a member of The Rolling Stones, nothing had been issued since his departure from the band: no solo recordings, no songwriting demos, nothing. His only released production was of the Master Musicians of Morocco playing flutes and drums, and chanting. A remote (rather than studio) recording, it sounded like cardboard. Whatever Brian heard—maybe it was the drugs he had taken—I couldn't grasp.

I saw *The Last Picture Show*, one of the best movies I've seen. The acting was natural and honest, and the story of high schoolers coming of age in a dying Texas town in the early fifties was authentically rendered through a black & white lens and a country and western soundtrack. Plus, Cybill Shepherd, in her acting debut, was a knockout.

I was looking forward to taking Terri to see Ten Years After at The Forum on November 11. Since viewing their dynamic performance in the *Woodstock* movie a year previously, and liking their new album *A Space in Time*—the first on Columbia—I was up for the concert. But my car broke down in West Hollywood in the late afternoon and I had to cancel my evening plans. Fortunately, I reached Terri, but calling her hadn't been assured. We were decades before cell phones, and there were no phones in the dorm rooms. I would call a pay phone booth on her floor. A resident had to be close enough to hear it. She would answer it and then knock on Terri's door, whereupon Terri would come to the phone. Sometimes I reached her, sometimes I didn't. Back in the days when girls were reluctant to call boys, she never phoned me. As time went by, I wondered if it was a reflection of her declining interest.

Procol Harum, one of my favorite groups, was playing on my home turf at the Ackerman Grand Ballroom on the fifteenth, and tickets were only two dollars. Unlike other groups with similar classical influences, Procol relied more on a cathedral, Bach-like organ sound than orchestral accompaniment. It was a warm-up gig for their performance three days later with the Edmonton Symphony Orchestra in Alberta, Canada, which was recorded for a live album.

The last time I had socialized with them was in August, at an evening party thrown on their behalf at the house of A&M Records' president Gil Friesen. The group arrived after spending the day at Disneyland. As it was a hot summer's evening, I wore a T-shirt promoting a new concert movie titled *Medicine Ball Caravan*. Drummer B. J. Wilson loved the slogan: "We have come for your daughters." He pressed me into trading shirts with him. At first I thought he was kidding, but he was serious. I ended up with the one he had bought at Disneyland, a long-sleeve dress shirt decorated with tiny Mickey Mouse images. That night Procol Harum performed at the Santa Monica Civic Auditorium and B. J. wore my T-shirt.

One of my favorite new groups, Grin, was the opening act at UCLA. Front man Nils Lofgren made a name for himself contributing to Neil Young's *After the Gold Rush*. I created an ad for Grin's new album that ran in the *Daily Bruin*. Although I was the college rep of Grin's label, the UCLA events person denied my request for a backstage pass. So, I wasn't able to visit with my pals Procol Harum, but did introduce myself to Nils during the sound check.

To coincide with the performance, the *Daily Bruin* published my Procol Harum interview from earlier in the summer (a version of which ran in the *L.A. Free Press* in August). From when I first met them, at the office of their publicists Gibson and Stromberg, their in-house lyricist Keith Reid impressed me the most. The band had begun when Gary Booker answered an ad to put Reid's poetry to music. Gary had been the singer and pianist in an R&B group named The

Paramounts. Keith had been a clerk in a London legal bookshop. In short order their pairing yielded a massive hit in the summer of 1967 with "A Whiter Shade of Pale," and a successful rock group was born.

Keith introduced to me the concept that art comes from emotional pain: "I don't believe anybody is a happy person. I've never met anybody who is a happy person. Being alive is not a happy experience. I write when I'm unhappy or troubled. It's an emotional release."

Terri was my date for the evening. She declined my offer to escort her to and from her dorm, suggesting that we meet at the Grand Ballroom. It was an excellent concert, and we embraced for longer than I would have hoped for after the show. I couldn't help but feel that our moment had passed, almost as if it were a goodbye embrace.

The UCLA basketball season started. One of my duties was to choose which Columbia and Epic half-page ads ran in *Hoops*, the program printed for home games. Rather than place the stock ads, and inspired by Stan Cornyn's copy, I asked Paul if I could create something better, which he encouraged, acknowledging their shortcomings. I illustrated Sly Stone to attract readers to the group's new album *There's a Riot Goin' On*, and created a new one for *The Chambers Brothers' Greatest Hits*.

I visited Grelun Landon, head of publicity for RCA Records. My relationship with him was based initially on my interest in Mike Nesmith and The Guess Who. The label was conservative, and didn't have much that appealed to me, but had gotten hipper by signing The Kinks and David Bowie. Occasionally there would be a worthwhile release from a new group, like Sky or Fresh. Landon was personable, although so soft spoken I couldn't understand everything he said. My first encounter with him made me question whether listening to loud music had diminished my hearing. His continuous smoking turned everything in his proximity grey, including his face and hair. He was far from dynamic, and too old to relate to the new rock groups. I had heard that he kept his job because of his close relationship with Elvis and his manager. His specialty was RCA's roster of country artists, but the country genre seemed too reactionary to interest me. One afternoon he introduced me to Barry Mann, sitting on the couch in his office. With his wife Cynthia Weil, Mann had written a number of the classic songs of the sixties, including "You've Lost That Lovin' Feeling," "On Broadway," "We Gotta Get Out of This Place," and "Kicks." I had heard Barry's newly released album, *Lay It All Out*, because it was on a CBS-distributed label. As he was visiting Grelun, I didn't want to pepper him with questions. It was cool to have met him.

I stopped off at the office to check in with Paul Rappaport. I picked up a copy of Bob Dylan's new single, "George Jackson," an impassioned tribute to the former leader of the radical Black Panthers who had recently been shot dead attempting to escape from prison. The song was more a reflection of how Dylan felt than an accurate account of the events. It wasn't among Dylan's best, but it was a welcome return to social commentary, absent on *New Morning*, his album of a year ago.

Mark Leviton had an extra ticket to see the Grateful Dead at UCLA's Pauley Pavilion on November 20. I wasn't a Dead fan, but was curious. The New Riders of the Purple Sage, a Dead offshoot, opened the show with their more conventional country repertoire. The Dead's set was marred by delays caused by problems with the sound system. Their long jams failed to interest me. We left early in their set. Bill Pique wasn't so lucky. He had to review the show for the *Daily Bruin*. He described it as "a never-ending jam from eight o'clock till one in the morning. It was all the same, long and monotonous. A drag."

The next week I ran into Phil Savenick, the cartoonist for the *Bruin*, who'd taken photos at the show. He'd seen Phil Lesh use his bass to whack a fan who tried to climb on the stage. Earlier, backstage, the new pedal steel guitar player for the New Riders shoved a girl into a urinal because she didn't recognize him from having played the first set. Actually, there was no "backstage." It was the arena's locker room. I guess the Dead weren't as mellow as they appeared to be. Half a dozen drug casualties were sprawled out, nearby, in front of the urinals, Phil reported.

A week later Mark and I went to see The Doors perform at the Hollywood Palladium. The group's new album, recorded after Jim Morrison's death in July, had just been released, and the single, "Tightrope Ride," was getting airplay. I liked the new album and enjoyed their set. They were a terrific band, but it was clear that, without Morrison, something was missing. Dr. John opened the show, but lacked the mystery I found so appealing in his voodoo-themed *Gris-Gris* album. Opening act Curved Air, an English progressive band with an attractive female singer, was too ethereal for me.

On November 30, Sweathog, a Columbia Records group, played a noontime free concert for the students in the Ackerman Grand Ballroom. "Hallelujah," their new hit single, was the highlight. I was a fan of the drummer, Frosty, who'd come to prominence accompanying Lee Michaels. The last time I'd seen the group, when they opened for Black Sabbath in Long Beach, guitarist B. J. Morris had lit his guitar on fire, which would not have been appropriate here. I composed an ad for the *Daily Bruin* and helped to promote the event. After the set I met them and their manager, Lenny Stogel, and escorted the band to KLA at the back of the hall to record an interview with one of the DJs.

On the turntable: Commander Cody and His Lost Planet Airmen's *Lost in the Ozone*, Van Morrison's *Tupelo Honey*, Don MacLean's *American Pie*, Herbie Mann's *Push Push*, Batdorf and Rodney's *On the Shelf*, The Who's *Meaty Beaty Big and Bouncy, Led Zeppelin IV*.

DECEMBER

ON FRIDAY, DECEMBER 3, I went with Sherman Cohen to see The Beach Boys in concert at the Long Beach Arena. Brian Wilson wasn't touring with the band, but they brought him out to play organ on an odd number, "A Day in the Life of a Tree," from their new album *Surf's Up,* with a recitation by their manager, Jack Rieley. I would have preferred to have seen Brian on one of his more familiar songs, but it was good to see him on stage, period. The Beach Boys played well, although the show was not well attended.

I had met Mark Leviton the previous year when, as a freshman, he came into the *Daily Bruin* office to inquire about writing for the entertainment section. Mark and I bonded over our mutual appreciation for the bands of the British Invasion, Frank Zappa, the Firesign Theatre, and private-detective novelist Raymond Chandler. With short, crinkly hair, a beard, and glasses, he couldn't pass for a wannabe rock star, but that didn't mean that the kid didn't have talent.

We wrote a couple of songs together—Mark supplied the music to my lyrics—with the intention of revamping my band, Mogan David and his Winos. "Street Baby" depicted a homeless kid living on the streets. "Party Games" reflected the frustration we felt as shy guys after approaching disinterested girls at the previous summer's Behemoth Festival, Heather Harris' annual party staged in her parent's backyard in Westwood.

We had a few rehearsals in preparation for going into the recording studio. I sang, Mark played guitar, and Jim Bickhart returned to play bass even though he had graduated. Matye wasn't into it—he was into his girlfriend—so he was gone. I didn't call Jon Kellerman, who was now in graduate school.

The last session with Kellerman hadn't ended well. After recording the two songs for our single, I wanted to run down a version of Betty Everett's 1964 hit "The Shoop Shoop Song," for backup, but Jon became bored and led us into playing surf instrumentals. As Paul Rappaport liked our first single and our musical taste, he was a natural for the lead guitar slot. Plus, he played the same guitar as Kellerman, a Gibson Melody Maker. I loved the tone. My friend Todd Schneider's younger brother, David, played drums.

Our first single had been produced at no cost: the instrumental tracks were recorded in Tom Matye's parents' living room; the vocals were recorded many months later in the bathroom of the student apartment we shared on Beverly Glen Boulevard using our neighbor, comedian George Carlin's, tape machine.

This time out we were recording in a proper studio, although a low-budget one. Paul and I knew Rich Fazekas through college radio. He engineered at Sound Sync in Riverside. On Sunday, December 5, I picked Paul up at his apartment in West LA and we made the seventy-mile trek. We recorded the two songs Mark and I had written. The main problem we experienced was that David had failed to fully rehearse the drum breaks we had written for him on "Street Baby," and we had to start the song sixteen times before we got it down. The studio wasn't glamorous, and was far from the happening environs of Hollywood, but we were excited to be recording in an actual studio.

I met Mark in Hollywood for a screening of Stanley Kubrick's new film, *A Clockwork Orange*. My enjoyment of this inspired example of filmmaking was compromised by the cruelty of violence. I felt shaken as we exited into the afternoon sun.

Among my classes, I made a mistake in taking the Perception of Music. I thought I would learn why music affects us, why certain melodic phrases or minor chords make a listener feel sad. It wasn't like that at all. It was mostly comparing different listening experiences and different musical scales from different cultures.

On Thursday the sixteenth, I was killing time in the lobby of the Continental Hyatt House waiting to interview the biggest pop star in the world, Marc Bolan of T. Rex, for *Phonograph Record Magazine*. Atomic Rooster, a British progressive band, checked in while I waited. The hotel was favored by visiting musicians as it was on the Sunset Strip and close to clubs, like the Whisky, where the group was booked.

Primarily because of Led Zeppelin's outrageous behavior as guests, it had become known as "the Riot House."

I would have been anxious over the time lost if I hadn't finished my final exams. Meeting Marc in person was an experience. He was a combination of rock star and animated character. With his big hair and little-girl shoes, he kind of looked like Minnie Mouse. I refer you to my chapter on Marc later in this book.

I had spoken to Terri before finals, and told her I would call her over the winter break. I contracted laryngitis, and couldn't speak. I had my mom call her mom to tell her why I couldn't call. I rested at home, listening to music and watching TV. In those days, prior to home video recording on VCRs, I didn't watch much, mostly old movies, but occasionally TV shows: *All in the Family, Sanford & Son*, and *60 Minutes.*

On the turntable: Badfinger's *Straight Up*, Mary Hopkin's *Earth Song/Ocean Song*, The Kinks' *Muswell Hillbillies*, Harry Nilsson's *Nilsson Schmilsson*, John Denver's *Aerie*, Alice Cooper's *Killer*, Faces' *A Nod Is As Good As A Wink...To A Blind Horse*, *The World of Johnny Horton*, John Prine.

JANUARY

I WAS EXCITED ABOUT the new quarter. I was taking two history-of-film classes, the American Motion Picture and Documentary Film; and a sociology class, Social Change. This year the UC Regents raised the undergraduate fees to $200 a quarter, double from my freshman year.

On January 6 the *Daily Bruin* published my career overview on one of my favorite bands of the British Invasion, Herman's Hermits. My feature on the Nitty Gritty Dirt Band finally ran in *Coast Magazine*. Although I had interviewed them in August, it was held pending the release of their *All the Good Times* LP. What I didn't include was an encounter with R&B singer Bobby Womack.

It was the first time I had been in a recording studio, United Artists' on Third Street in Los Angeles. The bass player and drummer were recording a rhythm track for the (Hank Williams–composed) Cajun standard "Jambalaya." I thought a band performed together, not just (in this case) two members recording separately. I was a fan of the group, and enjoyed talking with John McEuen and Jimmy Fadden. Bobby Womack breezed through the door in a buoyant mood. My friend Robert Wolfe and I were introduced to him, and when he shook Robert's hand, something fell out. He had slipped him a "red," a Seconal pill. Robert picked it off the floor and said, "You dropped this." Bobby responded, "No man, that's for you."

When we writers got together, most of the discussion was about music. We didn't talk much about politics or sports or even girls; we didn't talk about scoring or taking drugs—because we didn't. It was music, film, and what was happening on campus. We talked about Duane Allman's recent death in a motorcycle crash, and questioned if The Allman Brothers could stay together after having lost one of rock's best guitarists. We discussed Peter Frampton leaving Humble Pie, how in addition to his talent he provided a balance for Steve Marriott. We sought the meaning of lyrics. Paul and I speculated on Bob Dylan's "Desolation Row," especially the line, *They're painting the passports brown.* Mark and I talked about the tragedy that had befallen The Mothers of Invention. During a concert in Switzerland, a stupid fan shot a flare gun into the rattan-covered ceiling at the Casino de Montreux, which caused it to burn to the ground. A week later in London, another stupid—and jealous—fan pushed Frank Zappa into the orchestra pit during a performance at the Rainbow Theater. Frank's injuries were serious, and the future of his band was up in the air.

As a college rep, I was required to go to the CBS Records regional sales meetings at the Century Plaza Hotel on Saturday, January 22, and the following day. I hung mostly with Michael Ochs, Columbia's West Coast head of publicity. Forthcoming releases were presented, with the intention of inspiring the company to promote and sell the product when it hit the stores. One record spotlighted The Frogs—in suitable voice—performing a cover of Peter, Paul, and Mary's "I Dig Rock 'n' Roll Music." It was so awful, it tarnished the company's credibility. During the break I met *Rolling Stone* publisher Jann Wenner.

On Tuesday the twenty-fifth, I went with Todd Schneider to see the Nitty Gritty Dirt Band at the Troubadour. Opening act Jonathan Edwards was still high in the charts with his hit "Sunshine." I liked his pop-folk style and had his debut album at home. After his set, we chatted with the girls who were to our left, but when they told us that they were the wives of the members of the Dirt Band, we turned our attention to the two guys seated to our right, Bob Emmer and Leon Nirenberg. Bob was the college rep at USC for A&M Records. The set soon started. The Dirt Band played well, alternating instruments as they ran through bluegrass, Cajun, and country styles. I was reveling in "Mr. Bojangles," "Some of Shelley's Blues," and "Jamaica, Say You Will" when, two-thirds of the way through their set, an inebriated Leon, who sat to my immediate right, vomited. Some of the matter bounced off the floor onto my right sock. Bob Emmer made light of the situation by promising to buy me a new pair of socks.

I was leafing through the bootleg albums that were on sale at Lewin's Record Paradise on Hollywood Boulevard. In the 1960s the store was important as it was the only one in the area that stocked English imports. The original Beatles and Rolling Stones albums released in England were coveted because they had additional songs and different covers from their American counterparts. Only later were the imports also valued for their superior sound. By the early 1970s, with The Beatles having broken up, and with the same albums now issued on both sides of the Atlantic, the store was a shadow of itself, reduced to selling bootlegs. When I commented on the high prices to a fellow shopper, he alerted me to a guy who had a record concession in Santa Monica, who not only had lower prices, but who also took records in trade.

Bootlegs were records made by fans of an artist, usually recorded on nonprofessional equipment at a concert. They were illegal to make and sell—not own—because they were unauthorized, and the artists, songwriters, publishers and record companies received no money. The justifying attitude among bootleggers and fans was that the record companies and artists were making so much money already they weren't being deprived. As a record fan, you knew these pressings were illegal, but you wanted them to further your experience as a fan of the artist's music.

Apollo Electronics was on Broadway, across from a parking lot. Richard Foos had a section of the store in which he sold used records and bootlegs. With his curly hair and beard, he looked like a dusty prospector from an old movie. Richard was friendly, if low-key, and gave me a better deal than when I traded my promotional albums at Aron's Records in Hollywood. I picked up The Rolling Stones' *Beautiful Delilah*, an album of unreleased outtakes, among other items.

On Monday, January 31, United Artists Records hosted a "Legendary Sock Hop & Malt Party" at the Whisky a Go-Go to kick off their Legendary Masters Series. Fats Domino, Ricky Nelson, Jan & Dean, and Eddie Cochrane were the subjects of the first four releases. Each package contained lots of hits and comprehensive liner notes. It was rare to see such quality in a reissue of older music. Early in the evening, before the Nitty Gritty Dirt Band could make a surprise appearance, the electricity went off, and stayed off. The result was that Sherman Cohen and I felt less inhibited about talking to the girls who sat in the row in front of us: Shelly Heber, her younger sister Nikki, and their roommates. Sherman was impressed that Shelly worked in the charts department at *Billboard*. I was impressed that she had been president of one of The Yardbirds' fan clubs in the 1960s. The electricity never came on, which limited the fun that the evening promised.

On the turntable: David Bowie's *Hunky Dory*, Emerson, Lake & Palmer's *Pictures at an Exhibition*, Yes' *Fragile*, Colin Blunstone's *One Year*, The New Seekers' *I'd Like to Teach the World to Sing*, Billie Holiday's *God Bless the Child*, *The Concert for Bangla Desh*.

FEBRUARY

ON THURSDAY, FEBRUARY 10, Michael Nesmith played a free noon concert at the Ackerman Grand Ballroom, accompanied by Red Rhodes on pedal steel guitar. I went backstage and chatted with Mike before the show.

On Tuesday the fifteenth, T. Rex headlined the Hollywood Palladium. While Ballin' Jack performed, Marc Bolan was off the stage, on the left, dancing along. Nobody approached him. During his set, Marc was enthusiastic and confident, but his lead guitar playing was overly ambitious.

I enjoyed the oddball black comedy *Harold and Maude* and was taken by how well Cat Stevens' nine songs enhanced the mood. The music had a similar effect as Simon & Garfunkel's in *The Graduate*. I particularly liked the two new songs, "Don't Be Shy" and "If You Want to Sing Out, Sing Out," which were both life-affirming. Neither song was included on Cat's current album, *Teaser and the Firecat*, and there isn't a soundtrack album for the movie.

The English clerk at Discount Records had just returned from London where he had picked up an album, *Another Monty Python Record*, by a comedy troupe that had their own TV show. It was outrageous, and English! I'd never experienced anything like it. The jacket looked like a classical album, with lots of cross outs and the title handwritten in on the side. I heard two cuts, "Spanish Inquisition" and "The Architect," and made a mental note to get the record when it was released in the States.

On Thursday the seventeenth, my ad ran in the *Daily Bruin* for Redbone, a group that had climbed into the Top 30 with "The Witch Queen of New Orleans." In the 1960s, a successful advertising campaign in New York featured posters of obvious non-Jews—like an American Indian—eating rye bread with the caption "You Don't Have to be Jewish to Love Levy's Real Jewish Rye." As Redbone promoted their Native American ancestry, I featured a photo of Mark Leviton with "war paint" and a feather taking a bite out of a 45-rpm record pressed between two slices of bread. My title was "You Don't Have to be Indian to Enjoy Redbone." I plugged their album and an upcoming appearance opening for Ike & Tina Turner at The Forum.

Badfinger, with their Beatles-like, power-pop sound, were among my favorite artists of the early seventies. Their first four records were all hits: "Come and Get It," "No Matter What," "Day After Day," and "Baby Blue." In April 1971, Ben Fong-Torres, *Rolling Stone*'s music editor, called the *Daily Bruin* office looking for a writer to interview the group. Jim Bickhart, my editor, recommended me. It was my first professional assignment. They performed at the Pasadena Civic Auditorium on Friday, April 30, and on Monday I interviewed them at the Continental Hyatt House. They weren't stimulating conversationalists, but they were friendly, and I liked them. They seemed like humble, regular guys. They didn't flaunt their rock star success or Beatles connection. They weren't egotistical or pretentious.

I hadn't seen them in a year when they returned to the Los Angeles area to perform a number of dates. On Monday the twenty-first, they played a good set at the Whisky a Go-Go, after which I visited with them backstage. It was a large room on the second floor furnished with two black leather sofas. I sat on the carpet in front of the large window that looked down on the Sunset Strip. Guitarist Joey Molland expressed his frustration that their playing time in clubs, like the Whisky, was limited. They had to play two sets a night, and audience response was sedate compared to that in larger venues. I talked mostly with Pete Ham, the group's main vocalist, lead guitarist, and songwriter. I found his gentle demeanor appealing. I spent more time with him the following evening during a reception Capitol Records threw for the band at the Black Rabbit Inn on Melrose Avenue.

On Thursday the twenty-fourth, the *Daily Bruin* ran the ad I composed for the new Firesign Theatre album, *Dear Friends*. It plugged that evening's Firesign Fest, an hour of programming on KLA. I provided albums for the station to give to winners of a contest.

The next night, I joined Mark Leviton at the Valley Music Theater in Woodland Hills to see Badfinger headline over Pure Prairie League and Billy Joel. Mark had been assigned to write a feature on them for *Phonograph Record Magazine*, and I covered it for the *Daily Bruin*. We met them backstage and then joined them and their publicist at Charley Brown's restaurant, nearby, for dinner. Most of the customers were families. Nobody approached the band. Despite the prospect of a good meal, they weren't in the best mood. Although their most recent album, *Straight Up*, was a commercial success, and "Day After Day" their biggest hit, they were demoralized. George Harrison having vacated his producing duties halfway through recording the album had left them artistically dissatisfied. George had hired Todd Rundgren, whom the band found selfish and restricting. They complained that sometimes Todd would be playing piano for his own pleasure in a different room while the group was working in the studio. Harrison's departure, coupled with Paul McCartney's having himself departed— after championing the band and writing their breakthrough single "Come and Get It"—left them feeling abandoned. They also heard that John Lennon didn't like them. And, as with so many groups, where was the money? They still all shared a rented house in London with their fifty-nine-year-old manager.

On the way back, Joey and drummer Mike Gibbins piled into the back seat of Mark's Ford Fairlane; I rode shotgun. Joey marveled at the Troggs album Mark had. Mark pulled into the parking lot of the Valley Music Theater and greeted the attendant by thumbing in the direction of the backseat and, with an affected English accent, purposely uttering the novel phrase, "We're with the band." We dropped them off and, after parking the car, had trouble finding their roadies—Nicky and Fergie had to be the nicest in the business—before gaining admittance. Mark and I enjoyed the show, but the pacing was off. We joined them afterward.

Pete, frazzled, stormed into the dressing room and spouted, "It's fucked" (his assessment of the performance). They complained about the "shitty" sound, and having to play on a revolving stage. Badfinger loved The Beatles, were inspired by them, and created splendid singles, but when they toured the States they felt they had to cater to the audiences expecting their concert experience to be characterized by harder sounds and a heavier orientation—longer songs and long guitar solos. Because of equipment limitations, they weren't able to use a proper piano, which meant that they had to rely on up-tempo songs at the expense of their equally effective ballads. As a consequence, the rhythm of their set, which included two songs by Dave Mason that hadn't appeared on a Badfinger album, never found a proper flow. Those Mason songs, and a cover of Little Richard's "Lucille," failed to ignite the crowd. Upon departing, they gave me their address and phone number, and invited me to visit them when I made it to London.

On the turntable: Grin's *1 + 1*, Nitty Gritty Dirt Band's *All the Good Times*, The Coasters' *Their Greatest Recordings*, The Drifters' *Their Greatest Recordings*, George Carlin's *FM & AM*, Paul Simon, America, John Kongos.

MARCH

BIG BROTHER AND THE Holding Company were coming to town to play the Whisky, and a free noon concert was booked in the Ackerman Grand Ballroom on Thursday, March 9. Their *Cheap Thrills* was one of my favorite albums, but singer Janis Joplin had felt constrained and quit the group at the end of 1968. I didn't like the music she made with her next ensemble, Kozmic Blues Band, which incorporated horns. Big Brother reformed a year later with Kathi McDonald stepping into the void. Kathi, who'd sung backup for Ike & Tina Turner, had a different approach from Janis, but was capable. The band was tight rather than drug-addled, as their image might have promised. Afterward I escorted them to KLA to be interviewed by a DJ. Kathi was carrying her baby. I thought it must be tough to be in a touring rock band with such a young child.

That evening The Kinks played the Hollywood Palladium. Although I had seen them perform three times previously, tonight was extra special. Singer Ray Davies was resplendent in a green jacket and a red, white, and blue floppy bow tie. He camped it up, throwing kisses to the audience. Ray had a lot of fun with "Day-O (The Banana Boat Song)," a Jamaican folk song, which had been a big hit for Harry Belafonte in 1957, encouraging a call-and-response with the audience. When The Beatles and other rock bands were interviewed in the 1960s, they commonly cited musical influences of rock 'n' roll, rhythm and blues, and just plain blues. Here, Ray was flaunting a calypso-style song far removed from those genres. Similarly, Ray engaged the audience on "Alcohol," far exceeding the arrangement from their current *Muswell Hillbillies* album. He performed the song grasping a beer can as a prop, to the surprise of those pressed to the front of the stage, who endured a shower of suds. It was an exhilarating show.

Afterward I went to the Continental Hyatt House hotel for a party RCA Records threw for the group. I arrived early, when few people were present. I noticed singer Carly Simon. I thought she was alluring from the photos on her album jackets, but in person she didn't appeal to me at all. She was tall and gangly with big lips. That's when I understood the concept of being photogenic.

More people came, and later on as Ray arrived, our eyes met, and I nodded to him, but I didn't approach. Ordinarily, I would have. Ray was a hero to me. In writing songs with Mark, we were most influenced by him, The Who's Pete Townshend, and The Rolling Stones' Mick Jagger and Keith Richards. I had read a recent interview where the writer commented on how surly Ray was. His point was that it wasn't always a benefit to meet one's heroes, as often they'll disappoint you, and you'll feel less about them than if you never met them.

The next night I joined Bickhart and Leviton to take in a triple bill at the Fox West Coast Theatre in Long Beach. With the increasing popularity of motion pictures in the post–World War I era, ornate movie palaces—with stages for vaudeville performances—had been built. In the 1950s, as television viewing flourished, movie attendance declined. By the late 1960s, many of these movie palaces had fallen into disrepair. Some were retrofitted into rock concert halls, like New York's Fillmore East—converted from the Village Theater—Detroit's Eastown Theatre, and Elizabeth, New Jersey's Ritz Theatre. The Fox West Coast Theatre was the first in our area to be transformed and offer a consistent program of live performances. Since the mid-1920s, it had been the premier venue in that area, but by the early 1970s the Spanish Colonial Revival–designed building had lost its luster.

Opening the show were Daddy Cool who, the previous year, scored a number one album and single in their native Australia. Atypically for a 1950s revival band, they had good original songs that often incorporated contemporary arrangements. They were touring the US on the strength of radio play of their song "Eagle Rock." Next up was the Pure Food and Drug Act, which featured virtuosos Harvey Mandel on guitar and Sugar Cane Harris on electric violin. We had come to see the headliners, Captain Beefheart and the Magic Band, three members of which were former Mothers of Invention. Mark was a big Beefheart fan. The band performed material from their newest album, *The Spotlight Kid*.

The Magic Band members had strange names: Rockette Morton, Zoot Horn Rollo, Winged Eel Fingerling. And so did the song titles: "Woe-Is-Uh-Me-Bop," "Japan in a Dishpan," "I'm Gonna Booglarize You Baby." The band was good, and I enjoyed most of the set. I preferred Daddy Cool, however. The following month Bickhart, Stan Berkowitz—a film major and fan of Russ Meyer's sexploitation films who also wrote for the paper—and I trekked out to the Theatre to see Little Richard. Richard was nearing forty, and well past his prime. Despite his excessive self-aggrandizement, he still was a thrill to see.

Gibson and Stromberg were promoting Yes, so on Friday, March 17, publicist Bobbi Cowan arranged for a limousine to drive a group of writers eighty miles to the Swing Auditorium in San Bernardino to see the English band. It was a welcomed diversion, as I'd had final exams the past week. En route, Bobbi offered me a hit of cocaine. It was my first time, so I tried it. Fortunately, it didn't do much for me. It was a comfortable ride. But I wasn't fooling myself. I didn't feel like a rock star as our limo slowly rolled into the parking lot; I was more amused. Milling teenagers, thinking we might be on the evening's bill, gawked at us, offered goofy smiles, and flashed peace signs.

Backstage we met the members of Yes. Rick Wakeman, the group's gifted keyboardist, was changing into his stage gear. With his pasty pallor and long blond hair, he could have passed for a Viking except for his flabby body. I had heard that there was friction in the band between Wakeman, who was a drinker and an omnivore, and the rest of the band, who were vegetarians. I stepped out into the auditorium to see the end of Black Sabbath's set.

This first tour of the US has helped to propel Yes' current album, *Fragile*, into the Top 10 and their "Roundabout" single into the Top 20. The tour and royalties earned on the album—which cost $30,000 to record—will be the first big money the group will have made. Yes performed well in San Bernardino. The sonic quality of Jon Anderson's lead vocals was impressive, as were the group's three-part harmonies.

On Thursday, the following week, Emerson, Lake & Palmer played the Santa Monica Civic Auditorium. I had been a fan of Keith Emerson's keyboard playing with his former group, The Nice, but this was the first time I had seen him in concert. The group played an enjoyable set that incorporated classical and jazz styles. Their current album, *Pictures at an Exhibition*, was a live recording based on Mussorgsky's piano suite.

On March 25, the UCLA basketball team defeated Florida State to win the National Collegiate Championship, capping an undefeated season. I watched the game on TV. When I was in my teens, I was a big baseball and basketball fan, but my interest had waned as I was attracted to the music scene. I had attended only one game all season. Since The Beatles, there had been a divergence of sports and music fans. Sports participants tended to be physically oriented, masculine, and conservative. They were uneasy with the rock music world of long hair, drugs, undernourished bodies, flamboyant clothes, and, generally, a liberal way of looking at the world. A girl who would be attracted to a football player wouldn't be interested in me.

Steve Gabor owned the Music Odyssey, the best-stocked record store in West LA. UCLA contacted him about putting in a record store on the A-level of Ackerman Union. As the space was prepared, I met Steve and the store's manager, Michael Warner. I thought the new store was a bad idea. Ackerman Union's previous record store, located in another part of the complex, had seemed never to do much business. Ron Mael, later a member of Sparks, was behind the counter. In November 1970, when my first record, "Nose Job," came out, it was the store's biggest-selling single, which meant that it sold one copy in the two weeks it was stocked. Before the new store opened at the end of the month, Gabor had a small kickoff party, enlivened by the presence of his stunning young wife, who was very sociable.

I visited with Michael Ochs at CBS. He was always friendly and welcoming. I had just picked up copies of our new single, "Street Baby" backed with "Party Games." He put it on his turntable. Although he thought we had progressed from our first record, he wasn't enthused. He also admitted that he hadn't liked any of the singles Columbia had released the past year either. His eyes lit up when he replaced my single with a recent, rare acquisition. "Listen to this," he said. His excitement was apparent as he played "Baby Let Me Bang Your Box" by The Toppers. A 1954 release, it was an example of the novel, double-entendre records of the period. Even though he didn't like my record, I dug Michael because he was a real music guy.

Our single received good comments in the press. Mike Saunders wrote in *Phonograph Record Magazine*: "'Street Baby' is an excellent hard rocker in The Stones mold with Who overtones on guitar." Greg Shaw in *Creem* called it "exciting."

Classes for the spring quarter started on Thursday, March 30. I had a light schedule: Music of the United States, a history of rock music masquerading as a "survey from colonial times to the present"; Fundamentals of Learning, a psychology class on animal and human conditioning; Urban Sociology, which studied the characteristics of big cities in Western culture.

The next night I drove Mark Leviton, Jim Bickhart, and Stan Berkowitz to Knott's Berry Farm to see Paul Revere & the Raiders perform at the John Wayne Theater. Prior to the popularity of The Monkees, Paul Revere & the Raiders had been the most popular American rock group, racking up a slew of excellent hit singles that included "Just Like Me," "Kicks," "Hungry," and "Good Thing." As regulars on the *Where the Action Is* TV show, their popularity had been such that every member of the quintet was featured in the teen magazines. Since then, the personnel—except for lead singer Mark Lindsay and bandleader Paul Revere—had changed. They were older, more polished—and less crazy.

After a tasty fried chicken dinner at Mrs. Knott's Chicken Dinner Restaurant, we met the band backstage before the show. The Raiders hadn't had a hit in two years when "Indian Reservation" topped the charts in the spring of 1971. The set we saw showcased their more recent hits instead of the classics we had been expecting.

On the turntable: Todd Rundgren's *Something/Anything*, Fairport Convention's *"Babbacombe" Lee,* Neil Young's *Harvest,* The Conception Corporation's *Conceptionland.*

APRIL

ONE FRIDAY AFTERNOON IN the CBS Records sales office, Paul introduced me to a young friend of his, Justin Pierce, a senior at Fairfax High School. Justin would visit Paul, bring him pastries from the bakery where his mother worked, and Paul would give him promotional copies of new releases. Paul brought him into the shared office where I was sitting and suggested I help Justin with his writing for the school paper. The goal for me, and my fellow writers on the *Daily Bruin*, was to be good enough to make money writing. For those of us in the entertainment section, the promotional records, concert tickets, and movie passes were a bonus. In talking to Justin, I was taken aback that his primary motivation was to get the free stuff. He wanted to be a better writer—that's why he approached me— but he wasn't that committed to it. Still, I responded to his passion for the music, and gave him suggestions. As I got to know Justin, I could see that he was a good guy, and was inclusive as it related to people. He became one of my best friends, and we attended a lot of shows together.

Phil Savenick was in charge of putting together the yearbook for the graduating class. He had an idea for a companion book, *Your Book*. It had nothing to do with the university—which the first book covered. It was a collection of cultural images from our age group: elementary school, television, music, sports. He asked me to lend him trading cards from my collection to be reproduced in the book. I loved his concept and was happy I could contribute.

John Mendelsohn deserves a lot of credit for drawing peoples' attention to the quality of The Kinks' music, circa 1966-1970. To fans like me, *The Kink Kronikles*—the double album of hits, B-sides, and rarities he compiled and wrote the liner notes for—was sublime. The material was of a high quality, and many tracks hadn't been released in America previously. It sold extremely well, breaking into *Billboard's* Top 100, which was all the more noteworthy as The Kinks hadn't had a hit in almost two years. Also on the turntable: The Mothers' *Just Another Band from LA*, The Hollies' *Distant Light*, Michael Nesmith & the Second National Band's *Tantamount to Treason*.

MAY

IT WAS TIME TO reinvigorate my band. We'd made a couple of records, but we'd never performed live. We now had a sense of purpose. We were going to provide the entertainment for the year's *Daily Bruin* party. Bill Pique, a newer contributor to the music section, was willing to switch from guitar to bass. Compared to us Jews, he was like a mountain man. He had played football at Palos Verdes High School.

He was a good guy, but a bit uncouth. He suggested his friend, Rob Lampl, be the drummer. With his long hair and fuzzy beard, Rob looked like a typical hippie. He favored jazz-rock, and fingered a psychedelically painted guitar, but here his task was to pound the drums. He got a set from Bill's brother and was a natural on the instrument. We practiced after hours and on weekends at the *Daily Bruin* office, often having a meal afterward at Maison La Crepe in Westwood Village. Bill practiced his French, but it must have been Dirty Old Man French, as he kept asking the pert, young waitresses for their legs.

I enjoyed visiting Pete Senoff at Atlantic Records. With his short hair and body-builder physique, he was an anomaly for the music business. He may have been unhip on the outside, but he was hip on the inside, with excellent taste in music. He sponsored an annual bus trip to downtown's Olympic Auditorium to take in the wrestling matches, with burgers afterward at Original Tommy's at Beverly and Rampart. He gave me an advance copy—a white label pressing with no information—of *Take A Sad Song...* It was an ingenious production of contemporary hit songs—"Hey Jude," "Honky Tonk Women," "Dance to the Music"—performed in 1950s arrangements by studio musicians under the artist name Godfrey Daniel, after an expression of actor W. C. Fields.

Pete invited me to a showcase for new artist Bette Midler at the Paradise Ballroom in West Hollywood. A one-time bombsight factory, it was turned into a private club by Frank Sinatra and his pals in the late sixties. Cabaret acts, like Bette's, were more familiar on the East Coast. I was impressed with her pipes and personality, showcased best on her lively renditions of The Shangri-Las' "Leader of the Pack" and The Andrew Sisters' "Boogie Woogie Bugle Boy." Barry Manilow accompanied her on piano.

CBS had released a line of albums in the new SQ Quadraphonic format. With a decoder box and special amplifier, records played a mix of four channels through four speakers. With the speakers placed in four corners surrounding the listener, it was as though he were in the middle of the music. This month RCA launched its competing format, Compatible Discrete 4. When Quad was introduced, I heard a presentation that included Steam's hit "Na Na Hey Hey Kiss Him Goodbye." Stereo approximates a performance coming from the direction of the stage. Quad seemed like a gimmick to me.

One of the difficulties I had with the older—unhip—salesmen at the CBS office was that they didn't seem to care about the music they were selling. The expression bandied about was that "a [record] salesman could just as well be selling shoes" for all he knew about the music. A big offender to me was Frank Mooney, who concocted a promotion for the new Music Odyssey store, with the prize being a new multi-gear bicycle. The way it worked was for each Columbia/Epic album a customer bought, he would have a ticket deposited in a box from which the winning one would be drawn. It was explained to me that it was illegal to have a contest with a raffle based on purchases. Mooney thought the store was too small to bear any scrutiny. Not even the contest could drum up shoppers.

The girl who won bought over thirty albums and accounted for over 90 percent of the tickets in the box. After the contest, she attempted to return the albums for a refund. I don't know if she got to keep the bike.

The store was open less than a year when it closed in February 1973. Gabor failed to consider that there would be next to no business on weekends, holidays, and during school breaks, and little during summer sessions. Even though there were not many customers, Gabor estimated that he lost five thousand albums to theft.

I went on my first record company junket. It wasn't really a junket, just one night in a hotel room in Las Vegas traveling with other writers and publicists. B. B. King was appearing at the Casino Lounge in the Las Vegas Hilton. His set was proficient and polished, but I was surprised that it was the same act I had seen when he opened for The Rolling Stones two and a half years earlier. I took note that even the moments I had thought were spontaneous, were well rehearsed. I came home with the confidence that I could win in Vegas, having pocketed twenty-five dollars from the Hilton's two-dollar blackjack table.

A couple of days later, on Saturday, May 13, John Mendelsohn's band Christopher Milk played the Lindie Theater. The audience was sparse. John and the band showcased a lot of good ideas, but he was an ineffective singer and the music was too ambitious for the musicians' abilities.

On Tuesday, May 16, Randy Newman opened at the Troubadour. I first took note of him in 1967 from three songwriting credits on Eric Burdon and the Animals' *Eric Is Here* album. I enjoyed "Mama Told Me (Not to Come)" and "I Think It's Gonna Rain Today." He didn't perform often, so it was a treat to finally see him. Hunched over his piano, singing in a world-weary, Louisiana-blues style, he created an intimacy. Among the songs he debuted, I especially liked "Lonely at the Top" and the farcical sing-a-long "Political Science."

The next evening, my twenty-second birthday, went quietly except for taking in a performance by Chicago's Wilderness Road at the Whisky. The Conception Corporation told me about them, but I found their set of country- and gospel-influenced rock lacking. It did include a promising original idea, that of a mock revival show, but it wasn't developed enough for me.

I was now a regular at the Whisky. It had been three years since my first visit, when Tom Matye and I arrived at the club not long after it opened for the night. We were shown to a table behind a post, and were too intimidated to ask for a better seat. We nursed our soda pop until Danny McCulloch—the ex-Animals bassist who had a new solo album out—took the stage to a sparse audience.

I was familiar to some of the waitresses, and even to the doorman who called me by name, although not by *my* name. A good-looking black man who wore flashy suits that seemed at odds with his black-plastic-rimmed glasses, Albert was always in good spirits and greeted me with a wide smile. When it was my turn in line, I flipped my wallet open so he could see my ID. Facing it was an Elvis Presley pocket calendar. I was on RCA Records' press list and received one each year. Somehow, Albert identified the photo as singer Tom Jones, even though I corrected him the first few times. "Here comes Tom Jones!" he would say when I approached.

In the *Daily Bruin's* annual Rock Poll, The Winos placed fourth in the Weirdos category, tied with Sha Na Na, trailing Alice Cooper, Flash Cadillac, and the winner, The Mothers of Invention.

A new single on Epic, "Rub It In" by Dave Clark & Friends, came into the office. I was excited as it featured The Dave Clark Five's vocalist Mike Smith. Rounding out the group were noted session musicians Alan Parker on guitar and Eric Ford on bass. It was a cover of a country record and didn't sound like a hit to me, or like The Dave Clark Five. I much preferred the promotional poster of a beautiful naked girl.

At the office I also picked up a few tchotchkes—Yiddish for ephemeral objects—in this case ones used for promotion. The record division of the mighty CBS Corporation pandered to the drug culture with packets of (marijuana) cigarette rolling papers. The covers plugged the latest releases by the Jeff Beck Group, New Riders of the Purple Sage, Delaney and Bonnie, and Dr. Hook. There were small bags printed with Columbia Cement Works promoting Andy Williams' *Love Theme from the "Godfather,"* with a tag that read, "If you don't buy this record, there's more where this came from." A handy jean-carrying bag was printed with the Loggins and Messina logo.

On the turntable: Jethro Tull's *Thick As A Brick*, Janis Joplin's *In Concert*, Procol Harum's *Live In Concert with the Edmonton Symphony Orchestra*, Dr. Hook and the Medicine Show's *Dr. Hook, Raspberries*.

JUNE

DAVID BROMBERG WAS A folk singer who garnered notice because he had written a song, "The Holdup," with George Harrison on which George also contributed slide guitar. On Saturday, June 3, he gave a private performance in Lenny Stogel's backyard in the Malibu Colony. I was looking forward to seeing him play because I liked his debut album. Bromberg didn't have a technically good voice—it wasn't powerful and didn't have much range—but it was expressive. He had a natural way of incorporating stories into his songs. I knew few people there, so I introduced myself to Harry Shearer and his wife. I was a fan of his comedy group, the Credibility Gap, from when they satirized the news on radio station KRLA starting in 1969. Their debut album, *Woodschtick,* had come out a year before, and taken the concept of a Woodstock-like rock festival and created an in-door event with comedians instead of musicians. Harry told me that he had also written for the *Daily Bruin.*

On the following Tuesday, as I made my way through Westwood, visiting the record stores for the last time as a college rep, I appreciated the special qualities of the Village. It didn't give me a warm feeling, like imagining the good old days The Kinks were singing about on *The Kinks Are the Village Green Preservation Society,* nor were friendly, chirping blue birds guiding my path as in a Disney movie. The Village had its own self-contained feel: there was a Safeway supermarket and a Bullock's department store. It also had a sort-of old world feel—at least for Southern California. For example, the Bank of America— where I'd applied for my BankAmericard credit card—was housed in an expansive Moroccan-styled building with a dome. I passed the art deco Bruin Theater, where I'd seen a screening of The Rolling Stones' *Gimme Shelter,* with Jim Morrison sitting a few rows back. I attended afternoon showings of The Beatles' *Yellow Submarine* at the UA, and *Catch-22* at the National; the Fox, Regent, and Plaza were the other theaters. There were four bookstores: Westwood Books, Brentano's, Campbell's, and Hunter's Books. And plenty of places to eat: Mario's, Alice's Restaurant (inspired by the 1969 movie), the Bratskeller, the Pizza Palace, Hamburger Hamlet, Woody's Smorgasburger, Old World, and Wil Wright's Ice Cream Parlor for dessert. Sepi's submarine shop and Ships Coffee Shop were more affordable for my budget. As I walked, I took in the changes that were occurring with the architecture. The charm of the Spanish and Mediterranean styles was giving way to newer structures with less character. It was an area in transition. Already gone were the head shops, Headquarters and the Free Press Book Store, and Sat Purush, the Indian clothing boutique south of the Village where George Harrison romped in his underwear trying on clothes.

That night I saw a new Columbia group, Dr. Hook and the Medicine Show, at the Troubadour. Although they looked like a quintet of hillbillies on leave from *Li'l Abner*'s Dogpatch, they were actually a bar band from New Jersey. *Dr. Hook* included ten of Shel Silverstein's songs, one of which, "Sylvia's Mother," had just climbed to number five. It was based on a true incident whereby Silverstein had called his ex-girlfriend—not named Sylvia—and was told by her mother that she was getting married to a bullfighter. Despite the band's casual nature— given to horsing around and swearing —they were strong vocally and instrumentally, and a lot of fun.

I was looking forward to graduating, but little else. I had placed an ad in the *Los Angeles Times* to sell my gas-guzzling 1967 red Firebird convertible, but didn't get much response. I did get a call from a doctor in Beverly Hills who requested that I drive to his office so he could test-drive the car. I did, but he wasn't interested in buying. I made my way back to campus. It was dusk as I looked up at the lights coming from the dorms, and thought of Terri. I'd had few dates since I'd last seen her, which made me even lonelier.

Despite my feelings for her, it may not have made for a long-term relationship when I considered her tardiness, or that she was so irresponsible to have racked up thirty-two parking tickets on campus. In one of our conversations, she was sympathetic for her older sister's dilemma after having married a much older man. I wrote a song about it. Here are most of the lyrics to "Beauty Queen":

She was just twenty-one, she was a beauty queen
But she was getting tired of the same old scene
She looked fine, she was the Queen of Downey
She was Miss Orange County

Married to a man fifteen years older
He gave her everything, he tried to mold her
Every third day she cries on her bed
Love was lacking so her sister said

Beauty Queen, you're a rose (i.e. Roese)
You smile nice, but it's just a pose
Beauty Queen, you're so keen
You're unhappy, so what does it mean?

They had a kid and she found it hard
To break away and leave her yard
So she lives not knowing what to do
I'd hate to be in her position, how about you?

Not doing much other than completing my studies, I agreed to a publicist's request to interview Ozzy Osbourne, Black Sabbath's lead singer. Even though I liked some of their songs, like "Paranoid" and "Iron Man," I wasn't a fan of the group. Black Sabbath was one of the few examples of an artist making it primarily on their own efforts. There wasn't much of an initial marketing campaign, nor had they benefited from a hit single. The group had a unique sound that attracted fans who saw them opening for other bands on their first US tour. I was curious about their lyrical themes referencing the occult and religious horror imagery.

On Wednesday, June 7, I met Black Sabbath at 773 Stradella Road in Bel-Air. They were renting a large house from John du Pont, an heir to the Du Pont Chemical fortune. They had been swimming, and a still-wet-in-swim-trunks Ozzy met me in front of the pool house. He was friendly. His stringy hair was still dripping water. His nickname—his birth name was John—was tattooed on the back of the fingers of his left hand, O-Z-Z-Y. I'd never met anybody with a tattoo before. Tattoos were associated with negative character traits: the province of roaming sailors, juvenile delinquents, and criminals. In addition to tattoos on his arms, he had a smiling face on each kneecap.

Ozzy was a willing and engaging conversationalist. Considering Black Sabbath's droning sound and the dark imagery of their lyrics—most supplied by bassist Geezer Butler—I was surprised when Ozzy said that his favorite rock group was The Beatles. As a teen, he pasted pictures of them all over the walls of his room, and fantasized that his sister would marry Paul McCartney. When he heard the heavy guitar sound of The Kinks' "You Really Got Me," he said it was a revelation to him.

In talking with fans, drummer Bill Ward heard them describe the band's music as "downer rock," which referred not only to the overall bleak effect, but sedative drugs, such as Seconal, which were commonly consumed by kids—and called "downers." The group's instrumentation matched lyrics that were negatively expressed, drawing upon the occult, Satan, and the supernatural. The instrumental styles of Black Sabbath, Led Zeppelin, and Deep Purple, defined by loud, sustained, and grinding guitar chords, came to be referred to as heavy metal. The term was most likely adopted from Steppenwolf's 1968 hit "Born to Be Wild." The lyric *heavy metal thunder* referred to the roar of a motorcycle.

Ozzy understood the positive, therapeutic effect of fans leaving the band's concerts feeling relieved of their frustrations. I hadn't thought that a band with a gloomy outlook could make listeners happy. The album Black Sabbath was recording had references to Lucifer, nightmares, witchcraft, and the supernatural. It was more melodic than their three previous albums, Ozzy assured me, and he invited me to the studio that evening to hear what they were doing.

They were recording at the Record Plant on Third Street. Studio B looked more like an avant-garde artist's living room than a recording studio. A smoke-burned American flag hung on one wall. Parachutes were draped on the opposite wall. The room as a whole was composed of gentle combinations of orange and red, including tie-dyed baffles surrounding the drums.

"For the best coke, just ring 3-8-9-0-9-8, only one hundred dollars!" exclaimed Ozzy as he grinned stupidly from behind a microphone. "I'm so stoned," he moaned while gesturing like Frank Sinatra.

"Look at 'em," Geezer referred to the way the earphones squeezed Ozzy's brassy head. "He looks like he's in the Guards." Ozzy took out a hardbound book with hand-written lyrics to the song "Snowblind" and commenced chanting in his customarily determined Sabbath style. The other members joked that Ozzy was so wasted he couldn't remember the lyrics and had to resort to reading them from the book. Ozzy had written them, inspired by cocaine and a nightmare of Butler's. His voice was flat—although he didn't seem to notice—and the track had to be recorded again until he got it right. The first verse was finished and Ozzy sang again, matching the first take in order to give the (double-tracked) vocal more strength. He had trouble singing the next verse and the band agreed to take a break. The other members were low-key. Drummer Bill Ward was the friendliest. Tony Iommi impressed us as he tried different lead guitar runs—rather than merely a variation of one mode—until he came up with the one they used on the track. Because Ozzy was so wasted, probably due more to alcohol than any other substance, the group didn't want my friend Todd Schneider to take any photographs.

On Saturday, June 10, The Winos made their debut at the *Daily Bruin* party. We set up in a narrow space inside the family home of Heidi Yorkshire—*Bruin* editor David Lees' fiancée—on Tower Road in Beverly Hills. I was nervous, and my adrenaline surged, but we delivered a passable set.

I was excited about getting my degree, but I had no interest in attending graduation. For a school so large, I would have known few people. My parents didn't seem interested in attending the ceremony either.

I was a big Rolling Stones' fan and anticipated every album they released, but I had a hard time coming to grips with their latest, *Exile On Main Street*. Too few tracks were of a high standard. I was tired of "Tumbling Dice" because of its constant presence on the Whisky's sound system. "Happy" would have been so much better if sung by someone other than Keith Richards. The "songs" seemed more like uninspired jams, and the sound was muddy. Not having a playable Rolling Stones' album didn't portend well for the summer. Still, when Michael Warner and I attended their Sunday concert at The Forum on June 11, I had a good time. Our seats were next to the sound mixer, which meant that we were in the perfect place for good sound, in an arena that was built for basketball and not acoustically suited to music. The band performed with a lot of energy, and I didn't mind that the *Exile* songs didn't hold up compositionally.

On June 21 Mark and I went to the Whisky to see The Strawbs. Jim Bickhart had turned us onto the group when he worked at A&M, and we became fans. They had evolved out of the English folk scene, originally as The Strawberry Hill Boys, but adopted more of an electric rock sound that incorporated ominous, medieval influences by way of the organ—played by Blue Weaver after Rick Wakeman left to join Yes—and droning, monk-like choral vocals. Dave Cousins was a strong singer, and he also contributed the folk-like dulcimer. The cover of their new album, *Grave New World*, carried the motif with woodcut illustrations.

On Friday afternoon, June 23, I went to Gibson and Stromberg to pick up tickets for Jethro Tull's concert that evening at The Forum. As I waited for Mark to meet me, I chatted with Bob Gibson. Because I had just graduated, he recommended I go to law school. He reasoned that there were few lawyers who were savvy in the music business, and, as it was a growing field, there would be opportunities for a music fan like me. I thought it was good advice, but hoped to get a job in a creative area, working for a record company.

Mark arrived, and as Bobbi Cowan was giving us the tickets, she asked if we minded giving a ride to "a young writer." Bobbi had provided the tickets, so how could we not do her a favor? For most of the trip, Danny Sugerman was sedate, but at some point the drugs he had taken must have kicked in. Like a dog that relished the wind whipping through its face, Danny leaned his head out the window and howled, "Aauugghhh!" After we entered The Forum, at the top of the steps, Danny yanked off his shirt, unleashed an "aauugghhh!" and ran all the way down to the floor.

I had interviewed the members of British rock sextet Heads Hands & Feet—whose members included Albert Lee, Chas Hodges, and Tony Colton—around the pool at the Continental Hyatt House. They opened the show with a set of country rock, but the crowd barely paid attention. Before Jethro Tull was due to start, a gorilla (most likely a man in a suit) jumped around on the stage, followed by a handful of stagehands wearing caps and overcoats. When they finished adjusting the equipment, they removed their overcoats to reveal that they were not roadies but members of Jethro Tull. The group played well, featuring their new album *Thick As A Brick*. Lead singer/flautist Ian Anderson, atypically, looked more like an old man than a youthful rock star. Rather than combating his looks, he pushed in the other direction by assuming the persona of a deranged homeless man: his wiry hair bristled, and he wore what appeared to be a bathrobe over a leotard. Despite the seriousness of their music, the group injected physical humor by changing their clothes on stage, adorning animal costumes, and chasing each other in the manner of The Marx Brothers. They encored with "Aqualung," a fitting end to an excellent show.

During my time as a college rep, it would not have been proper for me to have written stories or reviews of CBS acts. With the job over, I wanted to write an article on Paul Revere & the Raiders. I interviewed Mark Lindsay and Paul Revere in a recording studio at CBS, on June 28, the day after a performance on Disneyland's Tomorrowland Stage. They were open and patient in responding to my fumbling, Columbo-like probing. I sensed a conflict of art versus commerce. Revere was more focused on the presentation of the live act and the economics of touring and Lindsay was more involved in the production and songwriting.

In the first few years, Revere, Lindsay, and the band had worked incredibly well. Paul the hustler, four years older than Mark, was like an older brother. Although Mark matured into a confident front man with matinée idol looks, at his core he was a gangly, bespectacled shy kid who hid behind his saxophone. Initially they had an outrageous, at-times-"gross" live act that attracted a fervent college-age crowd. When they became TV stars, they had to change to appeal to their new, younger teenage fans. Later still, as they and their audience matured, they had to retool again, and questioned whether the tour could accommodate their props, or whether they had to tone down their showmanship, as in the recent appearances I'd seen at Knott's Berry Farm and Disneyland.

At some point they lost their way. Mark wanted to go in the direction of The Beatles and other acts that had opened the door to artistic expression. But Paul was a blues and boogie-woogie piano stylist unmotivated to explore. Paul was pragmatic, feeling the band was better off touring than spending the increased amount of time recording that was now required. Consequently, session musicians were used. This was partly why the other three members left in the spring of 1967, to form their own band. Their popularity as Raiders didn't survive the transition, and their new band, Brotherhood, was a commercial flop.

As Paul receded musically, the band's producer, Terry Melcher, stepped up to partner creatively with Mark. But after Terry left, Mark was cast adrift, having to bear the burden of pushing for the highest quality The Raiders could muster. The new lineup fared less well on the charts, but had a reprieve with "Indian Reservation," which was recorded to be a Mark Lindsay solo release. It hit number one—the "group's" only chart-topper—in the spring of 1971. As a solo artist, Mark Lindsay had a Top 10 hit in January 1970 with "Arizona," but his subsequent efforts failed to make the Top 20.

On the turntable: David Bowie's *Ziggy Stardust and the Spiders from Mars*, Randy Newman's *Sail Away*, *History of Eric Clapton*.

JULY

ON JULY 3, PROCOL Harum performed a terrific set at the Santa Monica Civic Auditorium, where I had last seen them in March. They featured songs from their new album, recorded with the Edmonton Symphony Orchestra. It was their best-selling album, and spawned the hit single "Conquistador." The Eagles preceded them, in their first local appearance. Their harmonies were impressive, but their songs were just OK. After the show I went to a party held for them at a house on the beach. People weren't that sociable, so I didn't stay long.

I was curious to see Ramatam, who played the Whisky on July 19. I had loved Mitch Mitchell's drumming as a member of The Jimi Hendrix Experience, but here he was less engaging. April Lawton, a beautiful guitarist, fronted the band, but her visual appeal wasn't enough to make up for the mediocre songs and arrangements. Also on guitar and vocals, Mike Pinera, whom I'd interviewed two years before when he was in Iron Butterfly.

As school had ended, we relocated our Winos rehearsals to the Lampl family garage in Westwood. On a couple of occasions we checked out the bands at Gazarri's nightclub on the Sunset Strip.

On Saturday, July 15, The Winos played a party in the backyard of Shelly and Nikki Heber's house on Laurel Canyon Boulevard. For the special occasion I sprung for fireworks—just like The Who—but they failed to have the desired affect. The Roman Candle was positioned too close to Rob's drum kit, which meant that sparks flew no higher than the inside of his snare drum. John Mendelsohn, my original editor at the *Daily Bruin*, came to check us out, though I don't think he had been invited. We played much better than at the *Bruin* party. Afterward, as a special treat, I set up a projector and showed 8mm films—without sound—of The Beatles performing that I'd borrowed from Atlantic Records' publicist Pete Senoff. As I was setting up, I noticed Mark departing with his girlfriend. It bothered me that he didn't stick around for the camaraderie, and that he didn't say goodbye. It was a fun night.

Here's our summer set list:

> "I Can't Explain" (The Who)
> "You Really Got Me" (The Kinks)
> "Love Potion Number Nine" (our heavy arrangement of
> The Searchers' hit)
> "Nose Job" (first Winos' single)
> "Just Like Me" (Paul Revere & the Raiders)

"Glad All Over" (The Dave Clark Five)
"Do Wah Diddy Diddy" (Manfred Mann)
"The Last Time" (The Rolling Stones)
"Train Kept A-Rollin'" (The Yardbirds)
"Down the Road Apiece" (The Rolling Stones)
"Communication Breakdown" (Led Zeppelin)
"Street Baby" (second Winos' single)

On July 23, Alice Cooper played the Hollywood Bowl. Theatrically, it was the most amazing show I've ever seen. DJ Wolfman Jack came out to introduce the evening, riding on a camel, surrounded by a harem of six dancing girls. Doves were set free when the band hit the stage. During "Gutter Cat vs. the Jets"—a song that started out like The Stones, then transitioned into the Jets' song from *West Side Story*—the group chased each other on stage as though they were in a gang fight. It concluded when Alice was hung from the gallows, an effective stage piece that debuted on the previous year's *Killer* album tour. To show he was OK, Alice reemerged in white top hat and tails. The show ended with fireworks, bellowing smoke, floating bubbles, and what appeared to be confetti dropped from a helicopter, but were girls' paper panties like the ones packaged with the album. Because of the band's lackluster performance and the many negligible tunes from their new *School's Out* album—which wasn't as good as their previous two LPs—the show was more entertaining than musically engrossing. The *School's Out* album jacket is one of the best I've seen. It unfolds into an old-time school desk with initials of the band members carved into the wood. The vinyl record is wrapped in a pair of pink-paper, girl's panties. Truly inspired!

I discovered a sleepy record store on Market Street in Inglewood. Inglewood Music had an impressive stock of 45s, including years-old flops still in the bins. I bought singles I'd only read about (and hadn't heard): "Call My Name," "Don't Start Crying Now" (Them), and "She's

Coming Home" (The Zombies) among them. As I thought the owner would recognize me as a regular customer, I asked him for a job. I imagined it would be fun to work in a record store, at least until I could secure a record label position. The store never seemed to be busy, so I wasn't surprised when he turned me down.

On the turntable: Cheech and Chong's *Big Bambu*, The Strawbs' *Grave New World*, Mark Volman & Howard Kaylan's *Phlorescent Leech & Eddie*, Simon & Garfunkel's *Greatest Hits*, Stories, Spring.

AUGUST

THE NEW ISSUE OF *Phonograph Record Magazine* came out. Among the photos on the inside cover was one of me visiting with Procol Harum backstage at the previous month's concert.

Bob Emmer and I had become friends, even though he'd not fulfilled his promise to buy me a new pair of socks. We went to Ledbetter's on Westwood Boulevard a few times. Originally a folk music club, it had turned into a pickup bar with a pool table and cheap pitchers of beer. Contemporary, up-tempo music blared: Santana, Buddy Miles, Creedence, etc. Once we met beforehand at Bob's apartment. He had a waterbed.

August turned out to be a good month for music. I went with Bill Pique and his friends to see The Allman Brothers at the Hollywood Bowl (August 6). I'd first seen the group in January 1970 at the Whisky. There wasn't much of a buzz on them—the club was half-filled—but I was riveted by Duane Allman's guitar proficiency. At the Bowl they performed well, but suffered from Duane's absence. He'd died in a motorcycle accident the previous October.

Guitarist Peter Banks left Yes to form Flash, which sounded like a rocked-up version of his former group at their Whisky debut

(August 16). The Guess Who (August 2) and The Kinks (August 29) turned in good shows at the Santa Monica Civic.

The Faces played a sloppy set at the Hollywood Bowl (August 25), owing, no doubt, to the onstage bar setup which included a bartender who dispensed drinks to the band throughout. I found out later that keyboardist Ian McLagan had filled the white carnation he was wearing as part of his tuxedo ensemble with cocaine to sniff during the evening. The group's pacing was off and the performance was merely routine, but the evening was a lot of fun. A young woman threw one of her high-heel pumps onto the stage. Rod Stewart retrieved it, and it looked like he was going to throw it back. He then sauntered over to the bar and had the bartender fill the shoe with Blue Nun. He held the shoe aloft in a toast and the crowd cheered. He then drank the wine and heaved the shoe back into the crowd, to riotous applause. During the encore, he kicked soccer balls into the audience.

The Winos performed at this year's Behemoth Festival (August 4). The highlight for me was seeing Jerry Mathers (Beaver from the *Leave It to Beaver* TV show of the fifties and sixties) dancing during our set. Jerry's younger, attractive sister, Suzanne, was Heather's roommate. Shelly Heber had us back, on the next night, but to fewer people.

At one of our recent outings for crepes, I asked Paul about the possibility of Columbia signing the band. He shrugged it off, saying that Columbia was interested only in bands like Santana and Chicago. At the time, few clubs would have considered booking a band like ours. The Whisky and Troubadour, for example, favored acts signed to record companies, requiring the label to subsidize the box office by purchasing tickets for executives, writers, radio programmers, and store buyers.

It was obvious that the 1960s-inspired style of The Winos was out of favor. Look at a then-current Top 10 in *Billboard*: (1) "Song Sung Blue" by Neil Diamond; (2) "Candy Man" by Sammy Davis Jr.; (3) "Outa-Space" by Billy Preston; (4) "Lean On Me" by Bill Withers; (5)

"Too Late to Turn Back Now" by Cornelius Brothers & Sister Rose; (6) "Troglodyte (Cave Man)" by Jimmy Castor Bunch; (7) "Nice to Be With You" by Gallery; (8) "Rocket Man" by Elton John; (9) "I Need You" by America; (10) "Daddy, Don't You Walk So Fast" by Wayne Newton. How many of these would you say are rock records?

For me, I think it was taking the fantasy of gesturing in front of the mirror in imitation of my favorite rockers to the next step. Even though I knew my limitations as a singer, I failed to consider that I could improve by paying for singing lessons. I don't think any of us seriously thought we could make it. By the same token, I think we had potential. We had our own, identifiable sound, and the promising songs Mark and I were writing, but nobody recognized it because our British Invasion–inspired sound was out of time.

Now that I'd graduated, I wanted to work for one of the major labels, preferably CBS Records. Among the areas with which I was familiar, I didn't think I would be good in sales or in radio promotion. The department I dealt with mostly was publicity. Publicists, by their nature, were friendly with big smiles. When I visited their offices, they made me feel welcome, would always have time for a chat, and gave me copies of their new releases.

Considering they had the same job in the same business, they were not from the same cookie-cutter. The ones I dealt with were as disparate as characters in an Agatha Christie book, like *Murder On the Orient Express*: Judy Paynter (Columbia), from Texas, looked like an ex–beauty queen; Sharon Lawrence (Rogers & Cowan), once a good friend of Jimi Hendrix, had a pasty face and wore tent-like dresses that made her look like a dowager; Andy Meyer (college program head at A&M) affected a rumpled college professor look, complete with smoking pipe; Bob Garcia (A&M), short-haired Latino on the outside, hip on the inside; Judy Sims (Warner Brothers) cherubic ex-teen magazine writer and ex-school teacher; Pete Senoff (Atlantic), bodybuilder; Grelun Landon, (RCA) older, country fan. United

Artists' Michelle Straubing was the only one who dressed in a rock fashion, but with her shag hairstyle, hot pants, and laced-up boots, she looked more like a groupie. I liked them all.

I wanted to work in publicity. I knew this department best, and I was familiar with most of the music writers. As I visited the publicists on a regular basis, I felt like they were my friends, but none helped me get a job.

The other area I thought I could do well in was A&R, which was an abbreviation for artists and repertoire. In previous decades, an A&R man would sign talent, find them songs, hire a producer, and book the sessions. Though, with artists writing their own material, and with many producers operating independently, their duties diminished. I felt I could evaluate talent—and relate to it—and recognize good material. Columbia's Allan Rinde was the first A&R man I got to know. He was in favor at his label because he had signed Ten Years After, whose debut album for Columbia was a big seller.

Paul thought it would be a good idea if I went to New York to show the people who were head of the college department how much I wanted a full-time job. Frank Shargo, whom I had known in LA, gave me a brief tour. Although there was no job opening, he did ask me if I would be willing to relocate to New York. I told him I wouldn't. During the tour I ran into Sandy Pearlman, the comanager and coproducer of Blue Oyster Cult, who were signed to Columbia. Sandy was happy to see me and invited me to visit.

Junior high had been three years, high school three, and college another four. During my last year at UCLA, I had been restless. I felt it was time for me to make my way in the world. I couldn't relate to those underclassmen who delayed graduating until they had completed a fifth year. I was primed to get a job in the music business: I'd done a stellar job for CBS, I was involved in putting on concerts at UCLA, and I was writing for the *Daily Bruin, Rolling Stone,* and the rock magazines.

Nobody saw the potential I thought I had. I enjoyed my summer, but it was time to focus on getting a job. I checked the UCLA placement bungalow, but got no leads. I went to the Brown employment agency on Wilshire and La Brea because they didn't charge a fee. A line on the form asked for my ideal job. For clarification, I asked my counselor, who told me to state my ideal job regardless of how feasible it would be. I wrote in "Record Company President." He sent me on two job interviews, both to be a financial loan officer. At the second company, the man who interviewed me spoke for both of us when he questioned why they had sent me. I read through the *LA Times* classified section, and the best I could come up with was training to be a night manager at a Jack-in-the-Box fast food restaurant. I thought I would be unhappy in such a job.

When I dropped off my review of the new T. Rex album to the *Daily Bruin*, I picked up a letter that had been mailed to me from Peter Noone in England. He thanked me for the article I had written earlier in the year on his group Herman's Hermits, and suggested meeting when he next came to Los Angeles. I hadn't previously received a written response from any of the subjects I had covered, so getting this letter from one of my rock heroes provided a boost to my flagging spirits.

On the turntable: Rod Stewart's *Never A Dull Moment*, T. Rex's *Slider*, National Lampoon's *Radio Dinner*.

HERMAN'S HERMITS

N EXT TO THE BEATLES, I bought more 45s by Herman's Hermits than by any other artist. I liked their first record, "I'm Into Something Good," and their second, the more vibrant "Can't You Hear My Heartbeat," even better. Lead singer Peter Noone exuded a boyish charm that was easy for me to identify with because he was two-and-a-half years older than me, much closer in age than the other performers of the era.

One function of the arts—music, books, art—is to provide an escape from the drudgery and monotony of daily life. Rock 'n' roll provided such an escape in its first ten years. By the mid-sixties, the influences of the blues and the protest movement introduced heavier concerns. Consider these three hits, all on the charts in the summer of 1965: The Rolling Stones' "(I Can't Get No) Satisfaction," The Animals' "We Gotta Get Out of This Place," and Herman's Hermits' "I'm Henry VIII, I Am." The first is a frustrated complaint and the second an expression of despair. The third may be silly, but it's fun. It's a record that will bring a smile to your face and lift your spirits. Herman's Hermits' hits were well crafted and always delivered artistically. I liked them. They made me feel good.

As the senior music writer at the UCLA *Daily Bruin* I could write about (mostly) whatever I wanted to, and for an issue in January 1972 I composed a lengthy appreciation of the band. Many months later I was thrilled to receive a letter in the mail from Peter, thanking me, and suggesting we meet when he was in LA next year.

Richard Nader, a promoter who had staged successful oldies shows in New York, had an ambitious plan for a "British Invasion Revisited" tour. Herman's Hermits (four of the five original guys) headlined over The Searchers (three of the four originals) and these familiar lead singers fronting non-original groups: Gerry Marsden and The Pacemakers, Billy J. Kramer with the Dakotas, Wayne Fontana and the Mindbenders. I wrangled an assignment from *Rolling Stone* to write the story. The show did well in New York and in other cities, but advance ticket sales in Los Angeles and San Francisco were poor, so those shows were cancelled. By mid-July the tour arrived in LA anyway, to tape a *Midnight Special* TV show. As much as I was disappointed that The Forum date had been cancelled, I was at least able to attend the taping and see highlights of the show.

The day before, I met Peter and his wife, Mireille, in the coffee shop at the Beverly Wilshire Hotel. We had an easy rapport, and I conducted an interview with Peter in their room upstairs. He was scintillating, funny, and a delightful storyteller. It was a revelation hearing about the early years of the band and how they were transformed by success. He invited me to visit him when I was in London in the fall. It was the beginning of a lasting friendship.

Peter grew up in Davyhulme, a district of Manchester, in a musical family. He loved rock 'n' roll and was an avid record buyer and listener of the American Forces Network. He was attracted to humor and dialects. "I became an altar boy and learned to sing in Latin," he said, "making up most of the words and mimicking the Irish priests who spoke with a Dún Laoghaire accent." He studied acting and music at the Manchester School of Music, and at thirteen was plucked therefrom to act in a TV show. Peter became a minor TV celebrity when cast as Stanley Fairclough, the son of a popular character on *Coronation Street*.

"After my character was shipped off to Australia, no work came in for two years," Peter said, "so I had odd jobs: I played records at parties, I had a window-cleaning business, I'd sell programs at Old Trafford during Manchester United football games, and on Saturday nights I'd sell newspapers." (Throughout this chapter, unattributed quotes are Peter's.)

At a youth club, Peter was asked to sing with a group whose regular vocalist had failed to show. They liked him better than the other guy, and he joined the group, which included Karl Green on guitar. "I bought a silver lamé suit that didn't fit. It was advertised in the paper by a singer who wasn't making it. It cost me about twelve dollars. I thought, 'Great! I'm gonna be a rock 'n' roll star!' We did 'Be-Bop-A-Lula' by Gene Vincent and 'Well I Ask You' by Eden Kane. I tried to be a tough rocker and hated it because it wasn't me. I was fifteen at the time and I wasn't turning anyone on.

"There was another band around that was doing comedy impressions, and they were going down incredibly well. I thought, 'Great, let's be like them.' We did Buddy Holly songs with the 'a-ho-hoes.' I thought we did really well. I got rid of that suit and got a red one. I was buying loads of records at the time. I wanted to be a disc jockey more than a singer. So, I had access to a lot of music. We did Bobby Rydell's 'I'll Never Dance Again,' and musically were supplying a sound that was different from the other bands that were mostly into Chuck Berry and R&B.

"Between numbers we used to tune up for five minutes, and while at first I was self-conscious, I found that I could talk to the people and tell jokes effectively. Like, we played Manchester and learned all the new jokes there, and then when we played in our home of Bolton, no one knew any of the jokes."

Sometime later, the other guitarist left and Keith Hopwood replaced him. The group was big on Buddy Holly and named themselves Pete Novac (after Peter's favorite actress, blonde bombshell Kim Novack) and the Heartbeats (after Holly's song "Heartbeat"). "Sometimes we'd open the show with one of the members saying,

'I'm sorry ladies and gentlemen, Pete Novac can't make it tonight.' They'd all cheer because they didn't like me. 'But, fortunately, we have the biggest star around, here's Millie!' And I'd come out in a dress with balloons for the boobs, and I sang 'My Boy Lollipop' [a hit by Millie Small]. The people peed in their pants. Al Rigley, the bass player, popped the balloons at the end of the number. There were no fag overtones. I never realized until I was twenty-three that people must've thought I was bent."

Peter wasn't visually impaired, but wore black, plastic-framed glasses to approximate Holly's look. While rehearsing a Buddy Holly number at a local pub, the publican asked Peter why he was wearing those glasses. When he replied, the publican laughed, telling him he looked more like "Herman" (actually Sherman) on the "Mr. Peabody" cartoon from *The Bullwinkle Show*. His mates made fun of this new name, which led to the band renaming itself Herman & The Hermits. The band even wore hermit-like costumes made out of potato sacks— for one performance before they were abandoned. Remarkably, in February 1964 this early lineup was filmed for the regional TV show *Scene at 6:30* rendering "Fortune Teller" at Liverpool's Cavern.

"All the groups that were making it had Jewish managers, like The Beatles, so that's what we figured we needed. We were all Protestants and Catholics. Get a Jewish manager and win the world! We thought Helen Shapiro had a hit, not because she was particularly talented, but because she was Jewish. It was an incredible mentality." Harvey Lisberg and Charlie Silverman, appropriately, became the group's managers.

The band worked almost every night, but they hadn't interested a record company. EMI label manager Derek Everett (who later signed them to EMI's Columbia Records) suggested that Harvey Lisberg try to interest budding producer Mickie Most. The Hermits felt good about Most because in October 1963, at the Manchester Odeon, they had seen him on a bill with The Everly Brothers and The Rolling

Stones and thought he was a good performer. Peter noticed that few people seemed to like The Stones.

From a picture postcard of the group, Mickie thought Peter Noone could appeal to the American market as he resembled a young John F. Kennedy. He was also intrigued with his name because he thought it was pronounced "Peter No One."

"There was an R&B scene, which we were into as well. Manfred Mann had Paul Jones as a singer and he was cool and sexy. I wasn't, but I used to look like him, so I'd send him up perfectly. They had a B-side, 'Without You,' a Bo Diddley thing that I used to fumble on the harmonica, and I never did get it to my mouth. On ballads, like 'The End of the World,' I would camp it up with an exaggerated monologue in the middle, like doing Shakespeare.

"Mickie thought this was the most incredible act he'd ever seen. Mickie took us into the studio but we failed the audition. We were having success so we didn't notice it, but we were unrecordable. He offered to sign only me, but I looked upon myself as the leader of the band and wasn't interested. He wanted me to kick two guys out of the band, which occurred, typically enough, in a Chinese restaurant. They took it great and I took it bad."

Lisberg and Silverman auditioned a local trio, The Wailers, who impressed them with a vibrant rendition of "Hava Nagila." Guitarist Derek "Lek" Leckenby and drummer Barry Whitwam were game, but the bassist's father wouldn't permit him to go professional. As Lek was a better guitarist than Karl Green, Karl agreed to switch to bass. With this new lineup in place, April 1, 1964, the name was shortened to Herman's Hermits.

Derek Everett suggested Mickie consider "I'm Into Somethin' Good," a Goffin-King song, for The Hermits' debut. A record had been released in April in the US by Earl-Jean of New York girl group , but it struggled to get airplay. The Hermits learned the song and on July 26 returned to London to make a recording—like most of The

Hermits' subsequent records—at Kingsway Recording, which was located above a Midland Bank branch.

"Mickie Most didn't like the record and didn't want to release it. We were heartbroken. I knew it was good. We told all our fans and our mums that we were gonna have a record out, and then he wouldn't release it. We drove back to Manchester and were gonna break up the group, 'It's not worth it. We're not getting anywhere.' Fortunately, he took it home and played it for his wife and she said that it was the best record she'd ever heard. 'Okay, I'll release it, but I won't spend any money on it,' Mickie said. We called every record store and ordered three, which is illegal. We told our mums to tell the people they worked with to order it. Nothing happened for a week. Then, out of the blue, we did a *Ready Steady Go!* TV show on a Friday night. On Saturday it sold forty thousand and it was number one in three weeks."

The key to understanding Herman's Hermits' appeal and popularity was how naturally they projected their own identity, that of cute, fresh-faced schoolboys. Their newly acquired matching suits looked like school uniforms without the crests. Peter and his mates were able to attract younger kids. "I'm Into Something Good" shares a similar innocence with The Beatles' "I Want to Hold Your Hand." Other Hermits' songs, like "Mrs. Brown, You've Got a Lovely Daughter," fit right in. And a song about being in school, a cover of "Wonderful World" (recorded as a tribute to the recently departed Sam Cooke) was more convincingly rendered by seventeen-year-old Peter than twenty-eight-year-old Cooke.

The Beatles ranged in age from twenty-one to twenty-four. Freddie Garrity of The Dreamers was twenty-three and Gerry Marsden of The Pacemakers was nearly twenty-two. Both singers were similar to Peter, with big personalities and excellent voices. So The Hermits—Peter was sixteen, Karl and Keith seventeen, Barry eighteen, Lek twenty-one— looked the part. Other artists forged identities far removed from who they were. For example, The Animals' Eric Burdon, a budding graphic artist and film buff, cast himself as a black American blues singer.

Peter was cute, a good singer, but he wasn't cool. At times he acted like a goofy kid, and his smile revealed the retention of a baby tooth partially pushed out by a permanent one. His immaturity made it easy for the group's young fans to relate to him. He was just like them. "I didn't know what I was doing. My stage persona was a shy little boy, which is basically what I was." As he developed, he became more polished, more confident, and handsome. As a band The Hermits were certainly competent, looked cute, and their gently sung harmonies were spot on.

"I was an audio freak as a kid. I was trying to record directly into my Telefunken tape recorder from the television speaker when a play, *The Lads*, with Tom Courtenay, came on. Throughout they kept playing a new song, 'Mrs. Brown, You've Got a Lovely Daughter.' I listened to that tape and thought, 'Boy, that's a real fun song.' I was into twenties and thirties English music hall songs because of the sexual innuendo, and it sounded like one of those. Live, we played it with an introduction: 'My girlfriend's just given me the elbow, and I've just been 'round to her mother's house...' We set up each song and made them comical, because if the people danced and didn't watch you, you'd lose the contract. The people could just as easily dance to records. I was actually a window cleaner during the day, and we played 'When I'm Cleaning Windows' [George Formby, from 1936]. We'd make up our own lyrics. The humor was raw, very basic. After the song I'd give out my phone number: 'I go for six shillings and am the best window cleaner around.'

"'Mrs. Brown' worked especially well for non–rock 'n' roll gigs, like weddings and bar mitzvahs. Older people would hear it and uncover their ears and think, 'Oh, great, there's a song we can deal with.' We would change the name to the host's, like 'Mrs. Silverman, You've Got a Lovely Daughter.'" At times in the early days when The

Hermits performed it, Peter dressed up like a schoolboy, with cap and satchel.

"Mickie said that we had one day to record an album to capitalize on the hit single. Our first album was essentially our stage act, but straight, without any of the set-ups. We had eleven songs and we needed a twelfth. Mickie was one hundred percent against recording 'Mrs. Brown.' It was the only other song we could do. We couldn't perform 'Without You' because it was already a hit by Manfred Mann. We couldn't do 'Mashed Potato Time' as it was entirely a visual number that didn't sound all that good. So, we recorded 'Mrs. Brown' in two takes, complete with the bass out of tune. Part of the appeal of the song is the uncommon banjo sound, which was played by Keith Hopwood on a Gretsch Country Gentleman guitar that had a damper on it. 'Don't worry,' Mickie said. 'We'll hide it on side two.'"

The Americans at MGM knew what they were doing. When they released The Hermits' first album, *Introducing Herman's Hermits*, in February 1965—two months after "I'm Into Something Good" peaked at thirteen on *Billboard* magazine's Hot 100—instead of burying "Mrs. Brown," they placed it second in the running order. DJs looking to play more Hermits chose this track. MGM wanted to release it as a single, but neither the band nor Mickie wanted to, relenting only when MGM guaranteed advance sales of 600,000. "We thought it would ruin our image," said Peter. The single entered *Billboard* at number twelve, the highest chart debut in the first seventy-five years of the magazine's rankings. It was soon number one. Many months later when The Hermits' debut album was released in the UK, the song was programmed last.

Interestingly enough, when John Tobler and Stuart Grundy interviewed Mickie Most for a BBC radio series on record producers in 1981, Mickie told them it was the worst record he had produced, and claimed he couldn't even remember the recording session.

Most of the British bands tried to play authentic American rock 'n' roll, which meant disguising their accents. Paul McCartney approximated Little Richard on "Long Tall Sally," and on their harmonies The Beatles sounded like The Everly Brothers. Even R&B-styled combos like The Rolling Stones, The Animals, and Manfred Mann displayed this dedication. Could anybody really tell the difference between Ray Charles and The Spencer Davis Group's Stevie Winwood?

With the surprise success of "Mrs. Brown," the group saw an advantage to playing up their Englishness. Look at their names. Aside from Karl Green, you'd never find these in a high school yearbook: Lek Leckenby, Barry Whitwam, Keith Hopwood. Peter took endless amusement in rattling off "Peter Blair Denis Bernard Noone" when interviewed. Decades later, I've never met anybody else with those surnames, except for Peter's immediate family.

THE FIRST BLOW TO The Hermits' rising self-esteem came in January 1965 when Mickie Most elected to use studio musicians for their next planned single, a cover of The Rays' 1957 hit "Silhouettes." Similar to most of the chart-riding English acts of that time, The Hermits were covering 1950s hits like "Sea Cruise," "Kansas City," and "The End of the World." The group played it safe, like most of the other artists, by copying the original records almost intact. "If we were told to learn 'Silhouettes,' we would've copied The Rays' version, which I liked." Mickie had something else in mind, an up-tempo, original arrangement.

"We were in the wrong world. We were a performing act, and when we started having hits, we couldn't talk between numbers because of all the screaming, and we weren't the group we started as. When we tried to make records, we were lost. Our first LP and most of the second were, essentially, our live numbers without the set-ups.

Then we began to tour constantly and we didn't have time to work out new songs or record them." It took less time away from touring and other commitments, like TV and films, to have Peter come to the studio to record his lead vocals, and for Karl and Keith to sing the harmonies.

For "Silhouettes," the instrumental backing was provided by Vic Flick, guitar; Big Jim Sullivan, guitar; John Paul Jones, bass; Bobby Graham, drums. Flick had played the distinctive guitar melody on the original "James Bond Theme," which debuted in *Dr. No.*

I interviewed Mickie Most in 1972 for a feature in *Rolling Stone.* It was the first comprehensive interview he had given, and I found him open and candid. I asked him about using session players on Hermits' recordings: "I don't think they resented it. The Hermits could have certainly made the records, but making records is so competitive, I want to give it the best shot. If you have people in the band who are more talented than John Paul Jones or Jimmy Page [both later of Led Zeppelin] or the other studio musicians, let them play on their own instrumental backings. If you get the best people, it's much easier, and I don't think it's anything to do with the musicians in the band feeling hurt. I really didn't want to discuss it, because I was paying the bills."

Peter put it this way: "At first the band played, but after it was discovered that Barry the drummer had a problem with his timing, rather than replace him—he was a friend and a nice bloke—we substituted for him in the studio. When Karl Green faded, he was replaced on sessions by John Paul Jones, who was a genius and arranged a lot of our records. He even joined the band for a three-date German tour. The Hermits were afraid of him! The Hermits, in addition to the first two albums, played the backing tracks on 'Listen People,' 'A Must to Avoid,' 'Leaning on the Lamp Post,' the *Both Sides* album, and the songs they wrote."

This wasn't an issue for the fans as they didn't know. They saw a band performing on a TV show playing live or lip-synching, so why would they think otherwise? Only with the popularity of Cream in 1967 did music fans become more aware of the skills of individual musicians in a rock band context. Or as John Mendelsohn wrote many years later in referring to the US contingent of studio players known as The Wrecking Crew, "Am I alone in wishing I didn't know that so much music I loved was performed by persons in clueless haircuts and ghastly cardigan sweaters?" What mattered then, and matters now, is whether the record is any good.

"Mickie used The Hermits less and less. He and I discovered the process was faster, if not as much fun. We stupidly left The Hermits out of all the decisions, causing them to hate us and, I think, rightfully so. In the callousness of my youth [paraphrasing W. Somerset Maugham] I thought little of other people's feelings and destroyed my friendships in the name of super success, none of which I regret, sadly enough, because the recordings are of the moment, and I was in the moment and The Hermits weren't."

Herman's Hermits spent most of 1965 in America. Their first big American tour was in the spring as part of Dick Clark's Caravan of Stars. Joining them were Little Anthony and the Imperials, Freddie Cannon, Bobby Vee, Round Robin, Billy Stewart, Bobby Freeman, The Ikettes, The Hondells, The Detergents, Brenda Holloway, and Reparata and the Delrons. The tour stayed in hotels every other night, which meant sleeping on the upright seats in the tour bus, which was more like a school bus than one altered to provide comfort for the long distance travelers. Usually Peter would get on late, which meant that he ended up squeezing in next to the three-hundred-pound Billy Stewart or the three-hundred-pound Round Robin. Fortunately, he was skinny. Some of The Hermits tried to sleep on the luggage racks. When Billy and Round pulled real guns on each other—over a woman—The Hermits freaked out and were furnished with a station wagon and driver that followed the bus. Members of Bobby Vee's band introduced them to cherry bombs by throwing them out of the bus to explode in the path of the station wagon. The Hermits were hooked.

On August 7, they played a few dates on the West Coast, headlining a concert at the Pasadena Rose Bowl that drew thirty-four thousand people, the largest attendance until The Beatles drew fifty-five thousand at Shea Stadium a week later.

On August 15, The Hermits were wrapping up their American tour in Oahu when they heard that Elvis was on the island filming *Paradise Hawaiian Style*. Curious about the appeal these newly popular British groups were having, Elvis agreed to meet them. By the time arrangements were made, Lek, Keith, and Karl had already flown home, so on August 16, Peter, Barry, and Harvey Lisberg joined Elvis and his crew at the Hawaiian Polynesian Village. Elvis tossed off a few bars of "Henry VIII" for them. "He was making fun of me, but who cares?" said Peter "It was Elvis!" Peter asked Elvis, "How come you made it without long hair?" Elvis and his crew thought the Brits were goofy. Elvis met The Beatles ten days later.

As The Hermits visited with Elvis, "I'm Henry VIII, I Am" was at number one. Where did The Hermits find such an oddball song? Peter explained: "When my grandfather, Tommy Noone, got drunk he would get on the piano—I mean, literally, he would climb on top—and change from his Irish brogue to impersonating an Englishman, and he would sing 'Henry VIII.'" The song had been a music hall hit in 1910 for Harry Champion, who sang it in a Cockney accent. When "Winchester Cathedral" by The New Vaudeville Band became a hit in the fall of 1966, it ushered in a revival of 1920s music that had all manner of artists, including The Beatles and The Rolling Stones, joining in. It's hard not to think that Herman's Hermits primed the trend with "Henry VIII." New Vaudeville's mastermind Geoff Stephens also composed "There's a Kind of Hush," which first appeared on The New Vaudeville Band's debut album.

Herman's Hermits' popularity was so considerable in 1965 that among singles released that year they had six in the Top 10 to The Beatles' four. When the group returned home from Japan in February 1966, with (US) gold album awards for *The Best of Herman's Hermits*, the customs officials in Manchester demanded duty be paid on their "gold records," not realizing there was no value in the tinted metal plating.

When the Herman's Hermits/Animals summer tour hit Detroit on July 28, 1966, Peter visited Motown Records. On his way out, he ran into Stevie Wonder. "I was nonplussed that he knew my songs. He sang 'Mrs. Brown, You've Got a Lovely Daughter' with the most perfect impersonation of me I have ever heard. Being a quick-witted sort of chap, I told him that I was a huge fan of his work and that by an incredible quirk of circumstance, I had just purchased his latest album. He was duly impressed and signed it right there. Actually, the album was *The Moods of Marvin Gaye*, and he signed all over Marvin's face."

In 1966, Herman's Hermits made the US Top 10 with "A Must to Avoid," "Listen People," "Leaning on the Lamp Post," and "Dandy," and barely missed with "This Door Swings Both Ways." "Dandy" was written by The Kinks' Ray Davies about "a jovial person who's a womanizer," based on his brother Dave. Mickie Most recorded it with The Hermits after The Animals had passed.

Peter's favorite Herman's Hermits' record is "No Milk Today," which hit number seven in the UK and even made the Top 40 in America as the B-side of "There's a Kind of Hush." The song was composed by Graham Gouldman (also managed by Lisberg), who had previously hit the Top 10 with The Yardbirds ("For Your Love" and "Heart Full of Soul"), The Hollies ("Bus Stop"), and The Hermits ("Listen People"). His father, Hymie Gouldman, was a poet who occasionally chipped in with ideas or lyrics, uncredited. Hymie, visiting a friend, saw a note to the milkman on a doorstep and gave his son the idea for "No Milk Today." He even wrote the couplet, "The bottle stands forlorn, a symbol of the dawn." Graham fleshed out the song using a bridge he had written for an unfinished song intended for The Mindbenders. When The Hollies turned it down, he offered it to The Hermits. It became their biggest-selling record worldwide.

"I think it is Herman's Hermits' best recording and perfectly captures the moment and the feel of Manchester terraced houses and what was the end of a British era. John Paul Jones played two bass guitars (an upright and a Fender) on the track and also did a brilliant arrangement. I did the lead vocal and then Karl Green, Keith Hopwood, and I did the backgrounds."

Despite their clean image, The Hermits could be rambunctious and at times even destructive. This came to a head during a tour with The Who and the Blues Magoos. On the evening of August 23, 1967, at the Flint, Michigan, Holiday Inn, Keith Moon and Barry Whitwam celebrated their twenty-first birthdays with the touring party. (Keith turned twenty.) Keith initiated the mayhem when he started a food fight by flinging a piece from his five-tiered drum cake at a hotel manager who claimed the music was too loud. As it escalated, Keith slipped and broke his front tooth. In a 1972 *Rolling Stone* interview, Keith goes into much detail about how he, in an attempt to run away, jumped into a Lincoln Continental, put the car in the wrong gear, and backed into the swimming pool. Pete Townshend refers to the incident in his memoir *Who I Am*. It was such a great story it became part of Keith's oeuvre. In actuality, it never happened. Karl Green and John Entwistle accompanied Keith to an emergency dental clinic. Members of The Hermits sprayed cars in the parking lot with fire extinguishers that, by morning, had damaged the paint.

THE BAND CHEMISTRY WORKED well for two or three years before it began to unravel. There were a number of reasons. Initially it was exciting for these teens: traveling for the first time with numerous trips to America and other parts of the world, staying in hotels, filming TV shows and movies, with girls screaming at them, chasing them and pulling at their hair and clothing, and, in some cases, making themselves available for sex. But their intensive work schedule wasn't novel anymore, and they began to tire. The band members were more comfortable drinking alcohol than taking drugs, and this became a factor. Even though Peter described his behavior as having been a "brat" at times, he wasn't the only problem. Karl, who developed a drinking problem, antagonized Lek.

As a teenager trying to fit in, who are your role models? If the older rockers you hung out with drank, you drank. If they splurged on fancy cars, you did too, even if you couldn't properly drive. "I'd come straight from school into the world of big spenders," Peter remembers, "and I thought I should look the part." He bought a Jaguar, then a Cadillac, then a Chevrolet, then a Rolls-Royce. As a young driver, he crashed more than one.

As Peter was younger than everybody else on the scene, he "wanted to fit in and to be liked" and thought drinking would make him "more interesting." "We'd go to the Ad Lib club in London, and John Lennon would buy my drinks because he knew I was only sixteen and I wouldn't get drunk and try to beat someone up. It was a two-drink minimum and John said, 'You get two Cokes and I'll get two Bacardis [rum] and we'll mix them.' Because John drank Bacardi and Coke and smoked Larks, I did, too."

Wholesome-looking Peter developed a problem with alcohol. "I thought the more you drank, the more you were one of the boys. From seventeen until twenty—the big money days—I regularly drank a bottle of vodka a day." He attended an Alcoholics Anonymous meeting with his accountant father, also a heavy drinker. "I didn't think of myself as an alcoholic, but I had a job to do onstage, so I cut down."

Herman's Hermits considered themselves a band, yet the more articulate and personable Peter was the one who did most of the interviews with the media, the youngest band member asserting his position as leader. Peter wanted to stretch beyond being a pop singer. If he accepted an offer to act, as he did with *The Canterville Ghost* (an ABC TV play) and *Pinocchio* (an NBC TV movie), The Hermits couldn't work and he felt bad about that.

Peter also experienced an identity crisis of sorts. When he was a young teen, people called him "Stanley Fairclough," after his character on *Coronation Street*. With the success of the band, the media mostly referred to him as "Herman." For example, in 1965 the press reported that "Herman" had received an award from the British Clothing Federation for being one of the ten best-dressed men in the country. Who was "Peter Noone?"

Once they were kings of the hill. But then, in the fall of 1966, *The Monkees* debuted on TV, and The Monkees essentially replaced Herman's Hermits in the teen market. As Peter put it of his fellow Mancunian Davy Jones, "He does Herman better than Herman."

As rock music progressed, The Hermits were left in the dust by The Beatles, The Rolling Stones, The Who, The Yardbirds, and others. Much as they would have liked to have competed—and even pop singer Peter "brooded" about it—they were out of their element. And the band members never distinguished themselves as songwriters. "Because of the popularity of 'Mrs. Brown' and 'Henry VIII,' there was no way we could grow—even if we were capable—and when flower power and San Francisco and Jimi Hendrix came along, it just destroyed us." They tried, with Donovan's "Museum," an ill-guided attempt at psychedelia that misfired.

MGM Records had been considered a major label, but toward the end of the sixties it experienced financial difficulties, losing $18 million in 1969. Peter Asher, who had been an A&R executive with MGM that year, described it as "a fucked up, crooked, weird company." When Mickie Most offered his original productions (The Animals and Herman's Hermits) to American record companies, they all turned him down. Derek Everett was able to interest MGM because EMI distributed them in the UK. There was now less money for promotion and marketing. The tragedy is that the group was still making good records, but in America, its biggest market, after the summer of 1967, Herman's Hermits never again had a national Top 20 hit. In Britain they had eight, including four Top 10s. MGM was sold to PolyGram in 1972.

The group rebounded on the cabaret circuit of adult nightclubs. Peter was able to talk to the audience again, and he says The Hermits markedly improved as musicians. Still, where do you go from here when you're young and still want to express yourself? A split was inevitable. Peter wanted to do what he wanted, without the obligations to the band, and The Hermits wanted to develop their own sound.

"I didn't realize it at the time, but the others were resentful because I got so much attention. I was the one who was doing the interviews, and they wanted to be interviewed, but weren't invited. It came to a head when we played the Royal Variety Performance in 1970. Afterward, I was the one who met the Queen because not everybody in the show could. They went home and their mums told them how disappointed they were because they didn't meet the Queen."

Herman's Hermits broke up in 1971. Peter had a hit with "Oh You Pretty Thing" that David Bowie wrote and played piano on. Encouraged, he and Mickie next recorded Bowie's "Right On Mother," which flopped. Peter never had another hit.

When I spoke to Lek at *The Midnight Special* taping, he described the current Hermits (minus Noone and Hopwood) as playing country-rooted music "not unlike what Crosby, Stills, Nash, and Young were doing." The Hermits were signed to RCA in the UK. Two flop singles had been released, but not the album they had recorded.

Karl eventually left and established a ceramic tiling business. Keith had built a recording studio and provided the theme music for commercials and TV shows. Lek died of non-Hodgkin's lymphoma in 1994. Barry tours as "Herman's Hermits Starring Barry Whitwam." Peter and Mireille moved to Los Angeles in the fall of 1973. The following year I got to experience a proper Peter Noone show, first at Disneyland, and then at Knott's Berry Farm. I couldn't believe how good he was, incorporating the set-ups he had used in the days before screams made it impossible to be heard. And in his mid-twenties, his voice was stronger than it had been in his teens, most impressively on a cover of Frankie Laine's "Jezebel," a song The Hermits had recorded on the *There's a Kind of Hush All Over the World* album. It was an exhilarating show.

Throughout the seventies and eighties, Peter did TV, recorded a few singles for the French market, played dates, and acted in the theater. He was on Broadway and the touring company of *The Pirates of Penzance,* assuming the part of Frederic. When I saw the musical at London's Drury Lane Theatre in Covent Garden in 1983, the elderly gentleman sitting next to me remarked that he thought Peter was "the best Frederic" in the three productions he had seen, and that included Rex Smith in the original Broadway run.

I wish I'd been able to do for Herman's Hermits what I did for The Monkees at Rhino, revamping, restoring, and improving the group's catalogue. But ABKCO's Allen Klein had a policy of not licensing to other record companies so he could benefit from the increased profit if a consumer bought an ABKCO album. It didn't matter to him, as in this case and others, that he may have issued only a best-of collection, leaving the original albums unavailable.

Allen Klein was a shrewd businessman who early on represented Mickie's interests in the US and Canada. He produced *Mrs. Brown, You've Got a Lovely Daughter,* a mediocre movie, just like the band's previous *Hold On.* Later he also represented The Rolling Stones,

The Beatles, and other acts, cultivating a notorious reputation. In The Rutles parody of The Beatles in *All You Need Is Cash*, Klein is characterized by John Belushi as Ron Decline. When Mickie Most needed money to finance his new label, RAK, he sold his American ownership in Herman's Hermits and The Animals to ABKCO.

I did have an effect on Peter's professional life. I introduced him to the local new wave music scene. In October 1978 I took him to Chinatown, to Madame Wong's restaurant-turned-nightclub to see Gary Valentine and the Know. It reminded him of his youth, when The Hermits were just starting out, playing in clubs. He formed a group in that spirit, the Tremblers, and recorded an album for Epic.

I see Peter from time to time, and attend his concerts on occasion. His voice is remarkable and his band is capable and supportive. His show is very entertaining, showcasing much of the fun that is part of his musical personality. He very much values and cares about his fans, and I feel fortunate that I am one of them.

THE HOLLIES

THE STORY OF THE Hollies is a story of friendship. It started when five-year-old Harold Allan Clarke (hereinafter Allan) enrolled at Ordsall Primary School in Manchester, England. Allan Clarke: "The teacher asked, 'Who would like this young man to sit next to him?' Graham Nash raised his hand. There was an empty seat next to him. We got on naturally from then on. We started singing in school, and during the assemblies we stood out. We sang 'The Lord Is My Shepherd' in harmony."

Inspired by Lonnie Donegan, they sang and strummed guitars, billing themselves as the Two Teens—"in short pants and sparkly shirts." They joined a band that evolved into an early version of The Hollies in late 1962. "We were playing at the Oasis Club in Manchester on New Year's Eve," recalled Allan. "The manager asked what we were going to call ourselves. Holly was hung all around because of Christmas, so we said 'The Hollies.'" Drummer Bobby Elliott confirmed this account, and an illustration of a holly leaf accented the band's name on his bass drum head.

As the group was from Manchester, and only thirty-three miles from Liverpool, they appeared at the Cavern a lot, and developed a beat group sound (i.e. fast dance music) similar to that of The Beatles, The Searchers, and other Liverpool bands. Ron Richards, a one-time assistant to Beatles producer George Martin, saw them at the Cavern and signed them to record for Parlophone, the same EMI label as The Beatles.

On April 4, 1963, The Hollies entered the studio for the first time. Their repertoire was largely covers of American records, including their first two singles, which had been recorded by the Coasters. The group felt rushed during their early sessions. "Our first album was recorded in one day, the second in three days," Elliott recollected. "We were so naïve. The engineer would say, 'The echo machine turns off at half past ten' (so they could get to the pub before eleven). We believed him and rushed to get things done by then."

Among all the hit beat groups, The Hollies ranked near the bottom of the hipness scale, just above Freddie and The Dreamers and Billy J. Kramer with the Dakotas. The Hollies' two 1964 album covers showed Graham and Tony Hicks displaying pompadours when everybody else who tried to pass for hip looked like The Beatles.

Under Richards' guidance, in the UK The Hollies racked up eleven Top 30 hits—eight Top 10—before the lineup gelled in spring 1966. Allan Clarke was among the best of the beat group lead singers, as was Graham Nash of the harmony singers. Tony Hicks was an inventive rhythm guitarist who also provided a second harmony vocal. Bobby Elliott, a jazz fan, distinguished himself as one of the best of the beat group drummers. Bernie Calvert played bass and occasional keyboards. (Calvert's predecessor, Eric Haydock, introduced the six-string bass to rock 'n' roll.) All three instrumentalists had been members of Manchester group The Dolphins.

At a time when it seemed as though American teenage girls found any emaciated youth with an English accent appealing, The Hollies were added to a ten-day Easter show at the Paramount Theater in New York. Hosted by Soupy Sales and headlined by Little Richard, the April 1965 lineup included The Hullabaloos, The Detergents, Shirley Ellis, and Sandie Shaw. The Hollies played just two songs, five times a day. "Stay," a previous hit of theirs in England, was a number one for Maurice Williams & The Zodiacs in 1960 and a lesser hit by the Four Seasons in 1963. "Mickey's Monkey" had been a hit by The Miracles in

1963. Not many people were aware that Nash, a poor guitarist, played unplugged. "Our instrumental sound was best with only one guitar," said Allan. "But Graham could never just stand there and sing. He had to have his guitar to fall back on, like a prop."

It was the first time in America for The Hollies, and the first time each had his own hotel room. "I couldn't get over how the taps turned on in the bathroom and hearing the phone ring like it did in the American movies," Graham Nash wrote in his *Wild Tales* memoir. "And getting take-out food! There was no such thing in England, not even a hamburger stand."

Morris Levy, who promoted the show, hosted a dinner for them at the Roundtable. Even though they hadn't had a hit in America, he thought they were sure to break and wanted to make a deal for their publishing. The restaurant's décor was King Arthur and the Knights of the Roundtable, but that didn't stop Levy from booking a sensuous belly dancer. Despite Levy's charm, The Hollies were wary of his reputation and no deal was made. Nevertheless, their lust for the alluring dancer stimulated The Hollies to write their first hit, "Stop Stop Stop," which went Top 10 in eight countries. Tony created a Middle Eastern atmosphere on the very American banjo.

I first saw The Hollies on *Shindig!* in 1965, but I was more impressed by their appearance on *The Red Skelton Show* in February 1966. They performed "I'm Alive" and "Look Through Any Window"—in color—and I was hooked. These were two exciting records, dynamically recorded with strong lead vocals and soaring harmonies. Although both had been Top 10 hits in the UK, neither made the Top 30 in *Billboard*. To this day, they're among my favorite records.

The Everly Brothers were recording a new album in London in May, and liked The Hollies' songs so much they included eight of their original compositions. Early Clarke-Hicks-Nash credits were simplified on record labels as "L. Ransford," after Graham's deceased grandfather. It was a big deal for the whole group, who also sang backup. Allan and Graham had thought of themselves as bringing The Everly Brothers' sound to a rock combo. As eighteen-year-olds, they'd seen the Brothers in concert at Manchester's Free Trade Hall on April 22, 1960. Afterward, Graham and Allan—who had a cold—waited for hours in the rain until Phil and Don returned to the Midland Hotel. The brothers encouraged their musical ambitions and gave them autographs. Allan remembered having them sign a cigarette pack with a wet pencil.

As POP MUSIC EVOLVED, Graham Nash was right there in digging the new sounds. He expressed his enthusiasm to Keith Altham in an October 1966 issue of *New Musical Express*: "Pop music is moving forward at incredible speed. It's not just progressing, it's running full-tilt into tomorrow. I have never been so frightened, or excited, by the power which we have over young people." Citing The Beatles, The Rolling Stones, The Mamas and The Papas, The Lovin' Spoonful, The Beach Boys, Donovan's *Sunshine Superman*, and The Mothers of Invention's *Freak Out!*, he aspired "to make great albums" and "to make records that say something."

The Hollies finally broke through in America with two Top 10 hits in 1966. Graham Gouldman wrote "Bus Stop" after his father suggested that he write "a song about two people who meet at a bus stop and have an affair." His father even gave him the opening couplet. The Hollies' producer, Ron Richards, said that the group initially declined to record the song because "they thought it was a bit square." "Stop Stop Stop" followed.

In December, while supporting Herman's Hermits on a US tour, Graham Nash was filmed by CBS news for a TV documentary, *Inside Pop: The Rock Revolution* (which aired the following April), steamrolling Peter Noone with his vision of how rock can save the world. In a hotel room, Nash, sitting on one bed between songwriter

Graham Gouldman and Hermit Lek Leckenby, faces Peter Noone on the other, next to a wigless Bobby Elliott.

GRAHAM: "Pop singers get through to millions of people."

PETER: "What kind of people, kids or adults?"

GRAHAM: "They get through the kids who are going to become adults. I think pop musicians in today's generation are in a fantastic position. They can rule the world, man. Music is an expression of the younger generation. Paul Simon, John Sebastian, John Phillips, and especially Donovan, have got this great universal love, man. Today, because the kids are so tolerant and they really want to understand what people are trying to say, then they'll go with Donovan ninety-nine percent of the way. Because what he's trying to put over is best for everybody. What Donovan is trying to put over will stop wars dead."

PETER: "I believe that you're right about Donovan saying that love is a great thing. But ..."

GRAHAM [interrupting]: "Now we have the power, we have the tolerance, we can go in front of a television camera and we can go on the air and say with definition that Hitler was wrong, that Rockwell is wrong, that people who hate Negroes are wrong, right? And we can get up there and shout it to the world, Pete."

PETER: "I don't want to argue with you. I ..."

GRAHAM [interrupting]: "So, why don't we do more of it? That's what I'm saying. We can stop world wars before they've ever started."

PETER: "I disagree. I don't believe ..."

GRAHAM [interrupting]: "You know who starts world wars—people who are over forty. People are too old to realize that love rules the world."

Over the next eight months, "On a Carousel" and "Carrie-Anne," credited to Clarke-Hicks-Nash, were big hits on both sides of the Atlantic. Tony Hicks wrote the latter modeled on "Mr. Tambourine Man." Graham, quite taken with Marianne Faithfull, wrote the lyrics fantasizing about her. In Marianne Faithfull's autobiography she writes of first meeting The Hollies on tour (with other acts) in late 1964: "Graham Nash was my favorite. He was much more articulate and interesting than anyone else on the tour (but even then I was smart enough not to have sex with him). I'd have lunch with Graham and spend the night with Allan." Graham thought better than to use her name, so Tony's placeholder lyric "Hey, Mr. Man" became "Hey, Carrie-Anne." Allan contributed the bridge. Ron Richards suggested the novel steel drum for the instrumental break.

The group delved into the progressive, psychedelic sounds of the time. They got their feet wet with *Evolution*, a fine album recorded at Abbey Road while The Beatles were completing *Sgt. Pepper's*. Graham embraced psychedelia—he had even taken LSD—and this affected his relationship with the rest of the band, whom he dismissed as "a couple of beers and a game of darts with the boys." He was also "the only one who smoked dope in the band." Graham hung out with rock's elite at London's private clubs. Eric Burdon showed him a book on M. C. Escher when they were both on acid. He was captivated, and it proved to be the catalyst for Graham becoming interested in art, whereas he had formerly described himself as "a guy who never read a book... who never went to a museum."

During 1967's "Summer of Love," standards had shifted: The Beatles' "All You Need Is Love," Small Faces' "Itchycoo Park," and The Beach Boys' "Heroes and Villains" were all Top 10 in the UK. So, where did that leave The Hollies? Graham pushed them more in this direction for their next album, titled *Butterfly* in the UK and *Dear Eloise/King Midas in Reverse* in the US, released in November 1967. When "King Midas In Reverse" was issued as a single, few recognized it as Graham's plea for help as his marriage deteriorated. It was not the subject of hit records, and when it bombed commercially, it was a real blow. "We were knocked-out over it, but Ron Richards told us it wouldn't be a hit," Allan remembered.

The group thought they had made a good album, so they were crushed when it failed to make the British charts. Allan felt the band lost perspective: "It was the 'Flower Power' love-thy-neighbor period when everybody loved each other. Whatever you did was great, keep the good vibes going." In subsequent songwriting meetings, Graham felt as though The Hollies no longer trusted his commercial judgment. Allan confirmed, "We weren't turning onto his kind of music, which wasn't our kind of music."

In an effort to get back into the Top 10, Allan and Graham wrote a trifle about schoolboy romance. They titled it "Jennifer Eccles," after their wives: Allan's wife's first name and Graham's wife's maiden name. The girls even contributed to the lyrics, uncredited. It worked all too well, reaching number seven in the spring of 1968.

Graham, upon reflection, was bothered that it was a regression. It wasn't a song "about something," or one of the new songs he wrote that the band had rejected. The previous summer he and his wife had vacationed in Morocco. On the train trip from Casablanca to Marrakesh, he wrote an impressionistic song and titled it "Marrakesh Express." "The Hollies did 'Marrakesh Express' and 'Be Yourself,'" Allan revealed, "but they just didn't work as Hollies songs. We were thinking harmony all the time, and his new songs weren't suitable."

On February 14, 1968, The Hollies performed for free at the Whisky a Go-Go, the only time the group with Graham played in Los Angeles. It wasn't an advertised gig, just an impromptu showcase for friends and industry insiders. Afterward, Graham smoked marijuana with David Crosby and Stephen Stills in Stills' Bentley. At one point during their conversation, Stills said to Crosby, pointing at Graham, "Which one of us is going to steal him?" Graham refers to this moment as when he made up his mind to leave The Hollies, yet Stills was still in Buffalo Springfield—for a few more months—and there were no other plans afoot.

By the summer of 1968, The Hollies had been out of the US Top 30 for a year. "Our label executives on both sides of the Atlantic lost confidence in us," Bobby Elliott said. "They suggested we cover other writers." Manny Kellem, an executive for Epic Records in the US, suggested the band record an album of Bob Dylan's songs. It was an opportune idea. Both The Byrds and Manfred Mann had done well covering a number of Dylan's songs, with the latter's "The Mighty Quinn" a recent Top 10 record.

Graham was very much a part of the group during the initial recording of the Dylan covers album. But he thought the "Las Vegas" type of arrangements were "sacrilege." In July he took a vacation, back to Los Angeles' Laurel Canyon, where he would sing with Crosby and Stills for the first time. In early November, Crosby and Stills flew to London. Graham holed up in their Moscow Road flat for three weeks working on songs.

Allan Clarke: "A friend stopped me on the street and said, 'Did you know that Graham has a band together in the States?' I confronted Graham and he said, 'Yeah, I'm leaving.'" Graham confirmed his lack of tact: "I didn't have the balls to tell Allan or the other guys." On December 8, 1968, Graham flew to Los Angeles, leaving behind his home, his band, and his wife. Welcoming him was a California that he loved, a new band and support system, a new best friend in David Crosby, and a new love in Joni Mitchell.

Allan wasn't totally straight-laced—he believed in UFOs—but it was hard for him to relate to Graham's passion for the latest far-out music, and he didn't quite understand Graham when he pontificated about "the inner mind." They drifted apart, and it was a huge blow to Allan to lose his best friend. The Hollies also lost a spokesman who felt more comfortable talking to the press and engaging the audience during concerts. Terry Sylvester, who had been a member of Liverpool bands The Escorts and The Swinging Blue Jeans, was a perfect replacement. He could approximate Graham's tenor, and was a better guitarist. He rerecorded Graham's vocals on three of the Dylan tracks and finished the album. "I didn't even know what half the lyrics were about," Allan revealed.

Once again, the group's commercial instincts were right on the money. *Hollies Sing Dylan* (*Words and Music by Bob Dylan* in the US), released in May 1969, became the group's bestselling (non-hits) album in the UK. Recollections to the contrary, the album was well reviewed when it was released. John Mendelsohn writing in *Rolling Stone* referred to it as "a flying gas," while astutely realizing that it was "frequently insensitive to Dylan's material." Ken Barnes in *Phonograph Record Magazine*, Robert Christgau in the *Village Voice*, and I in the *Daily Bruin* all gave it, with similar reservations, good reviews.

The following month The Hollies recorded a song that Tony found at a publisher's office. Bobby Scott and Bob Russell wrote "He Ain't Heavy, He's My Brother" using a familiar phrase most associated with the slogan for Boys Town, a children's home. The record is a tour de force. Clarke's voice is magnificent, and the strings and harmonies tastefully complement the band's playing. Allan contributes the sensitive harmonica, and session man Reg Dwight (better known as Elton John) the piano. The record became The Hollies' biggest hit, a signature tune that rose to number three in the UK and returned the group to the Top 10 in America after a two-and-a-half-year absence. In 1988 The Hollies record was used in a Miller Lite beer commercial in Britain and reentered the Top 10, this time hitting number one for two weeks.

In fairness to The Hollies' collective judgment, none of the songs Graham played them became big hits. "Marrakesh Express," a favorite from *Crosby, Stills & Nash*, managed to get only to number seventeen in the UK and twenty-eight in the US when issued as a single.

WHEN IT CAME TIME for The Hollies to record their next album, Allan felt the band's demeanor had changed: "It wasn't about who had the best song, it was more like 'I have a new song and it's my turn.'" The band had gotten lazy, according to Terry Sylvester: "We'd copy the demos instead of working out more planned arrangements." Allan wrote "Long Cool Woman (In a Black Dress)" with Roger Cook (Cook's partner Roger Greenaway is also credited) in the style of Creedence Clearwater Revival. When The Hollies recorded it in July 1971, it wasn't earmarked to be a single. The song was sparingly produced by the group as their long-time producer Ron Richards was ill. There were no familiar Hollies' harmonies, and Allan even contributed the prominent rhythm guitar.

Seeing the success that Graham was having with Crosby, Stills & Nash, and imagining his share of the money from the millions of albums that they were selling, Allan was getting restless. He wanted some of that. As the group had rejected a number of his songs for the new album, titled *Distant Light*, he wanted to record a solo album.

Here's Bobby Elliott's take: "Because the LP didn't feature much in the way of strong harmonies, Allan took the spotlight. He was getting a big ego. People were taking him around, saying, 'Allan, you *are* The Hollies!' and he started to believe it. He saw Graham make his million and thought that if he went solo he'd make his as well. Although he might have stayed with the band, after he got his hit, he most assuredly would have left."

When The Hollies wouldn't let Allan record his solo album, he felt betrayed. "I really don't understand what transpired," he said.

"Graham Nash and I originally started The Hollies, and the others were subordinate to us." Allan left in October 1971. "I didn't want to leave, I had no idea if I would be successful, but I decided to take a chance. I titled the album *My Real Name Is 'arold* because I was stripping myself bare of the past."

Epic Records smelled a hit and released "Long Cool Woman" in May 1972. It became The Hollies' biggest record in America, hitting number two and going gold. Similarly, *Distant Light* became their biggest selling (non-hits) LP. The problem for The Hollies was that Allan was no longer in the band to sing their hit live. The problem for Allan was that he was immersed in recording his second solo album when his first hadn't sold well and hadn't yet been released in the States. With obvious disappointment, Allan said, "I was not in a position to tour America as part of The Hollies, or to get the recognition for writing and singing the hit." And, somewhat petulantly, he qualified it as, "It's not a Hollies song, it's my song."

When I met Allan the first time, in mid-September, "Long Cool Woman" was still in *Billboard*'s Top 10. "I'm a friendly person. I try to get along with everybody," he reasoned. "It's weird, but all my connections with The Hollies have been severed. It's as though they never existed, especially with 'Long Cool Woman' giving The Hollies a new lease on life in the States when it was done a year and a half ago. I said, 'You've gotta release that as a single.' They didn't initially because I was leaving."

The Hollies had been impressed with a Swedish band, Bamboo, they had toured with in Sweden. Tony even produced a few sides with them. They enticed the lead singer, Mikael Rickfors, to replace Clarke. Rickfors was an excellent singer, but Allan was a tenor and Mikael was more of a baritone and the revised sound deviated from that of The Hollies. "All through my career with The Hollies, I thought of retaining The Hollies sound because it was magic," Allan said. "I thought they should find a singer to imitate me."

Romany, The Hollies' album with Rickfors, released in September, had some good tracks, but with no hit single it didn't sell well. With two unsuccessful solo albums, Allan was motivated to return to the fold. He rejoined the band in July 1973. Rickfors went back to Sweden. In November The Hollies recorded a song that Roger Cook's secretary had recommended to Allan. "The Air That I Breathe," written by Albert Hammond and Mike Hazelwood, had been on Phil Everly's first solo album. The Hollies' most magnificent record, it was to be their last (newly recorded) big hit, charting in the Top 10 in the UK and US. They continued to issue albums throughout the seventies, recording the occasional track—like a cover of Bruce Springsteen's "Sandy"—that sounded like a hit to me. They even reconciled with Graham Nash, who rejoined the band for an album and tour in 1983, but by then the magic was long gone. In 2010 The Hollies were inducted into the Rock and Roll Hall of Fame.

I INTERVIEWED THE HOLLIES on November 21, 1972, for an article that *Rolling Stone* published the following January. I met them and their publicist, Toby Mamis, at the Beverly Comstock Hotel, just west of Beverly Hills. Although Tony Hicks, Terry Sylvester, and Bernie Calvert were all there and chipped in with comments, Bobby Elliott did most of the talking. I got to meet Mikael Rickfors the next night, when I joined the group at the E Club, Rodney Bingenheimer's first attempt at an English disco. The more I got to know Toby, the more I liked him. He was smart, knowledgeable in the music business, and we shared similar musical interests: the British Invasion and glam rock. Our friendship developed when Toby relocated to Los Angeles in June 1974. Although he doesn't live here anymore and I don't see him as much as I'd like to, he's still one of my best friends.

MANFRED MANN

BRIMMING WITH TALENT

CHAPTER ONE

IF I ASKED WHICH of the significant British Invasion bands you regarded as the most proficient musically, would you say The Beatles? The Rolling Stones? The Yardbirds? The Who? My answer: Manfred Mann, a band that should be in the Rock and Roll Hall of Fame. Known in America primarily for "Do Wah Diddy Diddy" and "The Mighty Quinn," and maybe for lesser hits "Pretty Flamingo" and "Sha La La," in England the group was big: thirteen Top 10 hits and three Top 10 albums.

Although lumped with other R&B and blues-influenced rock combos of the era, initially they were the odd men out: disheveled, bewildered 1950s jazz cats masquerading as rock stars and pulling it off because they were so good. Manfred, with his plastic-rimmed glasses, had the audacity to be the first rock star with a beard, a neatly trimmed, beatnik-like affair that recalled a 1950s hipster. The rest of the members looked like they'd just been awakened from a night sleeping on the floor. Manfred Mann weren't bad boys like The Rolling Stones, charismatic like The Beatles (except for singer Paul Jones), or flashy showmen like The Who. As a result, their renown has receded.

It all started with Manfred Lubowitz. He grew up in Johannesburg, South Africa, and was taught piano by an instructor from Julliard. At twenty he migrated to England because he was opposed to the South African government's apartheid (segregation) laws. Intent on working as a jazz musician, he felt he needed a pseudonym when writing for *Jazz News*, and adopted the surname of jazz drummer Shelly Manne, later dropping the "e." (He's listed this way in the September 26, 1962 issue of *Jazz News* as a tutor, right next to an ad for "The Rollin' Stones'" Saturday residency at the Ealing Club.)

With influences such as Charles Mingus and Ray Charles, Mann and multi-instrumentalist Mike Hugg formed the Mann-Hugg Blues Band in 1962. That ensemble evolved into Manfred Mann, the lineup solidifying around the time the group's third single was released in January 1964. Manfred switched from piano to organ to make up for recently departed horn players. The group also included Hugg, drums; Mike Vickers, guitar; Tom McGuinness—who looked just like Manfred, except for the beard—bass; Paul Jones, lead vocals, harmonica. They were less than two years apart in age.

Paul Jones (born Paul Pond) was, like others of the time, inspired by the blues and R&B: "When I was fifteen, I used to like Big Bill Broonzy and T-Bone Walker. R&B had the strongest beat I'd ever heard in my life, and I decided that was the style of music I wanted to be involved in. I picked up on Muddy Waters and Howlin' Wolf, who influenced my vocal delivery. I was also interested in The Exciters and The Miracles. It got to a point where all I wanted to do was sing the blues, and I neglected my studies and got kicked out of Oxford." Paul had studied for just over a year at Jesus College of the University of Oxford. Alumni included T. E. Lawrence and Prime Minister Harold Wilson.

Paul and Brian Jones made a tape with sidemen and presented it to Alexis Korner, hoping to play between Blues Incorporated's sets at the Ealing Jazz Club. The tape was "lousy," according to Paul, and they weren't accepted. Sometime later Brian asked Paul if he'd like to form a band with him and Keith Richards. Paul declined, saying,

"Nobody anywhere is gonna wanna listen to R&B." In 1963, Paul was the vocalist in a short-lived combo, The Roosters, whose guitarists were Eric Clapton and Tom McGuinness.

Back then the lead singer was a band's focal point. Musicianship and aesthetics were overshadowed by a sweet smile and glistening eyes. Onstage or off, Paul Jones was the consummate pop idol. He mugged while singing: smiling wide, rolling his eyes, pointing at girls in the audience. Handsome, with a strong jaw, he was photogenic. The effect of acne on his complexion only made him look rugged. Physically he looked like a male model: tall, thin legs, broad shoulders. His physical attributes notwithstanding, he may well have been the best lead vocalist on the scene, and he played excellent harmonica. He was effective at singing blues, with a gritty, urgent delivery, and could perform pop songs like a seasoned crooner.

The producers of the English pop music TV show *Ready Steady Go!* wanted an original theme to replace The Surfaris' "Wipe Out," and Manfred Mann got the commission. Jones, Hugg, and Mann delivered with "5-4-3-2-1," scoring a top five hit for the band from the exposure.

Unlike just about any rock group at that time, they included jazz covers in their repertoire: "Watermelon Man" (Herbie Hancock), "Sack O' Woe" (Cannonball Adderly), "Brother Jack" (Jack McDuff). Jazz elements were seamlessly incorporated into the band's rock songs. Take for example "I'm Your King Pin," a driving 1964 album track. Paul Jones sings and plays harmonica throughout. The instrumental breaks spotlight first Hugg's vibraphone, then Vickers' alto sax, and last Mann's piano. The group vocally answers Jones with the kind of call-and-response heard in jazz bands.

In addition to the members' fondness for blues and jazz, Mike Vickers was a student of classical music. It's a wonder, noting Vickers' and Mann's exposure to classical, that more of this form didn't creep into their music. Vickers' alto sax solos during the breaks were identifiable as jazz, as were his occasional flute solos. One would later hear echoes of his solo on "Without You" in the playing of Jethro Tull's Ian Anderson. As the group couldn't find a guitarist, Vickers supplied that too. Although he was adequate, this was the group's weakest point—his wind solos were more impressive. Overdubbing on the record, he performed sax duets with himself.

When I met Manfred and Mike Hugg in April 1970, when they were in Los Angeles appearing at the Whisky a Go-Go in their new band Chapter III, I was surprised that Manfred didn't consider the earlier lineup's musicianship exceptional. I thought they cohered well and their arrangements were incredibly good, better than anyone else's.

A good example is the band's summer 1964 single, "Do Wah Diddy Diddy," brought to them by producer John Burgess, who was also having hits with Peter and Gordon and Freddie and The Dreamers. Jeff Barry and Ellie Greenwich had written (with Phil Spector) "Da Doo Ron Ron," a big hit for The Crystals. They composed "Do Wah Diddy Diddy"—also nonsense words—angling for the next single, but Spector declined. The Exciters released it in January 1964 hoping for a follow-up to "Tell Him," their hit from a year previously, but it stiffed. The Exciters' was a typical girl group record. Manfred Mann's cover was much more thought-out, a dynamic recording structured with bursts and accented with tympani-like rolls on the drums. Paul's powerful lead vocals alternated with the band singing the catchy chorus in unison. The record topped the charts on both sides of the Atlantic.

In December 1964 the group toured the States for three weeks with Peter and Gordon and taped a *Shindig!* TV show. "We didn't enjoy the US tour and we made no money," Manfred said. Instead he decided that they should focus on the rest of the world, which probably limited their chart success in America. Manfred Mann became the first British rock band to perform behind the iron curtain, in Czechoslovakia.

Manfred, a pragmatist, concluded that the band had to release commercial singles to maintain its popularity as a live act. In his words, "It was jazz men trying to make a living." Bob Dylan has gone on record to say that he thought Manfred Mann was the best interpreter of his music. Manfred looked upon Dylan's songs as raw material for hit records, but the group's first cover had nothing to do with that ambition. Prior to rock groups covering Dylan being in vogue, the group, in January 1965, recorded a dramatic and effective "With God On Our Side," even though it was little more than a piano and vocal recital. Mann's approach to covering Dylan's songs necessitated cutting verses "in trying to make it work for us" rather than being faithful to the original song. Of course, most pop artists who covered the verbose Dylan did the same thing. In June, Mann and McGuinness were at their respective homes viewing Bob Dylan's live-in-the-studio BBC TV show. They were both impressed with "If You Gotta Go, Go Now"—Dylan singing accompanied only by his guitar—and had the band work up a full arrangement. Recorded three weeks after the TV show aired, Manfred Mann scored a number two hit in the UK.

Having seven big hits wasn't enough to prevent Mike Vickers from leaving in October 1965. Being in a pop group was a detour for him. He always wanted to compose and arrange for an orchestra. He later conducted the orchestra that accompanied The Beatles when they performed "All You Need Is Love" live on the *Our World* telecast, and he programmed the Moog synthesizer for them during the recording of *Abbey Road*. Stateside, the long-running *This Week in Baseball* used one of his pieces as its theme.

Rather than getting another guitarist, Tom McGuinness reverted to his natural instrument. In December Jack Bruce stepped in on bass, leaving John Mayall's Blues Breakers for more money in the Manfreds. Jack complemented the musicians well: he contributed cello on one song and brought to the band "Driva Man" by jazz percussionist

Max Roach. Because Mann missed the brass contribution from the band's earlier incarnation, he hired Henry Lowther on trumpet and Lyn Dobson on tenor sax, but they lasted only four months. Of this lineup Paul said, "I most enjoyed playing 'Black Betty,' an old Lead Belly number that featured Jack Bruce and me singing and blowing harmonicas together. It was a real rave-up, something like the early Yardbirds."

Away from the screaming girls in concert, Manfred noticed that his newfound stardom made people interested in what he had to say, seemingly for the first time. But fame also intruded in unexpected situations. Early one morning the band was returning home from a gig in the east of England when their car ploughed into a parked car. Most of the members weren't harmed. Paul had a broken collarbone and bleeding lip. Manfred had difficulty breathing and was in pain, with bruised ribs. Manfred remembers men racing over from a small hut where they had been eating: "What do I hear from these men as they rush over to assist? 'Is everyone alive?' or 'They seem to be OK but this one is unconscious.' Or perhaps 'Frank, call an ambulance, these guys need immediate help!' No, what I hear is 'Fucking hell, it's Manfred Mann, can I have an autograph?'"

In "Pretty Flamingo," built atypically for the group around a strummed acoustic guitar, Paul Jones' expansive vocal conveys the sunny mood in a fantasy of a beautiful, sexy woman walking down the street. It became their second number one in England; only twenty-nine in the States. (Bruce Springsteen performed it as part of his set during his 1975 tour.) It still wasn't enough to satisfy Paul: "The group's spirit was lifted for a time, but then it plunged. We all became disenchanted because the fire had gone out. That lineup existed from December 1965 to July 1966. When I left, the band transformed." It was the last song Paul recorded with the band.

As the lead singer and star, Paul Jones had basked in the glow of pop stardom. He was also interviewed as he was considered a pop intellectual: he had gone to Oxford, collected avant-garde poetry, married a novelist, and had worn a Campaign for Nuclear Disarmament badge. (When signing autographs, Paul wrote "CND" next to his name.) Despite the attention, he was upset because the band was named after someone else. It was a blow to his ego when fans approached him on the street thinking his name was Manfred. Paul finally left to star in a movie, Peter Watkins' futuristic drama *Privilege*. Of his time in the band, Paul told me that he enjoyed performing the blues and R&B songs, but not most of the singles. "Looking back, I liked the silly songs that were about the group," he said, "like '5-4-3-2-1' and 'Man in the Middle,' and also 'If You Gotta Go, Go Now.'"

In *Privilege*, Paul portrayed pop idol Steve Shorter, who achieved godlike popularity and then is manipulated by the establishment—politicians, religious leaders, corporations—to control Britain's youth. "I'd never done any acting and I never intended to," Paul said. "Somebody rang me up and asked me if I'd be interested in appearing in this Peter Watkins movie. I'd read in the papers how Eric Burdon was offered the part, and being vain, I wasn't going to take a small part in an Eric Burdon movie. It turned out that it was Eric's part I was offered, for no other reason than someone thought it would be great to have Jean Shrimpton for the female part, and Eric wouldn't look good next to her. They wanted somebody who was tall and thin for the male lead."

Paul, a fan of "way out movies," was familiar with Watkins' heavy docudramas. "It was great being offered a film of substance when everything one was offered before was sort of Robin Hood musicals with rock groups cast away on desert islands or sent to the moon, horrible stuff like that that Manfred and I used to laugh at when we were sent scripts to read. I enjoyed the part tremendously."

The film's opening scene has a tormented Shorter dragged onstage by handcuffed guards who beat him with nightsticks and then lock him in a cage. Girls scream hysterically as he sings "Free Me." The drama made a big impression on Alice Cooper, who was inspired to create theatrical set pieces for his group. Patti Smith was so moved she led off side two of her 1978 album *Easter* with her version of the song. The film was partially based on *Lonely Boy*, a revealing 1962 documentary short on pop singer Paul Anka. Watkins even recreated certain scenes for his movie. In Paul's estimation, the documentary format backfired: "I think I was pretty damn ordinary in the part, and I didn't feel that Steve Shorter could be identifiable with anybody. That's because of Watkins' quasi-documentary presentation. One identifies more with fictional situations. Steve Shorter was the product of many hours between Watkins and myself, discussing the extent to which teen idols are manipulated. Like, there were some who signed contracts stating that they wouldn't marry."

Paul summarized the message of the plodding picture: "I view the film as a noble failure, one that dealt with important questions. All his films are talking about the immediate future. The whole thing was that everyone should decide things for himself and not rely on others just because they may have certain educational qualifications. There's no politician in the world who knows more than you or I. He was saying 'never accept what politicians say.'"

Within months after filming, Paul scored two top five UK hits: "High Time" and "I've Been a Bad Bad Boy." The latter was from the movie. There was even a better record on the soundtrack album, "Privilege," the intended title song that wasn't included in the film.

Then it all fell apart. Given how briefly his solo stardom flared, it seemed almost as if Paul had ended up on the reverse of the Crossroads pact for abandoning the blues. *Privilege* bombed and over the next three years he had six flop records. Of special note is the talent behind the best of those, a cover of The Bee Gees' "And the Sun Will Shine": Peter Asher produced; Mike Vickers arranged; Paul

McCartney contributed drums; Jeff Beck, guitar; and Paul Samwell-Smith, bass.

Paul: "At that time, shortly after the movie, I was going for fame. I wanted to be the biggest thing. I didn't make it. I lost direction and sight of what made me successful, which was being raucous and simple." Paul cobbled together a living mostly by acting in films and plays. In 1979 he returned to his blues roots—with Tom McGuinness joining him—in The Blues Band. As of 1991, he and most of the members of Manfred Mann—but not Manfred—reformed and have revived the group's catalogue in concert. Billed as "The Manfreds," in 2015 they played over thirty dates in the UK and twelve in Australia. Paul's also been the host of an excellent BBC radio show dedicated to his first love, the blues.

CHAPTER TWO

FOR THE REST OF the band it was devastating when Paul left, even more so after their label signed him to a solo deal, casting them adrift. "We were so nervous about the whole success thing," recounted Mann. "Our big lead singer star of the sixties had left and everyone thought the band would fold. We were so worried about getting a new lead singer and some more hit singles and not failing and landing up delivering milk in the morning." The band replaced Paul with Mike d'Abo of A Band of Angels. Both acts were performing on the *A Whole Scene Going* TV show, and the Manfreds were impressed with d'Abo's singing and hired him away.

Jack Bruce also left, to form Cream with Eric Clapton and Ginger Baker. Klaus Voormann was recruited to replace him. A fine musician, Voormann was better known as The Beatles' Hamburg friend who designed the album jacket for *Revolver*. Years later this lineup was referred to as the second chapter of the band, or "chapter two." The group reestablished itself with "Just Like a Woman," their second UK Top 10 with a Bob Dylan composition. With Vickers, Bruce, and Jones gone, the blues, R&B, and jazz styles were largely absent in favor of pop rock.

The band wasn't thought of as progressive, yet Manfred was an earlier adopter of the Mellotron, an electronic instrument popularized by The Beatles and The Moody Blues. Manfred Mann's October 1966 single "Semi-Detached Suburban Mr. James," which barely missed the top spot in the UK, was the first hit to feature the Mellotron. In 1967 Mann and Hugg formed a company to compose soundtracks, produce other artists, and provide jingles for British European Airways (BEA), Hovis bread, and Dulux house paint, among others.

Because of their success with Dylan's songs, they got a copy of the unreleased *Basement Tapes* as the publishing demos were subsequently called, and thought "The Mighty Quinn (Quinn the Eskimo)" had potential. It was another fine arrangement from the band, characterized by Voormann's signature flute line and Hugg's resonant drum rolls. The record hit number one in England and returned the band to the US Top 10 in the spring of 1968.

The Mighty Quinn LP is the most indicative solid work of this lineup. Even with a new lead singer, the sound was still distinctly Manfred Mann. Although Manfred didn't consider chapter two a good live band, there were some positives. Mike Hugg had grown as a songwriter. (In 1965 he cowrote "You're a Better Man Than I," a much-lauded Yardbirds B-side.) One of the LP's songs, "Day Time Night-Time," was a top five hit for Keith Hampshire in Canada.

They had another handful of hits in England and then decided to dissolve. "I don't think the first two chapters had that much of a following—those who went out and bought every record," observed Mann. "People more or less just bought a song that they heard and liked. The first two chapters were aiming for success more for its own sake and were prepared to compromise in order to attain it. Each record as the years went by was just a step further away from what we originally wanted to do. By doing those records we got into rock. We were never into rock before. We picked up new influences and got into new things. After five years of making pop records, we ended up feeling part of that scene and not in any sense feeling part of the jazz scene."

Mike d'Abo had success as a songwriter. In the year Manfred Mann folded, he had a big hit with The Foundations' "Build Me Up Buttercup," which went gold on both sides of the Atlantic. That same year Rod Stewart recorded "Handbags and Gladrags" for his debut album. (The Stereophonics 2001 cover of the song went gold in the UK.) D'Abo acted in the theater, and later also composed music for TV commercials. Klaus Voormann became an in-demand session musician, with credits on albums by members of The Beatles, James Taylor, Carly Simon, and Lou Reed, among others. In 1982 he produced the debut album for German group Trio, resulting in the worldwide hit "Da Da Da" that broke through in America in 1997 when used in a Volkswagen commercial. In 1970 Tom McGuinness cofounded McGuinness-Flint, with a repertoire borrowed from the American South, similar to The Band, and had two more top five UK hits. In 1989 McGuinness coproduced and codirected a documentary on Jimi Hendrix for *The South Bank Show*. I thought it was excellent and gave him a call in England to discuss having him direct one for Rhino, but it never transpired.

CHAPTER THREE

MIKE HUGG, TOO, WAS disenchanted being in a pop band: "What we were doing before was almost like a day job, and to make those hit records was like going into the office every day and working hard." Hugg and Mann both missed performing live, performing the jazz that so energized them before they started having hits. Mere months after Manfred Mann dissolved, they attracted six musicians to their new ensemble and named it Manfred Mann Chapter III. The new direction, a drastic change from the previous two groups, emerged as a jazz-rock hybrid. With a horn section, the music reminded me of Charlie Mingus and Don Ellis. Hugg switched to piano and sang in a deliberate, hoarse manner similar to Dr. John. Mann and Hugg furnished their group with exquisite arrangements—mostly of Hugg's songs—resulting in a solid debut. "A 'B' Side," the flip to Manfred Mann's last hit "Ragamuffin Man," was reprised as "Traveling Lady."

It wasn't long before the brass started to take over and Mann realized that Chapter III was more Hugg's baby than his. The subsequent album, *Volume II*, pushed free form jazz, as rock receded. Subsequently, some of the brass was dropped and two girl singers were added, but Mann still wasn't happy and dissolved the project after two years.

CHAPTER FOUR

SOMETIME BEFORE THE RECORDING of that second album, though, Mann confessed his doubts to me: "We could do things that would likely make the group more successful. We could drop the brass and get a hip swinging guy up front to sing and play guitar—hey, that's not a bad idea!" We both chuckled. Little did either of us know at the time, but that's precisely what Manfred did. In 1971 Mann collected vocalist/guitarist/hip swinger Mick Rodgers, bassist Colin Pattenden, and drummer Chris Slade in a progressive rock band named Manfred Mann's Earth Band. I thought the group sounded like Free, a band

Manfred liked from the beginning. The group's first single, "Please Mrs. Henry," another Dylan song, sounded similar to "All Right Now." It took time, but Manfred hit pay dirt again. The band scored three Top 10s in their familiar UK turf, but Manfred had his biggest success yet in America. A cover of Bruce Springsteen's "Spirit in the Night" hit number one in 1977, and the accompanying album, *The Roaring Silence*, became his first—and so far only—gold album.

Manfred claimed that this band was his best live group. He still tours with a version of the Earth Band, mostly in Europe. Manfred's expressed desire of decades past still rings true: "I want to get out on stage and play, play good rock music so that it is an enjoyable evening for everyone."

THE YARDBIRDS

"The band was extraordinary, not only because of its musicianship, but because it was a band of ideas."

—Chris Dreja

I WAS A BIG Yardbirds fan. *The Yardbirds' Greatest Hits* was one of my most-played albums in high school. I later bought their albums and UK imports, and tracked down their obscure singles. The early-seventies band I had at UCLA included one of their songs in our set, and we recorded an original composition much in the group's style. Jim McCarty, The Yardbirds' drummer, was the second interview I conducted as a young rock journalist when he was in town promoting Renaissance, his new band with The Yardbirds' singer Keith Relf. I was inspired to write a lengthy overview on the band that became a cover story for *Rock Magazine*'s March 15, 1971 issue. In the early days of Rhino Records, I interviewed Jim and guitarist Chris Dreja and produced a Yardbirds picture disc. Most of the quotes in this chapter are from that February 11, 1982 discussion.

Although other artists of the British Invasion had more hits, I rank The Yardbirds third to The Beatles and The Rolling Stones on artistic innovation. Internal problems kept the group from ever reaching their commercial potential, and they ended up falling quite short, being instead remembered for leaving an indelible mark on the evolution of rock, especially in terms of technique and electronic experimentation, and for the development of the lead guitar (and lead guitarist). It might also be argued that, when they occasionally flashed the brilliance they were capable of, The Yardbirds produced some of the best rock 'n' roll of the sixties.

In May 1963 members of two groups formed The Yardbirds: Keith Relf (age twenty), lead vocals and harmonica; Paul Samwell-Smith (twenty), bass; Jim McCarty (nineteen), drums; Chris Dreja (seventeen), rhythm guitar; Anthony "Top" Topham (fifteen), lead guitar. Keith, who was fond of beat literature, came up with "The Yardbirds," a term for hobos who hung around railroad yards, after seeing it in Jack Kerouac's writings. The band's passion was to play American blues and rhythm and blues of performers such as Muddy Waters, Bo Diddley, Jimmy Reed, Blind Lemon Jefferson, Jelly Roll Morton, and Lightnin' Slim. "The names they had were extraordinary," observed Chris, "'Jelly Roll Morton,' 'Lightnin' Slim,' and 'Howlin' Wolf.' What's a 'Howlin' Wolf' when you live in Surbiton?"

The group was gigging regularly at London clubs when the members decided to devote more time to their music. Topham, still in school, had to quit because his parents wouldn't allow him to turn professional. He was replaced by an art school acquaintance of Dreja and Relf's, eighteen-year-old Eric Clapton, solidifying a lineup that Jim McCarty distilled into "three art school boys and two grammar school boys." Clapton, whose role models were guitarists Buddy Guy, Freddie King, and B. B. King, made his debut on October 19 at the Crawdaddy club. "What I immediately liked about The Yardbirds was that our entire reason for existence was to honor the tradition of the blues," he wrote in his autobiography.

Chris Dreja welcomed Eric into the group, and shared his room with him: "It seemed like Eric would go through a style every six months. During that time it was novel to pretend one was an American, and dress in an Ivy League style with a crew cut like Steve McQueen. After that he wore his hair in a bouffant and wore a plastic mac [a cheap Mackintosh raincoat]. Eric was moody and quiet, but he shared our sense of humor." Similar to Keith, Eric enjoyed reading beat literature, and was a fan of French and Japanese movies.

With his natty blond hair, Keith Relf resembled The Rolling Stones' Brian Jones. He was the natural star of the group and would later receive the most fan mail. His singing voice was ragged, slightly nasal, and uncultivated, and sounded like a harmonica, an instrument at which he excelled.

During performances at the Crawdaddy, the Marquee, and other clubs, Eric Clapton came into his own. When Clapton first auditioned for The Yardbirds, he couldn't play the usual melody lines and ended up improvising "as an excuse," because he didn't know what else to do. Clapton used lightweight guitar strings that broke frequently. While he changed them, the impatient crowd would slowly handclap in unison, resulting in the nickname of "Slowhand" from "slow hand clap(ton)."

During this early period, Jim kept his day job in a stockbroker's office. He would show up at gigs wearing his pinstriped suit, a cymbal under one arm, the *Financial Times* under the other. "I would change clothes in the lavatory and come out as a blues player, like Superman," he said. "We called him 'the accountant,'" added Chris.

The proprietor of the Crawdaddy, Giorgio Gomelsky, had been a champion of The Rolling Stones. He wanted to manage them, and even made a film of them performing (which has never turned up). Instead, the group signed with Andrew Loog Oldham, who accelerated them into venues larger than the modest backroom of the Station Hotel where the Richmond club was based. Giorgio had the similarly styled Yardbirds replace them as regulars, and soon signed them to a management contract.

Giorgio Gomelsky, twenty-nine, was a real character, a charismatic, bearded, bear of a man who sprinkled his Russian-accented English with "Baby." He grew up in the Russian (SSR) republic of Georgia, was schooled in Switzerland, and had contacts throughout Europe. His day job was that of an assistant film editor. He loved jazz and R&B.

The group signed with EMI (CBS label Epic in the US), and throughout 1964 recorded three singles (two issued in Britain) and a live album at the Marquee Club. Recorded in March and not released until December, *Five Live Yardbirds* was one of the few live rock albums then recorded. It was not all that it could have been. Some clown had had the idea of speeding up all of the ten tracks so they would fit on a single LP disc. Years later this was corrected, resulting in forty-five minutes of astonishingly (for its time) energetic, fast-paced rock 'n' roll. During the verses on the album's opener, "Too Much Monkey Business," Clapton's guitar sounds restrained, releasing a little energy by sneaking in notes here and there; then as soon as the break comes, all his power is forcefully unleashed. The whole album's like that. Clapton's irresistible playing sounds at times like a chicken chasing a fire engine, and at others like a staggering drunken rooster. Although Clapton was the only stellar musician, what strikes me more is how well the musicians jelled, forging a unique sound based on intense drives and climaxes that came to be called "rave-up."

To everyone's frustration, nothing sold. "Our contemporaries all had hits," said Jim, "and we wanted one as well." As The Rolling Stones and other R&B groups like The Animals and Manfred Mann got a head start on The Yardbirds, there were fewer songs to cover if they didn't want to repeat what those other artists had recorded. The goal was to have a hit record, not only for the revenue it would generate, but, as Chris pointed out, "to increase our popularity so we could draw a crowd beyond the fifty-mile radius of London."

While The Yardbirds were hanging out with The Beatles as special guests on their Christmas shows at the Hammersmith Odeon, John Lennon suggested Chuck Jackson's "The Breaking Point" as a potential single. They also met with a publisher who played them a simple demo with just bongos, a guitar, and a vocal. The composer, Graham Gouldman, was inspired to write songs by The Beatles. He was a guitarist in Manchester band The Mockingbirds. When the group's label declined to record "For Your Love," he offered it to The Yardbirds. They liked it. They thought it was different.

Samwell-Smith asked Giorgio to appoint him the band's "musical director." In arranging the song for the February 1 session, he kept the bongos on the demonstration record, now performed by Denny Piercey, and hired harpsichordist Brian Auger and standup bassist Ron Prentiss. The band as a whole was restricted to playing during a middle break. As soon as it was finished, they all believed it was that elusive hit.

Even before the group recorded "For Your Love," a bone of contention for blues purist Clapton, he exhibited passive-aggressive behavior. He showed up late for gigs, and skipped one entirely. He became increasingly argumentative and withdrawn. He quit the group—or caused Giorgio to fire him—days before the single was released.

Despite his expertise, the others were relieved when he left, and felt no longer restricted to the blues. Clapton's last appearance with the group was on March 3 at Uncle Bonnie's Chinese Jazz Club. "I didn't want to be part of a group that was going to be on TV doing Tin Pan Alley songs," Eric said. A month later he joined John Mayall's Blues Breakers. "For Your Love" became a big hit, soaring to number three in the UK and number six in the US.

Gomelsky asked Jimmy Page to replace Eric, but he was making too much money as a session guitarist, and recommended Jeff Beck (twenty). Jeff had played with fifteen groups through the years, but was then a member of The Tridents. He wasn't making much money—he had holes in his shoes—and he was married. He recalled two guys corralling him between sets when The Tridents appeared at the 100 Club, telling him to be at the Marquee on Tuesday at two o'clock. "There's a ratty van outside with 'Keith' written all over it with lipstick," Jeff recalled. "I'm thinking, 'It's The Stones!' I enter and realize my mistake, that it's an audition for The Yardbirds. I see Keith

Relf puffing on an atomizer. He tells me he has asthma. I thought, 'I'm joining an asthmatic blues band.'" Jeff took the job in part because it meant more money. He debuted with the group wearing Eric Clapton's suit on March 5 at Fairfield Hall in Croydon. "It was horrible when I first started with The Yardbirds," he recounted to the *Daily Bruin*'s Salli Stevenson, "because Clapton's playing was so irresistible that I found myself playing like him. On top of that, Keith Relf told me to play the same way because I was a new guitar player. The first night I ever played with them, I got an ovation of the standing variety for an instrumental I can't remember the title of. If I hadn't played that tune, I probably would still have been underdog to Keith."

Chris was put in charge of cleaning Jeff up, taking him shopping for mod clothes and getting his hair cut: "He was very shy and a bit of a rough diamond, pretty scruffy, working on his car all the time." Jim added, "Jeff's really a strange person because basically he's quiet and nice. He's got a big insecurity thing. He freaks out on stage, sometimes turning into something else, almost like a monster movie. I think he was uptight following Eric, but then he became a temperamental person anyway."

When I interviewed Jim and Chris in 1982, they described a promotional film Giorgio had directed of them lip-synching "For Your Love" in a field in Windsor. Their description of the band dressed in medieval costumes and suits of armor was so ridiculous, I thought they were pulling my leg. Years later, in the era of YouTube, it was posted for all to see. The Yardbirds marveled at Giorgio's ingenuity, but not all of his ideas were good ones.

"Heart Full of Soul," another Graham Gouldman song, became the group's next single. Because Giorgio thought a lot of the appeal of "For Your Love" was the prominence of the uncommon harpsichord, he had the idea of introducing novel Indian instruments to a rock arrangement. He hired a sitar player and a tabla player, but the former couldn't quite get the tempo down and the instrument sounded thin. Jeff Beck stepped in, plugged his guitar into a Tone Bender fuzz box, and came up with a paralyzing electrical riff that made me think of an enormous maniac bee working its way into someone's flesh.

The group was now playing more concert than club dates, and toured with The Kinks and The Beatles. During the summer, "Heart Full of Soul" climbed to number two in the UK and nine in the US. The group embarked to America for three weeks on September 2. Problems with the American musicians union caused dates to be cancelled.

A factor that affected The Yardbirds on their first tour, as well as limiting the flow of British bands to the US, was a rule enacted by the American Federation of Musicians union. In order to protect the jobs of their members, the AFM restricted foreign musicians from performing in the US unless there was a trade out with that country. For example, if a five-piece rock band from the UK wanted to tour in the States to promote their new record, five American musicians would have to be guaranteed employment in the UK. Those bands hoping to skirt by undetected, or whose management was uninformed, risked having dates cancelled—which is what happened to The Yardbirds— when brought to the attention of the US Labor Department and the Immigration and Naturalization Service. Here's AFM president Herman Kenin's position in 1964 regarding The Beatles: "We don't consider them unique. They are musicians and only sing incidentally. We can go to Yonkers or Tennessee and pick up four kids who can do this kind of stuff."

While in Los Angeles, The Yardbirds taped a couple of Shindig! shows, and on September 9 performed a scene-making party in the Hollywood Hills where they set up behind the living room sofa. Phil Spector, Jackie DeShannon, Peter & Gordon, and members of The Byrds attended. While Jim was packing up his drums into a van, comedian Lenny Bruce hurled a dirt clod at him from an upstairs window. Much more impactful, this is where Jeff met and fell head over heels in love with Mary Hughes, a statuesque blond beauty who had been a featured extra in the beach party movies. Compared with England, Chris Dreja described California as going from "black and white into Technicolor."

Jim: "Loads of people asked us if we were The Beatles." Chris: "We used to tell people we were salesmen, that we were selling long hair." It was a good joke, but it wasn't so funny when the group was denied entrance to Disneyland because their hair was too long.

With dates now available, Giorgio booked sessions for them in two legendary recording studios. At Sam C. Phillips Recording Studio (also referred to as Sun Studio) in Memphis, they recorded "Train Kept A-Rollin" and "You're a Better Man Than I." The legendary Sam Phillips, who had produced Elvis, Carl Perkins, and Jerry Lee Lewis, interrupted a fishing trip to engineer the session. Despite the special circumstances, Keith Relf got drunk and pissed everybody off. He redid his vocals a week later in New York. At Chess Recording Studios in Chicago—the home of Muddy Waters, Chuck Berry, and Bo Diddley—they captured Diddley's "I'm A Man," which had been part of the group's live set the past two years. In addition to the magical experiences, the band felt they got a better sound than they had previously in England.

That fall they did lots of gigs in the UK, some in Germany and Belgium. In October the third Graham Gouldman single was released. "Evil Hearted You" boasted fine group vocals, powerful guitar chords, and Beck's blistering lead. It got up to number three in the UK. Of equal interest was the B-side's "Still I'm Sad," composed by McCarty and Samwell-Smith in the mode of a thirteenth century Gregorian chant. Giorgio helped out on the low notes. Despite its unconventionality, it got considerable airplay in both the US and UK. Instead of "Evil Hearted You," Epic Records in America released "I'm a Man." It's the group's recording that best captures their speeded-up rave-up style, a frenzy of rapidly strummed, muted guitar strings. It made it to number seventeen.

In December The Yardbirds were back in the US for three weeks. At Chess Recording Studios they recorded "Shapes of Things," which group members—Jeff Beck included—consider their best record. Paul—with Jim contributing later—wrote the song in a Chicago bar about the destruction of the planet. It's a great record and a distinctly Yardbirds-sounding record. The pulsing guitars discharge a very electric sound, almost as if they were plugged into the power grid. The break spirits the listener away onto an exhilarating magic carpet ride via the Indian melodies of the vocals and lead guitar, which Jeff played on one string. The March 1966 single rose to three in the UK and eleven in the US.

A highlight for Jeff was when Giorgio took him to see Howlin' Wolf perform in a club that looked like it had recently been converted from a drug store. Jeff: "There were Negroes standing and sitting everywhere eating chicken and rice. And up on the stage was Howlin' Wolf dressed in a black dinner jacket and sitting on a stool playing some battered old guitar." Jeff met Howlin' Wolf and sat in with his backing group.

Attendance on the winter dates was mixed. Only ten fans turned up for a show on Christmas night at the Peppermint Stick Club in Wheatfield, New York. Traveling by small planes in the Midwest during hunting season provided novel traveling companions, according to Jim: "Next to you would be these guys who had been hunting and their dead moose was in the front seat."

From their numerous tours of the US, The Yardbirds got a good glimpse of the cultures in different parts of the country. The first time they arrived in Los Angeles, they unintentionally drove through Watts, with buildings still smoldering in the aftermath of the riots. Chris: "We were touring the US during a period when aluminum coffins were coming out of the back of the plane at the same time as our luggage, and servicemen were everywhere. Ninety percent of the country was conservative: Bible belt, military, crew cut types, or businessmen. Businessmen with briefcases would see us and walk back for another look."

Giorgio had an idea to make The Yardbirds the first rock band to play the San Remo Music Festival, held at the end of January in San Remo, Italy. He thought it would be good exposure, and it would ingratiate the group to the Italian record company. A month before, The Yardbirds had recorded the two Italian-composed pop songs (with English lyrics) at RCA Studios in Hollywood, but they weren't happy about it. Jeff even refused to contribute to one of the songs. The appearance was a misfire and no good came out of it.

The Yardbirds nonetheless had a good relationship with Gomelsky, whom they considered a sixth member of the band. Chris: "We had a good time with Giorgio. He used to look just like Fidel Castro, so we got him an army jacket and the type of peaked hat that Fidel wore. We used to have him paged at the airport: 'Would Fidel Castro please come to TWA check-in.'" But after one too many bad ideas—San Remo—it was time to make a change. More to the point, where was the money? They were having hits on both sides of the Atlantic, earning more from live performances, but they were making the same wage as a year ago. They didn't think Gomelsky was cheating them, but that he was bad with finances. When they informed him, he was heartbroken. In order for them to get out of their agreement with Gomelsky, the group agreed to forfeit their artist royalties on all their previous recordings.

At the time, recent hits weren't thought to have much value, so it was an easy decision to make. Only years later were the group's masters considered classics, generating income not only from record sales, but from films, TV shows, and commercials. For example, in 1986 Rhino produced *The Yardbirds Greatest Hits, Volume One: 1964-1966*. It sold around 130,000. For simplicity sake, if the royalty was a dollar an album, $130,000 was paid to Gomelsky with, presumably, no money paid to the band.

Paul's sister worked for novice manager Simon Napier-Bell as his secretary and recommended him as a replacement. When Simon met with the group, he liked them. He was anticipating meeting "bloody monsters like The Rolling Stones," but he found them "gentle souls with good manners." He took over in April 1966. "He worked hard in the beginning," Jim said, "got us our first-ever advance from the record company. But where Giorgio over-related to us, he couldn't relate to us at all."

On May 31 the group entered Advision Studios to record an album for the first time, with Samwell-Smith and Napier-Bell coproducing. Most of the songs were written in the studio—Relf supplied a majority of the lyrics—with the band sharing the credits. *The Yardbirds*, also known as *Roger the Engineer* from Chris' cover illustration of studio engineer Roger Cameron (and, minus two songs, as *Over Under Sideways Down* in the US), is considered a near-classic, ranking at number 350 on *Rolling Stone's* "500 Greatest Albums of All Time." It is, indeed, an exceptional album, but not because of the songwriting. Sonically, it's among the best albums of the period: with extraordinary dynamics, and clarity of both instruments and voices. The band's sound is consistent through a variety of influences: Indian, African, Australian, chants, blues, and country. There is also a song about suicide, Relf's "Farewell."

The album provides a showcase for Jeff's resourcefulness on nearly every track. Take for example "The Nazz are Blue." Jeff sings new lyrics over an energetic reworking of "Dust My Broom," a delta blues popularized by Elmore James. Jeff was a fan of hipster comic Lord Buckley who referred to Jesus as "The Nazz" because he came from Nazareth. (George Harrison's 1977 hit "Crackerbox Palace" was also inspired by Buckley.) For the solo, Jeff essentially plays one note, using vibrato and controlled reverb to sustain the volume. It's brilliant, it's effective, it's original, and it's totally Jeff. Its only fault was Beck's horrible moaning—he insisted on singing instead of Keith.

"Over Under Sideways Down," developed after jamming around Bill Haley's "Rock Around the Clock," was recorded in mid-April to be released as a single in June. A group composition, Jeff contributed the bass and came up with the sinuous violin-like riff on his fuzz-tone guitar. The flip, "Jeff's Boogie," showcased Beck's multiple guitar styles in a swing rhythm.

Jeff was brilliant. In my opinion, the best playing of his career was with The Yardbirds. Regardless on how shaky the ground he perceived himself to be, Jeff rose to the challenge as a member of a team. Rather than taking delight in how well he excelled, though, Jeff felt pressure. It was an internal dilemma, not because his bandmates were unreasonably demanding. In his post-Yardbirds career, his personal dynamic was different. As a bandleader he had more say in his repertoire, and his musicians were more beholden to him.

On June 18 The Yardbirds were hired to headline the Oxford May Ball, a prestigious and well-paid end-of-the-school-year formal dance. Keith had been drinking heavily and his performance deteriorated. He blew raspberries into the mic and rolled around on the stage. He was incapacitated for much of the second set during which the band played instrumentals. It proved to be the last straw for Paul, who was also fed up with touring. "At twenty-three I'm too old for all these screaming kids leaping about," he said, not long after the gig. "I don't think I'll be missed—no one really noticed me on stage. I might just as well have been a dummy."

"Paul was invaluable, articulate, and bright," Chris said, "but he was also nervous and high-strung. He was a lovely man, but a square peg in the round hole of rock and roll. Most people thought of him as uptight and officious." When Samwell-Smith left, they lost the creative heart of the band. He produced their last big hit: "Over Under Sideways Down" climbed to ten in the UK and thirteen in the US.

As it happened, Jimmy Page (twenty-two) had ridden with Jeff to the dance that night. On the way home, he offered to step in and play bass. The timing was finally right for Jimmy to hit the road as a member of a hit rock band. Although Jeff got along with the other members of the group, he felt that McCarty was the only one he could talk to, and was lonely. Having Jimmy join would mean that he finally had a friend in the band, an ally. "Jimmy made a point of getting the right clothes to present the right image," said McCarty. "We played a gig in Scotland where Beck and Page were wearing old military jackets with German Iron Crosses and they got spat upon. Jimmy seemed interested in instruments of perversion. Every now and then he'd talk about the Marquis de Sade."

Page wasn't much of a bass player, but he was too good a guitar player to remain on that instrument. After two months, Chris moved to bass. Jeff: "Jimmy can't play the bass for toffee; Chris was better." Jeff and Jimmy got the idea that they could perform Jeff's previous lead guitar lines in tandem. On September 23, 1966, at the Royal Albert Hall, after a handful of dates without Jeff, The Yardbirds debuted Jeff and Jimmy's dual guitars, or "stereo guitars" arrangement. When they were focused, it worked brilliantly. But Beck was an undisciplined *feel player* compared with Page's precision, and quite often it didn't work. As Jimmy Page told *ZigZag* magazine's Pete Frame in 1972, "That was all well in theory and at rehearsal, but on stage Beck would often go off into something else." In addition, Jeff hadn't anticipated sharing the guitar hero spotlight: "I didn't want my territory being encroached upon. I wanted to be *it*."

Not able to articulate his concerns with words, Jeff acted out: he missed dates, played inconsistently when he showed up, and was prone to destroying malfunctioning amps. He even complained of asthma sufferer Keith Relf's "coughing and sputtering" and the hissing from his inhaler during his solos.

Rumors had been circulating for months that Jeff was going to leave the group. In September, Barbara Sims wrote a letter to the *KRLA Beat*: "I am a Yardbird fan and as one who follows them as much as I can I would like to ask this. Where is Jeff Beck? He has not played with The Yardbirds on this whole tour but I see him on the [Sunset] Strip with Mary Hughes. Is he no longer in the group and is the rumor true that he is married?"

The Yardbirds toured extensively over the summer, taking a few days off in October to record a new single, "Happenings Ten Years Time Ago," and to film and record a song for Michaelangelo Antonioni's *Blow Up*. "Happenings Ten Years Time Ago" was Keith's idea of reincarnation, according to McCarty. Page, McCarty, and John Paul Jones (on bass) recorded the basic track. Beck arrived late and added his parts. In a flood of confusion—sounds of a jet plane taking off and a throbbing European police car siren—two lead guitars lash out. During the instrumental break Jeff mocks a clueless acquaintance, "Why do you got long hair?" At a period when few groups were yet knowledgeable about feedback, the record seemed eons ahead of its time. Now considered a psychedelic masterpiece, it was a commercial flop, managing to get only to thirty in the US and forty-two in the UK. The long guitar solos and jamming were a precursor to what would later be termed the "progressive era" in rock. Many now think of The Yardbirds as founders of "psychedelic rock." On the UK flip side "Psycho Daisies," Jeff sings, "California's my home with Mary Hughes."

Antonioni wanted a group to smash one of their instruments in a recreated Ricky Tick Club in his new movie. The Who, his first choice, passed. The Yardbirds' performance, a messy appropriation of "Train Kept A-Rollin" rewritten as "Stroll On," was representative of a Yardbirds concert except for the tranquil audience and Beck smashing a guitar during an amplifier malfunction, which was more

Antonioni's vision. Decades later fans can appreciate how good the band looks in the well-shot film.

The band was back in the States on October 21 to record a Great Shakes (milkshake powder) radio commercial, and play a number of dates before joining the Dick Clark Caravan of Stars tour on October 28. The Yardbirds were third-billed and felt out of place with the other acts: Gary Lewis & The Playboys, Sam the Sham & The Pharaohs, Bobby Hebb, and Brian Hyland. If you were Jeff Beck, would you want to be stuck on a bus for a month-long grueling tour of the South and Midwest—for little money—or be back in LA snuggling with "the Brigitte Bardot of Malibu," as Mary Hughes was sometimes called? Jeff claimed he had tonsillitis and hightailed it back to California three days after the tour started.

Soon after, Beck was no longer a Yardbird. As brilliant as Jeff could be as a guitarist, at this point it was good riddance: no longer having to put up with his tardiness, his absences, his sulking, his amp smashing. Jim: "He was a nervous guy who had trouble expressing himself. He kept it all bottled up. I don't think Jeff fit in. He did with our sense of humor, like doing impressions of Roger Moore in *The Saint*. He was more from a car mechanic background." Chris: "Jeff is a man of his emotions. He's a slightly out of control egomaniac." Jim: "Jeff and Jimmy would switch off playing lead guitar. Then Jeff started to get worse and kept on packing in tours before we'd finished, so it became the four of us. We'd kicked Jeff out. It was his own fault because he kept on letting us down. But the way we were at the end, the four of us was the best combination we'd had."

ONCE AMERICAN TEENS HAD been energized to form rock bands in the styles of The Beatles and The Rolling Stones. Now it was The Yardbirds' turn. Count Five, from San Jose, California, copied The Yardbirds' playing on "I'm a Man" so effectively that they scored a top five single with "Psychotic Reaction" in 1966. Todd Rundgren's first recorded band, Nazz, even took their name from a Yardbirds B-side. When Vincent Furnier and his bandmates—all big Yardbirds fans—became aware of the other Nazz, they changed their name to Alice Cooper.

Simon Napier-Bell, who successfully managed Wham! in the eighties and took them to China, had his fill of The Yardbirds. He referred to them as a "miserable bloody lot" and singled out Paul Samwell-Smith and Jimmy Page as the most troublesome. He made an arrangement with Mickie Most to take over production, and Most's partner Peter Grant to take over management, retaining a percentage for himself.

Most tried to "resuscitate" (his term) the group, but was unsuccessful. He recorded four singles with them of which "Little Games" charted the highest, reaching only fifty-one in the US. As a result, the *Little Games* album was released in America but not the UK. "My involvement with The Yardbirds was nothing, really," Mickie told me. "It was toward the end and the fire had gone out. It was more out of contractual obligation than anything else. They liked doing the songs."

It wasn't as if Most wasn't trying to have a hit with the group, or that he wasn't successful with other artists. During the year of recording The Yardbirds, he had nine Top 30 hits in the UK and six in the US. He even hit the Top 20 in the UK with Jeff Beck's debut single. Mickie recalled Jeff turning up in his office when he was supposed to be on tour in the States with The Yardbirds, telling him that he met a girl who didn't think he should be in the band anymore. Mickie: "Jeff said, 'I want to be a pop singer.' I played him 'Hi-Ho Silver Lining' and he said 'Let's do it.' Jeff recorded two guitar solos, almost identical. I liked them both, so I stuck them on."

It's clear Mickie wasn't right for The Yardbirds. "Mickie Most was just impossible to talk to because he was the big producer star,"

Jim said. "When you'd start criticizing him, he'd tell you how much money he'd made. Instead of recording singles, we should have been making an album. We hadn't realized that the market had changed from singles to albums."

Keith and Jim's lifestyle eventually caught up with the psychedelic culture that had embraced their music. "When we first went to California we were straight as a die," Jim said. "We might drink half a pint of beer, but that's it. We had this great following of hippies and freaks. From the music we were playing, they thought we were acidheads." Chris added: "People did misconstrue that we were about drugs, when we were really about the music." But after a while both Keith and Jim got heavily into LSD and smoking pot. Chris continued: "Keith got more involved than the rest of us. He burned incense and candles and turned his hotel room into a Buddhist temple. He bought himself a projector and projected stars on his body to see what they felt like. He'd play *East-West* by the Paul Butterfield Blues Band or *Freak Out!* by The Mothers of Invention."

As Jimmy was new to the band, he was still fresh and had energy. The other three were tired. Chris: "Keith was a sensitive man who wrote great lyrics, but like many alcoholics, he had a schizophrenic aspect to him." Jeff weighed in: "I think he was manic-depressive. He wanted to kill everybody. He used to read *Guns & Ammo* [magazine] to work out how to commit the perfect murder." During their last US tour, even Jim McCarty succumbed. He had a minor breakdown and was replaced for a couple of performances.

On March 30, 1968, the band recorded a live album at New York's Anderson Theatre. It was finally issued in September 1971. The band performed well and, as at most shows, some numbers were better than others. The standouts for me are "Heart Full of Soul" and "Over Under Sideways Down," both of which are more powerful than their studio versions. *Live Yardbirds Featuring Jimmy Page* was available only for a few months. Page convinced CBS to cease shipping the

LP because the title attempted to exploit his popularity with Led Zeppelin. Among the new material the band performed, Chris regrets they never made a proper studio recording of "Dazed and Confused" as it was an audience favorite. (Curiously, the song was titled "I'm Confused" and had no songwriting credit.) It's more familiar as the fourth song on Led Zeppelin's January 1969 debut album. The song was credited to Jimmy Page, but he didn't write it.

On August 25, 1967, The Yardbirds headlined the Village Theater in New York. They took in folksinger Jake Holmes' opening set, entranced with a song he performed from his new album *"The Above Ground Sound" of Jake Holmes.* The next day McCarty bought a copy from a Greenwich Village record store, and the group worked up their own version, with Keith doing a lyric rewrite. When *Led Zeppelin* was released with his song—with Page's new lyrics—Holmes didn't initiate legal action. He was making a lot of money writing music for commercials for major companies. His most memorable jingles are Dr. Pepper's "Be a Pepper" and the US Army's "Be All That You Can Be." Only decades later, under the threat of legal action, did Page agree to a settlement; the song now credited to "Jimmy Page inspired by Jake Holmes."

The group completed its US tour on June 5, 1968, and then played a final date on July 7 at Luton Technical College in Bedfordshire before breaking up. Jimmy wanted to continue with the band, but only Chris was onboard. The pair auditioned new members, and it was reported in the press that the new lineup included Robert Plant on vocals and Paul Francis on drums. But Chris had second thoughts, determined he didn't want to do it any longer, and elected to pursue a career in photography. In September Jimmy's new band fulfilled an already-booked ten-date tour of Scandinavia as The New Yardbirds. The band played a few newly booked UK dates the following month, and a tour was in the works for the US. Jimmy changed the name to

Led Zeppelin only after Chris threatened to sue if he continued to use "The New Yardbirds."

Despite the creativity of the group as a whole, The Yardbirds are most remembered for having three of rock's best guitarists passing through their ranks. Jim described how they compared: "Eric impressed me the most, he was a neat player. Jeff, on a good night, had more guts. Jimmy is very adaptable. He can play a wider range than the other two, but won't. I don't know why."

In the decade after the group's demise, The Yardbirds influence was apparent in Led Zeppelin, Aerosmith, Alice Cooper, Cheap Trick, Rush, Stevie Ray Vaughan, and others. Jeff Beck recorded "Shapes of Things" on his *Truth* album; Todd Rundgren recreated "Happenings Ten Years Time Ago" on *Faithful*; David Bowie covered two of The Yardbirds' songs on *Pin Ups*, so did Rush on their 2004 tribute EP *Feedback*.

"The Yardbirds never quite made it," Jim said in 1970. "They made it in one way in that they made a sort of fame, but they missed out slightly. If we knew then what we know now, we could have been one of the biggest things."

Chris: "It was one of those bands where the ingredients were just right. We were an emotionally bound together group of people."

The Yardbirds were inducted into the Rock and Roll Hall of Fame in 1992.

AT RHINO WE PRODUCED a couple of anthologies and reissued *Five Live Yardbirds*, with the speed corrected. We also tried to do other projects. When The Yardbirds broke up, Jim and Keith formed a group, Together, because they wanted to go in a musical direction like The Turtles. The Turtles' vocalists Howard Kaylan and Mark Volman wished that their group had a guitar virtuoso like Jeff Beck. I thought of realizing their one-time desires by combining the relevant elements of each group. As The Yardbirds (except for Relf, who died in 1976) played well when they reunited to record as the Box of Frogs in 1984 (with Beck on three songs), I thought of flying Kaylan and Volman over to London to record an album with remaining members Beck, McCarty, Dreja, and Samwell-Smith. It took some persuasion to convince Samwell-Smith, who preferred producing to playing bass. (He had produced the two Box of Frogs LPs, as well as five gold albums and one platinum for Cat Stevens, and a gold album for Carly Simon.) During my phone conversation with him when I was in London in September 1987, he expressed his frustration regarding Jeff: "Sometimes he showed up for a session, other times he wouldn't." As this would have been an expensive endeavor for us, I didn't want to risk our finances if Beck was unreliable, and didn't proceed.

I also met one of my best friends because of The Yardbirds. In 1973, a few months after I settled into my own apartment and got a listed phone number, I received a call from a stranger: "Are you the Harold Bronson who wrote the cover story on The Yardbirds in *Rock Magazine*?" Bill Stout was an artist, an illustrator, and a Yardbirds fan. We met and hit it off. In addition to sharing a love of rock 'n' roll and going to shows together, I tried to involve him as much as I could in Rhino projects. Bill created the original Rhino logo. Over forty years later, we remain friends to this day.

THE SPENCER DAVIS GROUP

I GOT A CALL from Marty Cerf, the director of creative services at United Artists Records. UA had generated a new music periodical, *Phonograph Record Magazine*, that would feature their own artists as well as ones not affiliated with the label. He wanted me to interview Spencer Davis for one of the initial issues. As part of a new acoustic duo, Spencer had a new album coming out on Media Arts Records. The Spencer Davis Group's catalogue was on UA.

The Spencer Davis Group were a mid-sixties R&B band from Birmingham, in the West Midlands area of England. The city, second only to London in population, was England's biggest manufacturing region and supported a rich rock music scene, spawning The Moody Blues, The Move, Electric Light Orchestra, Black Sabbath, and half of Led Zeppelin. In America, The Spencer Davis Group had only two Top 10 records, but in the UK they had five big hits—including two number ones and a number two—and three Top 10 LPs, in just fifteen months. Then Steve Winwood left to form Traffic, and The Spencer Davis Group never recovered.

When I interviewed Spencer in January 1971, he voiced his disgust with the whole London pop music scene. He had hit records, yes: "Gimme Some Lovin'" and "I'm A Man," among them. But he was tired of being recognized on the street and having his phone ring constantly. Mostly, he was discouraged with the way The Spencer

Davis Group had been going. He found that he was losing sight of his musical ideals and decided to chuck it all during a US tour in 1969.

Feeling that he had to get away, Davis packed his guitar and his family and migrated to a house just north of Hollywood. With no furniture in the living room, we sat on the carpet for our interview. Spencer was enthusiastic, jumping from one subject to another, and seemed just as willing to discuss the old Spencer Davis Group as his new career.

For Spencer, who grew up in Swansea, Wales, it all started with the blues: "When I first heard the blues—like when I heard Big Bill Broonzy or Jesse Fuller on the *Six-Five Special* TV show—it was a revelation. When I saw Bill play his guitar and bend a guitar string, I thought, 'Maybe that's something I can do.' I immediately went out and bought a guitar. There were thousands of kids who could play better than me, and even better than Broonzy or Lead Belly, but they didn't communicate the emotion or the blues experience.

"The thing about blues is its emotion: the intense feel, the spirit and the drive, and the lack of pretension. It was primeval, a cry of help. But the blues could also be happy music, like Gus Cannon and the jug band sound. I fell in love with Lightnin' Hopkins, Sonny Terry and Brownie McGee, Willie Dixon, and so many others. So, that's what inspired me to be a musician. At one point, I had a blues duo with my girlfriend, Christine Perfect [Fleetwood Mac's Christine McVie]. Toward the end of 1962, when I was a student in Berlin, I played bohemian-type coffeehouses. I used to sing the blues, and folk songs by Woody Guthrie ('900 Miles,' 'Ramblin' Blues'), Joan Baez, and Ramblin' Jack Elliott.

"I did a gig in Birmingham where I went to the university. There I saw the Muff-Woody Jazz Band. Muff Winwood played guitar. Stevie Winwood played piano like Oscar Peterson, and he was incredible. He played the melodica in addition to singing. He was doing a Ray

Charles solo and it just knocked me sideways. He couldn't have been more than fifteen.

"I played an interval spot at the Golden Eagle in 1963, my final year in university. I tore everybody up—the song was 'Got My Mojo Working' by Muddy Waters—so they offered me the residency as headliner at the club. This meant taking over from an out-and-out rock and roll band with dyed hair whose guitarists played their guitars behind their backs. I felt that I needed a rock band to compete.

"I rounded up Steve and said, 'Let's form a band, because I know so many songs and you know so many.' So he agreed to join on the condition that his brother Muff came as well, regardless of musical value. Muff came along because he was Steve's older brother and he had the driver's license. Steve was too young to drive. We got Peter York, who had been playing in various trad jazz and mainstream bands, to play drums." The band formed in April 1963.

For a time they were billed as the Rhythm and Blues Quartet or RBQ, then Muff suggested "The Spencer Davis Group" as it was a nice-sounding name. He also thought that, as Spencer was the most outgoing, he would do most of the interviews so the others could sleep late. The band's popularity soared. "We could have played the Golden Eagle eight nights a week," said Spencer. Robert Plant and Noddy Holder (of Slade) saw The Spencer Davis Group there and considered the band an inspiration.

On June 1, 1964, Chris Blackwell saw the group while on tour promoting Millie (Small). Chris had formed Island Records two years previously to promote talent from Jamaica. In some cases, where he felt a record had potential to sell beyond his one-man operation, he leased the master to a bigger company, as he had with Millie's recording of an obscure 1956 R&B 45 by Barbie Gaye. Released on Philips Records' Fontana imprint, "My Boy Lollipop" became a number two hit. He auditioned The Spencer Davis Group in a hair salon, signed them to Fontana, and released their first record in August 1964.

The band had a unique sound, mostly attributable to Stevie's (as he was called then) uncanny ability to sound like Ray Charles, but also in its repertoire of country blues. The group performed covers of blues and R&B songs originally recorded by Don Covey, Muddy Waters, Rufus Thomas, Elmore James, Bobby Parker, Ike & Tina Turner, The Coasters, and, of course, Ray Charles. The problem was a number of other bands also sampled the same sources. Their first single, John Lee Hooker's "Dimples," had been recorded by The Animals on their first LP. Their third, Brenda Holloway's "Every Little Bit Hurts," had also been covered by Small Faces. The bigger problem was The Spencer Davis Group's first four records had all flopped.

Jackie Edwards was a successful recording artist in his native Jamaica, often referred to as the "Nat King Cole of Jamaica." Blackwell appreciated his talent, and in 1962 lured him to England to help out at Island. Jackie recorded, wrote songs for himself and other artists, and even delivered boxes of 45s by bus to London's suburban record stores. Blackwell had him write a song for The Spencer Davis Group.

They liked Jackie's "Keep On Running," but didn't think the ska beat fit their style. "We arranged it with a guitar riff inspired by The Stones' 'Satisfaction,'" noted Spencer. Singer Jimmy Cliff attended the recording session, and was so excited he can be heard shouting in the background. Initially rejected by Fontana, it was released in November 1965 and climbed all the way to number one. Even The Beatles sent a congratulatory message. The group was so well thought of that in January 1966 producer Joe Boyd enlisted Steve and Pete to join Eric Clapton, Jack Bruce, and Paul Jones to record three tracks for an Elektra Records multi-artist album titled *What's Shakin'*. Billed as Powerhouse, Blackwood insisted Winwood use Steve Anglo as an alias.

"Somebody Help Me," written by Edwards, followed in the spring and also hit number one. "It was sort-of Beatle-ish in approach," said Spencer. The group's summer 1966 single, "When I Come Home," cowritten by Steve and Jackie, barely missed the Top 10. The band had hits throughout Europe and was especially popular in Germany. Spencer, a German language major, had attended the University of Berlin for a year, and was fluent in German.

The group were now pop stars, with photo spreads in all the music publications. Writers referred to Spencer as "the cute one," and said he resembled Paul McCartney. Do you recall in the Manfred Mann chapter when Paul Jones talked about the type of movie scripts he and Manfred had been offered? The "sort of Robin Hood musicals with rock groups cast away on desert islands or sent to the moon, horrible stuff like that." Well, the Spencer Davis group starred in one. In *The Ghost Goes Gear* the group's manager turns his haunted house into a tourist attraction. It failed to get distribution in America.

Brooklyn-born soul-drummer-turned-producer Jimmy Miller took over from Blackwell to oversee the group's next record, "Gimme Some Lovin.'" Spencer: "Muff came up with the riff. I had the melody, but played it in a minor key. Steve suggested we play it in a major key. He went off with a friend and wrote the lyrics." That said, the throbbing rhythm of the song that provides much of its appeal was appropriated from "A Lot of Love," a May 1966 45 by soul singer Homer Banks. Although Winwood's singing rendered the lyrics mostly unintelligible, it hit number two in the UK and became the band's first Top 10 in America. The next single, "I'm A Man," was modeled after a descending chord pattern in the chorus of Mel Tormé's "Comin' Home Baby." Steve wrote the music, Jimmy Miller the words.

Steve Winwood had been talking about leaving for months, but with hit after hit, it was easy for the rest of the band to focus on the current success and the demanding work schedule. So, in the spring of 1967, when he announced that he planned to depart following the tour the group was on with The Hollies, it was devastating. Even more so as "I'm A Man" was in the Top 10. "I'm not sure why he left," Spencer admitted. "We never said, 'Well, goodbye, it was great working with you.' I would have liked to because it was great working with Steve. We didn't even quarrel. Musically, I suppose, Steve was more advanced than me. That might have had a lot to do with it. When Steve expressed his wishes to leave, we had a meeting and the only one who wasn't there was Steve. It was weird. Blackwell said that he needed time to think.

"He was so young coming into this big thing, maybe he wanted time to grow up or whatever. I don't know. Muff went with him. I don't think he relished the idea of sticking around when Steve left. Muff was only an adequate bass player, but he was a pretty good guitarist. He played bass because there wasn't anybody else. Peter stayed with me." Muff took a job in A&R at Island Records.

In addition to wanting to stretch musically, Steve complained about how hard he was working, and the discomfort he felt from having to travel in the back of a van for vast distances at night. Spencer referred to 1966 as "the year of minimal sleep." More than anything else, he probably longed to play and socialize with musicians closer to his age. When he left the group, he was almost nineteen; Spencer was twenty-seven, Pete twenty-four, and Muff twenty-three.

Steve formed Traffic with musicians he met while jamming at Birmingham's Elbow Room club. Dave Mason was twenty; Jim Capaldi and Chris Wood both twenty-two. All were also from the West Midlands. Mason roadied a bit for The Spencer Davis Group and sang backup on "Gimme Some Lovin'." Capaldi added percussion to the recording.

Spencer got replacements, good ones, too. (Elton John, then Reg Dwight, showed up for the audition in a milkman's outfit. According to Spencer: "We didn't think that was cool.") The band embarked on a Scandinavian tour in June, but it was never the same. Spencer: "I can pin the demise of The Spencer Davis Group down to a date in July 1969. We were playing in Bellefontaine, Ohio, and I just decided the group was over. Ray Fenwick, Dee Murray, and Nigel Olsen [the latter two became members of Elton John's band] were in the group then. It came to a head between Ray and myself. I just decided to kill the group myself before it was killed by outside forces. In peoples' minds there was only one Spencer Davis Group, and that consisted of Steve, Muff, Peter, and myself. They just didn't allow for the possibility of another Spencer Davis Group.

"I went back to my manager, Peter Walsh, and said, 'I want to go out on the road with two acoustic guitars and a piano player.' My manager said, 'No.' He said that it wasn't going to work and he wanted me to go back to the States with the group lineup, and I just dug my heels in. He didn't give me any support. So I just said 'fuck it' and I got out.

"You have to understand one period in my life that I never want to go through again. The days when I used to get up and see the accountant, go and see the lawyer, see this man and that, were all chaotic. I wouldn't say there was crime involved. It's just that I hadn't been paid. Accounts were in terrible condition. On paper I had a lot of money, in the bank I had nothing. Where was it after all those smashes?

"In the meantime, Ray and Peter Walsh decided to take over the group. They wanted my name and were going to send over a group called The Spencer Davis Group without me, and I refused to go along. They said I was 'bitchy.' People have been called ugly and horrible things and I didn't want to get into that. So, the whole idea of going out with an acoustic band was an economic thing as well as an artistic one." Later in the 1970s, Spencer became a record executive for Island, representing Chris Blackwell's interests in California.

Spencer looked back at his original group with fondness: "I loved that band. Pete York to my way of thinking is still one of the finest drummers around. Unfortunately, we never made the States with that lineup. I think it would have been great to have toured the States because, and I'm sticking my neck out, I think Steve never sounded as good with Traffic, Blind Faith, or Air Force, as he did with us. It was a great band."

THE KINKS, RAY DAVIES & LARRY PAGE THE TEENAGE RAGE

I THOUGHT IT WAS unusual when Larry Page suggested a semi-clandestine rendezvous at the Kensington Hilton Hotel. Larry set the meeting for the afternoon, thereby avoiding the expense of hosting me for lunch. He had called me before I left for London in October 1987. He was excited. He had something for me, but he wouldn't tell me what. Larry zipped into the small car park in his sports car and welcomed me into the passenger seat.

Starting in 1965, ABC aired a Saturday morning animated show of The Beatles as cartoon characters. The Beatles had nothing to do with *The Beatles* except that their records were featured. Although the series had been voiced by actors, Larry claimed the cassette he was about to play me—a copy of a tape that someone had retrieved from a trash bin—was that of The Beatles themselves reading from the script before they became bored and actors were hired.

As he drove around, with my finely honed ears as a Beatles fan, I could tell it was the actors rehearsing their lines and not John, Paul, George, or Ringo. Surely, as the manager of 1960s hit bands The Kinks and The Troggs, Larry must have crossed paths with The Beatles a number of times. At the very least, having grown up in West London, he could recognize English accents much better than I. In offering to deal the tapes, was he trying to pull one over on this Yank, or did he really believe the voices were The Beatles?

Although born Leonard Davies, he became pop singer Larry Page the Teenage Rage in the mid-1950s. He had released four singles that failed to hit, and was realistic in keeping his day job of packing records at EMI's Hayes, Middlesex factory as they came down the conveyor belt. On one of his last days, he even prepared his own singles for shipment. Fortified from his experience as a pop performer, he became a behind-the-scenes man, first as a promoter, then as a producer and manager. As he put it, "No one was aware of rock 'n' roll management. It was theatrical agents managing jugglers. I was aware of an artist's feelings. I was in a position to look after them."

Before The Troggs, Larry comanaged The Kinks. He was responsible for arranging a publishing deal with Eddie Kassner and for naming them. Initially the group was called the Ravens. Larry thought a provocative name would get them attention in the crowded pop music world. The term "kinky," hinting at sexual perversity and outrageous behavior, was in the zeitgeist. It had recently been in the news tied to the Profumo affair, and as a description for *The Avengers* actress Honor Blackman's leather outfits (created by fetish clothes designer John Sutcliff).

Unlike his comanagers, he knew his way around the business, and excelled at old-school image making and publicity stunts. He also had a good ear for hits. The Kinks were signed to Pye Records. As the company pressed and distributed Warner Brothers Records in the UK, a reciprocal arrangement was made whereby Warner label Reprise Records released The Kinks' recordings for the States.

When The Kinks' "You Really Got Me" blasted from radios in the fall of 1964, listeners were riveted by a unique sound: loud and raw, characterized by a distorted guitar. Although simple, The Kinks' first hit was a powerful and rhythmically infectious record. I became a fan, and loved their follow up, "All Day and All of the Night," even more.

The sound and drive of the group's early records caused them in later years to be referred to as "the fathers of heavy metal."

They looked like characters out of a Charles Dickens novel when performing on such TV shows as *Shindig!* They were among the less attractive English hit-makers: singer/rhythm guitarist Ray Davies (pronounced Davis) had a gap between his teeth; Ray's brother, lead guitarist Dave, had the longest hair seen on a boy; bassist Pete Quaife's hair was short and on the verge of crinkly. Drummer Mick Avory had the good looks of a male model, but he was stuck in the back. In contrast to their facial disparity, the choice of their unhip matching ensembles was perplexing. The red hunting jackets with frilly shirts spilling over seemed from another era, but were nonetheless appealing.

Ray's voice wasn't technically good, but he projected a warmth and sensitivity. He had his own style in the same way Bob Dylan had his. In concert they were peculiarly unprofessional: Ray tended to let his guitar dangle rather than enhance the sound by strumming it, and Dave's intense play was sloppy. At times they traded verbal barbs.

As savvy as Larry Page was, he wasn't accomplished enough to control the feuding members' unprofessional and self-destructive behavior. By feuding, I don't mean that occasional insults were passed among them. This was a band in which fistfights were not uncommon. Shortly before leaving for the group's US tour, on May 19, 1965, during a concert at the Capitol Theatre in Cardiff, Wales, Dave kicked Mick Avory's bass drum across the stage. Mick's frustration at being pushed around culminated in him heaving his high-hat pedal at Dave. Dave went down, drawing blood. Mick thought he had killed him. In fear of arrest, Mick fled the scene, ending the concert.

A month later, Larry was at the end of his rope after a draining afternoon trying to coax Ray out of his Hollywood Bowl dressing room to perform at that evening's concert. He returned to England, leaving the group in the capable hands of their trusted road manager Sam Curtis. The group felt abandoned and fired Page. For a number of transgressions, the American musicians union banned The Kinks from returning to the States. (In The Kinks' 1970 album *Lola Versus Powerman and the Moneygoround, Part One*, their biggest selling non-hits record to that time, Ray expressed his bitterness toward Larry and the original Kinks' comanagers, by name, in "Moneygoround.") In April 1998 I saw Ray perform a concert featuring material from *The Storyteller* LP. As he delivered an account of the early days of The Kinks, he made fun of Larry, impersonating Page's nasal "Hello Cock" greeting (British slang for "Hello Friend"). Page also surfaces as a character in *Sunny Afternoon*, Ray's West End musical based on The Kinks.

As a consequence of being unable to work in America, Ray set his sights on England as a milieu, writing wonderful nostalgic and melodic songs that filled four of The Kinks' best albums. Unfortunately, three—*Face to Face, Something Else,* and *The Kinks Are The Village Green Preservation Society*—sold little more than ten thousand apiece in the States.

John Mendelsohn, writing initially in the UCLA *Daily Bruin* and later in *Rolling Stone*, had a lot to do with spreading the word on the magnificence of these little-heard Kinks' recordings. Warner Brothers hired him to execute a "God Save The Kinks" campaign. In contrast to the rocking sounds and simple messages of the majority of the group's mid-sixties material, here Ray's writing was literate and his conception artful.

Ray did not write love songs, or frustrated-by-love songs, but portraits of British society. They contained humor, cynicism, and irony, and were wistful for previous times, going all the way back to the reign of Queen Victoria. Class consciousness was a topic, no doubt aroused by Ray's exposure to upper-class society through the group's first managers, Grenville Collins and Robert Wace. At the same time, those hunting jackets gave the impression that The Kinks were members of an upper-class club about to mount horses in chase of a fox. In August 1966 George Harrison got a lot of press for his diatribe against his government's onerous tax policies directed at high earners—which included rock stars like himself and the other Beatles—in "Taxman," the lead track from The Beatles' *Revolver.* But two months earlier Ray voiced a similar resentment in "Sunny Afternoon," which became a UK number one hit.

THE KINKS WERE PERMITTED to play in the States again in 1969. I saw their show in the gym at UC Irvine. The admission price was a buck, and The Kinks were paid $1,000. It was exhilarating to finally see them perform, but they were the sloppiest band I had ever experienced. I saw the group nine more times in the 1970s, by which time they were presenting costumed musical plays. The material wasn't always great, but the shows were the most fun a member of the audience could have, second to seeing Flo & Eddie.

Although The Beatles are my favorite recording act, The Kinks are much closer to my heart. When an artist has a following in the thousands such as The Kinks, one's bond is more intimate than with an artist who has millions of fans, like The Beatles. It's not an exclusive or snobbish attitude, but a *simpatico* one. Noted music writer Paul Williams said he related to each Kinks' song as "a friend."

Years later the impact of the early Kinks' records held their sway. "You Really Got Me" was in my band's set list during 1972–73. We even rehearsed a B-side, "I'm Not Like Everybody Else." Later in the seventies, I produced a cover of a US flop, "Till the End of the Day," with local band the Makers.

In 1965 Page produced an album of orchestrated renditions of Kinks' songs: *Kinky Music by the Larry Page Orchestra.* Partly an attempt to get exposure for The Kinks' compositions (mostly Ray's), it also followed in the footsteps of similarly orchestrated releases of The Beatles' and The Rolling Stones' songs. Page's concept was hipper, with jazz-styled arrangements. In early 1983, I contacted him to license the album to Rhino for the US market. As it was the rarest Kinks' (associated) record, I thought that every ardent Kinks' fan would need this to complete his/her collection. As there were no Kinks' picture discs, I also issued the album with a striking Kinks' color photo comprising the A-side. Sales were unimpressive; I had miscalculated the number of hardcore Kinks' kollectors. Larry got paid, and a relationship developed.

In November 1984 I was in London and Larry welcomed me at his Ruston Mews home/office. Larry wasn't flamboyant or eccentric, but he was a character. He wore oversized black-rimmed glasses, like Jerry Seinfeld's father on the TV show, and his deliberate manner made me think that he was always assessing. What I liked most about him was his candor. From having been fired by The Kinks and involved in a subsequent lawsuit, it seemed that Larry was bemused when Ray called him out of the blue in the spring about managing the group again. At the same time, he was realistic enough to sense that it wasn't going to be long term.

He was bemoaning his morning call from the mercurial Ray. The Kinks had been approached by writer Jon Savage who wanted to write a book about the group. Ray had signed off on the final draft, but now that *The Kinks: The Official Biography* was about to be published, he— too late—tried to retract his approval.

In February 1987 after attending the MIDEM music convention in Cannes, I flew to London. I initiated negotiations with Precision Records and Tapes—Pye's successor—for their British Invasion artists, most importantly The Kinks. Our *Greatest Hits* album sold much better than reissues of The Kinks' original albums, racking up sales of 250,000. (Reprise retained the rights to a handful of albums.) It was only natural for us to augment this catalogue with that of their subsequent label, RCA Records.

The Kinks recorded six albums for RCA, and shrewdly negotiated to have the rights revert to them ten years after their last release. Early in 1989 I made a deal with Larry for an advance of $125,000. A few months later he was fired. Without Larry involved, our relationship with The Kinks deteriorated. It seemed that Ray's old resentment of his brother, for usurping his position as the adored little brother in a family with five older sisters, had reared its head. Larry explained that Ray wanted to negate the deal, as a good chunk of the advance would go to Dave, who was always in need of money. If the Rhino deal didn't happen, Dave would still be in a diminished/dependent position. Ray didn't need the money. His coffers were bulging with songwriting royalties, to the tune of $14 million, according to Larry. Astonishingly, the brothers revealed their hostility toward each other in 1991's "Hatred (A Duet)," one of their few late-period highpoints, in my opinion.

As a passionate Kinks' fan, I wanted to do an outstanding job of issuing the RCA albums for the CD format. My main inspiration was to produce an elaborate package combining the two *Preservation* albums, acts one and two, and adding a bonus track of "Preservation," which had been released as a single in the US, but not on an album. I wanted to make the booklet look like a libretto, with lyrics and an introductory overview from Ray. Ray had approval of such an expansion, but he wouldn't respond to phone calls, faxes, or letters. Because of our uncertainty, by November we still hadn't released any albums when I received a letter from Ray requesting that I hold off on *Preservation* as he was hoping to mount a musical or television special. He had written songs for a musical based on Jules Verne's *Around the World in Eighty Days*, which had been staged the previous year for six weeks at the La Jolla Playhouse (near San Diego). Ray didn't offer any concessions: he didn't offer to extend the duration of our deal, to buy us out, or give us replacement masters.

A year later, Ray was in town to write another musical. He gave me a call. I picked him up at the Continental Hyatt House and drove up the street to Cravings on Sunset Boulevard. The weather was nice for the first week of December, so we sat outside and ordered breakfast. I didn't want to push my agenda or come across as threatening. My intention was to be friendly, hospitable, and communicate our passion as Kinks' fans desiring to do the best for his catalogue. I wanted to make a positive impression, and for Ray to feel comfortable with me for future dialogues. I suggested that our intended package might help him gain interest in mounting *Preservation* as a musical. Ray was shy, awkward, and scratched out notes on a small pad.

Given the $125,000 I had advanced Ray, I could have expected him to reciprocate and pick up the twenty-five dollar breakfast tab, but knowing his reputation as a skinflint, I abandoned my usual languid response and grabbed the bill folder. I gave him copies of the four albums we had released, all but the *Preservations*.

In their original release, none of the RCA albums benefitted from a hit single. "Celluloid Heroes," the song that was most familiar because of its play on FM radio, bolstered sales of *Everybody's In Show-Biz*, a double album with one disc recorded in concert. During the performance, Ray went into an impulsive segment of "Day-O (The Banana Boat Song)," leading the audience in the call and response. It was picked up by the sports world, and "Day-Oh" has been a fan rouser for the last few decades.

Emotionally I was caught between being a fan who wanted to make my hero happy and being a responsible businessman. We Rhinos felt that, as passionate devotees, we had the objectivity most artists lacked when assessing their own careers. Without approval for my plan and at an impasse, I combined the two albums anyway and used the existing art in a superior package for a July 1991 release. Although RCA had benefitted from additional sales by issuing *The Kinks Greatest Celluloid Heroes,* Ray would not grant Rhino the rights to release a similar best-of album. As of this writing Ray has yet to mount a *Preservation* musical.

It wasn't as if I didn't know what I was getting into, or that I was unaware of Ray's reputation as a curmudgeon. When I interviewed noted session man Nicky Hopkins in 1973, he had this to say about Ray: "After The Kinks' *Village Green* LP, I stopped working with them. They didn't pay me for the sessions, and I did a lot of TV work with them as well. I'm really pissed off. The album's got Ray credited as guitar, vocals, and piano. I thought, 'Jeez! I did seventy-five percent of the keyboard work and I didn't get the proper credit.' I'll never work with him again. They're greedy bastards. Ray Davies is so tight his arse squeaks when he walks."

Fans of musical artists can express themselves in various ways. Some can be irrational: during performances, The Beatles were confronted by massive screams and a barrage of jelly babies (jelly beans). Some can be calculating: sneaking into hotel rooms or backstage areas so they can talk to their idols. Some offer up gifts of baked cakes and stuffed animals, or write fan letters. Many endure long lines at a signing to be able to tell an artist how much they like his work. Others are content to merely buy an album, a poster or T-shirt. For those of us at Rhino, our fandom was best expressed in producing a product of high quality. It was our way of showing how much we valued the music and the creators. In this case our affection for The Kinks was restrained.

Although I received no compliments from Ray, in Dave's 1996 autobiography *Kink*, he referred to our packaging and sound quality as "great." He also complained that the advance we had paid The Kinks was too modest. They had received a million dollars when they signed with RCA Records in 1971. Given that The Kinks did little touring during the term of our license, and did no promotion for our releases, I thought we did an admirable job. They earned another $125,000 in royalties, for a total of $250,000 on the deal.

THE TROGGS

THE STORY OF THE Troggs is unlike any other band. It has twists and turns and improbable episodes. It all started with Larry Page. He was incensed. Not only did The Kinks fire him as their manager, but they also sued him. In happier times, Larry and Ray Davies had written a song together titled "Revenge" for the group's first album. Now Larry was seething with revenge against The Kinks. But he wasn't malicious. He vowed to get back at them by developing another band and turning them into hitmakers. It was serendipitous when music publisher Pat Mills recommended the Troglodytes. Mills told Page that their version of "You Really Got Me" was better than The Kinks.

Reg Presley explained the band's origin: "Ronnie got into a group and bought drums on the never-never [installment plan]. The group disbanded and he was left with all this equipment to pay for. He asked a friend to play lead guitar, and then he asked me to play bass. I'd never seen a bass before, but I did learn to play at least a little bit. Then Chris, who played lead guitar, joined from another group along with Peter who supposedly played bass better than I, although I wonder about that now. We were playing R&B at the time. The Rolling Stones had just started playing Richmond, and Andover kids would rent buses to go see them. So we got loads of Chuck Berry and Muddy Waters records, and that's what we learned to play."

Page signed the band—the name shortened to The Troggs—and molded them into contenders. First, they needed new names. Page, his own name having been changed from Lenny Davies, subscribed to the Larry Parnes school of management whereby new, masculine monikers were given to budding pop stars. Singer Reginald Maurice Ball became Reg Presley. (When I first saw the songwriting credit on a record, I wondered if he was related to Elvis.) Credit *New Musical Express* writer Keith Altham, who suggested the change. Drummer Ronnie Bullis became Ronnie Bond, as in James Bond. Guitarist Chris Britton and bassist Pete Staples didn't require revisions. Second, Page needed to establish a unified look for the mod Reg, beatnik Chris, and rocker Ronnie. He had the Take 6 clothing boutique design gaudy striped suits for the band. They're on display on The Troggs' first album cover.

The Troggs were from Andover, a small city southwest of London in the county of Hampshire. Residents of Andover were considered "country bumpkins" or "hicks from the sticks," and The Troggs were no exception. With all the pop groups vying for media attention, how was Larry Page going to promote his new charges, without intellect, without big-city savvy, without much personality other than being nice guys? In order to mask their country yokel accents and naïveté, Page coached them to be extra polite, including standing when women walked into a room, and escorting them to the door. He also had them all show up for interviews, rather than favoring a single member, as was often the case.

CBS Records released the debut Troggs' 45, "Lost Girl," but dropped the group when it failed to chart. Reg Presley: "We got these two publishing demos, 'Did You Ever Have to Make Up Your Mind' by The Lovin' Spoonful, and 'Wild Thing' by a guy named Chip Taylor. We weren't in The Spoonful bag, so I looked at the sheet music of 'Wild Thing' to play along. 'Wild Thing, you make my heart sing, you make everything groovy.' I thought it was a joke. What kind of crap are they sending us? Then I played the demo, and it was incredible. I knew it was going to be a hit."

The composer, Chip Taylor, was born James Voight, the brother of actor Jon Voight. Taylor had cowritten "I Can't Let Go," a number two UK hit for The Hollies earlier in the year. He composed "Wild Thing" for a New York group called the Wild Ones. United Artists released the record in October 1965, but it stiffed. The record embarrassed Chip because the vocalist sang with a near redneck affectation, approaching the comedic style of Larry Verne in "Mr. Custard."

With one failed single, Larry Page wanted to avoid the financial risk of booking a studio, so he thought he could have The Troggs use the remaining time—if any was left over—of a session for the Larry Page Orchestra. The group waited outside Olympic Studios in their van for two hours. Reg picked up the story: "With forty-five minutes left, we noticed musicians leaving. So we rushed our gear in there. It took us fifteen minutes to set up. So, in twenty minutes we recorded 'Wild Thing' and 'With a Girl Like You,' both live, and they balanced it there. I used the ocarina in the break because there was one on the demo." The group also recorded The Lovin' Spoonful's "Did You Ever Have to Make Up Your Mind," but it was never released.

"Wild Thing," with its pounding drums, super-serious vocal, and absurd ocarina solo, provided a blast of simplicity in 1966 as rock music was progressing. It corresponded perfectly to images of primitive cave dwellers conjured up by the group's moniker. "It took off so fast, I was still laying bricks for a living when it was number twelve on the chart," said Reg. It rose to number two in the UK and number one in the US. At the time Graham Nash said, "They're so behind, they're in front."

"With a Girl Like You," composed by Reg, followed. "We'd never rehearsed 'With a Girl Like You' all the way through before," said Ronnie Bond, "because we didn't know we were going to record it. When we came to the middle break, I was nervous because I didn't know what drum pattern to use." Flush with the success of "Wild Thing," the group spent a frustrating day in the studio trying to improve on their initial recording, but were unable to do so. Reg noted that even Mick Jagger tried helping out. "With a Girl Like You" hit number one in the UK at the same time that "Wild Thing" was number one in the US. Larry Page's forty-five minutes of leftover studio time yielded two big hits.

The group's first LP—*From Nowhere* in the UK, *Wild Thing* in the US—was recorded in three hours. Ronnie Bond: "Some of the songs weren't completely written yet. On 'Jingle Jangle' and four other tracks, Reg wrote the lyrics and the music while we were recording the instrumental backing."

In Britain The Troggs became big stars, with five Top 10s and two Top 20s in little more than a year, from May 1966 to October 1967. The chart positions were even more noteworthy when one considers that England's main radio station, the BBC, banned three of the group's hits—"I Can't Control Myself," "Give It To Me," and "Night of the Long Grass"—for being too suggestive. Fortunately, they received airplay on pirate stations. Of note, "Night of the Long Grass" was Reg's proof that one didn't need to take LSD in order to concoct trippy lyrics. "I wrote that on a cup of tea," he said.

Although The Troggs' outrageousness bordered on comedy, their recordings were successful because they delivered them with an unpretentious honesty. Reg, who wrote most of the songs, sang in the manner of the ordinary working class teen who cared only about girls. But whereas The Beatles and others usually limited themselves to falling in love, The Troggs made their mark as lust-driven, sexually unsatisfied cavemen intent on ripping the dress off the nearest appetizing girl and having a go at it.

Titles such as "I Can't Control Myself" or "I Want You" are more implied than graphically stated, but when the lyrics were coupled with the group's unself-conscious musical interpretation, there was little doubt of their intentions. Presley didn't look much like a typically svelte lead singer: baby fat hung on his cheeks and his figure was trim but round. To me his accent sounded almost Irish, a cross between a jolly leprechaun and a lecherous gravedigger. He sang in a subtle but direct manner, sneering each suitable vocal.

Of all the British Invasion groups, their musical influences were less recognizable. The instrumental backing, hard and markedly simple, was sloppy, characteristic of the we're-tough-we-don't-care punk attitude. Chris was so good in creating the group's sound no one would have ever guessed that he had taken four years of classical guitar lessons. "Simple" is used a lot, by the group as well as others in describing their sound—simple, yes, but effective. For a parallel, consider the rudimentary styles of Black Sabbath and the Ramones.

What's interesting was how much the band's new musical direction emanated from the success of "Wild Thing." A handful of the group's subsequent singles were built on suggestive lyrics delivered with serious intentions. Prior to recording the song, the group's rock 'n' roll and R&B repertoire was similar to that of other groups, and included covers of Chuck Berry, Bo Diddley, Lee Dorsey, Wilson Pickett, Slim Harpo, Little Richard, and Muddy Waters. For comparison, take one of Reg's early songs, "With a Girl Like You," that he knocked off during an extended break from a construction job. It's a sweet—if simple—romantic song, without any hint of suggestiveness.

One of the best examples, and one of The Troggs' best songs, is "I Can't Control Myself." Reg was inspired to write it "by a girl we saw at a gig in Stevenage. She was wearing bright scarlet hipsters that were very, very tight." Writer Ken Barnes described the number two UK hit as "a lewd and lip-smacking ode to sexual volatility replete with leering lyrics and climaxing with a frustrated scream." The Troggs' last good single, "Strange Movies," recounted watching a porno movie. Note that "groovy" is part of the lyrics in both "Wild Thing" and "Strange Movies," although composed eight years apart.

Chip Taylor wrote "Any Way That You Want Me" for The Troggs as a thank you for making "Wild Thing" a smash. It became the group's fourth 1966 release to hit the UK Top 10. Page's Troggs bested not only The Kinks, but also The Beatles, The Rolling Stones, The Dave Clark Five, Herman's Hermits, The Who, and The Hollies. They fared less well in America, with only two big hits overall, but they distinguished themselves from being just another exponent of the British Invasion's second wave.

Relaxing at home one evening, Reg saw The Joystrings Salvation Army vocal group perform a song, "Love That's All Around" on TV. Inspired, he wrote "Love Is All Around" in fifteen minutes. A gorgeous paean to the "Summer of Love," it was a perfectly hummable love song, with Presley revealing a lightness, innocence, and sensitivity. The song became a big hit, number five in the UK and seven in the US.

The Troggs were offered $80,000 to tour the States for concerts and TV appearances (including *The Ed Sullivan Show*), but Page turned it down because, with only one US hit at the time, he thought the trip would lose money. The Troggs still hadn't made it to America, wanted to go, and were upset that he didn't discuss it with them. This was a last straw as they bristled against Page's control of the group.

Page slyly stuck his songs on the group's B-sides, earning extra money for himself. If, as a manager, he was working in the best interests of his clients, he would have selected the group's own compositions. Ronnie Bond: "Our manager decided to write songs for the bread, and it wasn't The Troggs as much. It was The Troggs doing their manager's songs." Bond also pointed out that the group was angry that Page released a second album, *Trogglodynamite*, composed of inferior material, without their consent. Page's commercial instincts were sound: *Trogglodynamite* followed *From Nowhere* into the UK Top 10.

They also felt uncomfortable with Page's publicity stunts. His goal was to constantly have them in the papers. The Beatles were photographed with boxer Muhammad Ali at his training camp in 1964. Two years later so were the stripe-suited Troggs. One saga, which ran in three consecutive issues of *New Musical Express* in

April 1967, had Chris leaving the band. He was quoted as saying that he was "sick of the long-haired, drug-taking image." Almost like the feigned, heated exchange in a professional wrestling match, Larry countered with a threat of a lawsuit if Chris left. A substitute guitarist was photographed arriving to join the group as they were leaving for a tour. Of course, it was all a hoax. The Troggs fired Page as their manager in June 1967, although their product continued to be released on Larry's Page One Records until October 1970. After firing him, they never recorded another hit.

Often referred to as "Britain's only punk band," at least as of the 1960s, The Troggs were also a prime influence of Britain's first wave of heavy metal bands. Ozzy Osbourne, then with Black Sabbath, told me: "The very sexual and driving aspects of our music came from listening to records like The Troggs' 'Wild Thing' and The Kinks' 'You Really Got Me.' I'd never heard anything like those records before. They were very important." (In 1972 The Troggs recorded a single with Sabbath's original producer, Roger Bain, that was musically effective but a stiff commercially.) Jimi Hendrix provided another example when he made a heavy version of "Wild Thing" an integral part of his act. In the *Monterey Pop* film he closed his set with it as he set his guitar on fire.

In 1968 Tony Murray replaced Pete Staples on bass. Reg explained: "We were always classed as basic and simple, but this guy was one step simpler than we were—he was an idiot. When music started to progress and we wanted to progress, he couldn't come with us. It reached its low ebb at a club date in Switzerland when he'd been making more mistakes. That night he played a tune different from 'With a Girl Like You' and didn't know it until we'd told him afterward."

Chris Britton added: "We played on this stage seven feet off the ground and he was so rigid that once he planted his feet he wouldn't move. Some fan tugged his shoelace and he went over like a falling statue. It's a shame because he's a nice guy." Although the lineup improved musically, The Troggs were victims of a lack of direction, and dropped off the charts. They even recorded bubblegum tunes in a misguided effort to get a hit.

During a recording session in 1970, studio engineer Clive Franks was so frustrated by The Troggs arguing with one another that he ran a backup tape as the band worked on a song called, of all things, "Tranquility." The resulting twelve-minute tape, a real audio-verite of the recording process, was passed around England's rock elite and became all the rage to quote from. Eric Clapton, Pete Townshend, and the like made phrases like "duba-duba-duba-cha" and "put some fairy dust on it" part of their day-to-day chatter. (Jim Bickhart made me a cassette copy from one that he got from Dave Pegg of Fairport Convention.) Despite the wrath Reg heaped on Ronnie in the studio, their unbroken professional relationship remained intact. Although the group was embarrassed by the disclosure, through the years they acquired a new cachet and got more work. (They even played at Sting and Trudie Styler's wedding reception in August 1992). "The Troggs Tapes" inspired a scene in *This Is Spinal Tap*. Director/writer Rob Reiner had gotten his copy from Mason "Classical Gas" Williams. I included an edited segment on *The Rhino Brothers Present the World's Worst Records, Volume Two* in 1985.

In November 1971 *Cream* magazine editor Lester Bangs, portrayed by Philip Seymour Hoffman in *Almost Famous*, ranted on The Troggs for twenty-four pages in the *Who Put the Bomp* fanzine. Sure, he went on tangents galore, but it was clear that he loved and understood The Troggs' music. This was followed by Richard Meltzer's one-page appreciation of their early records.

I was in London for three weeks in late summer 1973, but didn't want to extend my trip an additional week to attend an October 19 taping of *The Midnight Special* TV show at the Marquee. Billed as *The 1980 Floor Show*, David Bowie starred and picked Marianne Faithful and The Troggs as his guest stars. Their appearance and Bowie's endorsement did much to revive their career, resulting in better-paying gigs, if not a return to the charts. Although Bowie didn't cover a Troggs' song on his *Pin Ups* album, he did reveal that the band influenced his 1984 hit "Blue Jean."

In October 1973 The Troggs released their last great single, "Strange Movies." I liked it so much that in 1978 I auditioned Martha Davis, then between lineups of the Motels, with the intention of recording it with her, but the project went no further.

I saw The Troggs on April 22, 1980, at the Whisky a Go-Go, where they amazed the audience with a steamy set that probably sounded as they had in 1966. Los Angeles record buffs and future Rhino staffers Gary Stewart and Danny Perloff called it "The best show I've ever seen." I reintroduced myself to the group the day before when they played at the Rhino Records store. Ronnie Bond gave me his phone number and told me to give him a call when I was next in Britain. In 1984 I produced a *Best of The Troggs* for Rhino, which sold twenty-eight thousand copies.

Similar to The Kinks reuniting with Larry Page, The Troggs asked him back into their lives eight years after they had given him the axe. One of Larry's ideas resulted in a March 1992 Rhino release. Members of R.E.M. were big Troggs' fans and often included a Troggs' song as part of their set. They performed "Love Is All Around" on *MTV Unplugged* and released a live recording of it as the B-side of a cassette single. Larry produced an album in Athens, Georgia, with Reg and Chris accompanied by R.E.M.'s Bill Berry, Mike Mills, Peter Buck, and regular sideman Peter Holsapple. R.E.M. was hot. The band's current album, *Out of Time*, had sold over four million copies. Although R.E.M.'s vocalist Michael Stipe didn't participate, we thought there would be a lot more loyal R.E.M. fans who had to have everything the band recorded, and were dissatisfied with only five thousand sales.

In 1994, Wet Wet Wet's new recording of "Love Is All Around" was featured prominently in *Four Weddings and a Funeral*. On the strength of the hit movie, the record topped the British chart for fifteen weeks. By this time Reg was heavily into studying crop circles and the paranormal. He hosted *The Reg Presley UFO Show* on local cable TV. The British press reported that he looked forward to the financial windfall to enable him to hire helicopters to look at newly discovered crop circles, and to travel the world to investigate stories of UFOs and alien encounters. In 2004 he published his findings in *Wild Things They Don't Want Us to Know*. In *Rolling Stone* magazine's 2004 poll of the "500 Greatest Songs of All Time," The Troggs' "Wild Thing" was ranked 257. Reg passed away in 2013; Ronnie in 1992.

THE HISTORY OF THE DAVE CLARK FIVE

T HE DAVE CLARK FIVE were among the better bands of the mid-sixties British Invasion. As with The Beatles, it took them a few years before they developed their sound and had success. They had no grand ambitions. The band formed for the temporary goal of making enough money to afford passage to Holland for Dave's youth club soccer team. Members of the team played instruments, but there was no drummer, so Dave bought a drum set for ten pounds (twenty-eight dollars) from a Salvation Army outlet and learned the rudiments.

The band was good and gained a following, appearing often at the Tottenham Royal Mecca Ballroom. As exciting as the group was live, they weren't convincing when they auditioned for record companies. There were few labels interested in signing the group, and those that did wanted to furnish the songs and define how they were to be recorded. Dave, though, believed in the band's ability to make exciting records. He realized that he could control the repertoire if he paid for the sessions himself. He used the £300 ($840) he made for two days of stunt driving in a movie—crashing cars for a character played by singer Adam Faith—to pay for the recording. He then made a deal with EMI's Columbia Records in the UK (and Epic in the US), and bluffed the label into giving him a high royalty by asking for three times the going rate, thinking that would give him more room to negotiate when the company made a lower counter offer. Columbia didn't have to risk the expense of recording, so, to his surprise, they agreed. He also asked for the masters to revert to him after ten years, and they agreed to this as well. Nobody thought that this music would have longevity.

Dave left school at fifteen. His family was poor. He wasn't academically inclined. Somehow, though, he had a natural instinct for making good business decisions. He learned from his agent, Harold Davidson, and others. This led him to form a publishing company for the band's compositions. Income from songs was usually split 50 percent for the writers, 50 percent for the publisher, which meant that Dave made money not only from the songs he helped to write, but also from the publishing. It's one thing to take note of what songs dancers respond to, and another to eavesdrop on them between sets to pick up on phrases around which to build songs. Such eavesdropping resulted in the band's first two big hits, "Glad All Over" and "Bits and Pieces."

The importance of band-composed songs was brought home in October 1963 with their first charting record. The group loved American rock 'n' roll, and recorded a cover of The Contours' 1962 hit "Do You Love Me," which skirted the Top 30 in the UK. Dave had seen the Motown vocal group perform it live on tour in Britain. But it was bested by a contemporary, beat group (i.e. like The Beatles) arrangement by Brian Poole and the Tremeloes, which made it to number one. In contrast, The Dave Clark Five's version was slower, more rhythm and blues in feel, and superior. If the band relied mostly on their own songs, they wouldn't risk being beaten out again. (Seven months later, "Do You Love Me" became the group's third hit in America, rising to eleven. Brian Poole's version failed to chart.)

Dave was a controlling person. He was disciplined in the martial arts (including karate), and as a stunt man he was used to being precise. It was unheard of for a member of a rock band to also be the producer of their records, which Dave was. On the first few releases, unsure of how his attribution would be perceived, he credited the producer as Adrian Clark, utilizing his engineer Adrian Kerridge's first name and his own surname. Kerridge was on staff at Lansdowne, London's first independent recording studio. He worked with Dave to create a sound that was unique to The Dave Clark Five (aka DC5), utilizing four-track recording machines. Reverb featured prominently on their records. Rather than relying on an in-place echo chamber, Kerridge placed a microphone in the stairwell of a concrete bunker at the back of the studio. Reverb provided a novel hook to the group's next single, "Glad All Over," which topped the charts in England.

Dave was also the band's manager. It was a function he'd provided from the beginning, and he didn't feel a need to change when the group became popular, to give control to somebody else, even if he were more experienced. Having aspired to be a professional soccer player, he was, as a member of the band, more like the captain of a team that worked well together. He made good choices in solidifying the band's lineup. Mike Smith was the musical genius of the group. In addition to having a superb voice, he was classically trained on the piano, and cowrote many of the songs with Dave. Lenny Davidson played guitar, Rick Huxley bass, and Denis Payton sax.

The longhair era of rock signaled attitudes that were antiestablishment and free-wheeling, and skirted the rules. In contrast, in February 1964 Dave had his group members sign conventional, five-year employment contracts, almost as if they were in a 1940s dance band. Each member received a weekly salary of fifty pounds, four weeks of paid vacation a year, but no artist royalties on the records. They were on call twenty-four hours a day, were responsible for maintaining their own instruments, and had to follow Dave's guidelines on hair and dress. His lineup stayed intact for the nine years of the band's duration.

Ed Sullivan had a highly watched variety show in the States. His ratings soared when The Beatles were guests, and he thought The Dave

Clark Five would be a good follow-up. American teens, especially girls, loved these British newcomers. They looked different with their long hair, their English accents were novel, and they seemed polished and charming compared to local grown talent. Handsome Dave was the epitome of charm, whether he was addressing girls with "luv," or complaining that he couldn't get a good cup of tea in America.

When Ed's people contacted Dave's agent, he turned them down. Dave had no interest in going to America. From performing at US air bases in Britain, where off-duty soldiers had a good time getting drunk and behaving badly, he thought America "would be the pits." He was persuaded when the show offered a fee of $10,000 and a luxurious, all-expenses paid trip. It was an enormous amount of money compared to the fifteen pounds a day Dave had made as an extra in films and TV. It proved to be a turning point.

Ed loved the band. It wasn't so much that he related to their music, it was more how clean cut they all were. Displaying black and white matching stage clothes, neat haircuts, dazzling smiles, and matinee-idol chins, The Dave Clark Five were the best looking and most stylish of all the bands of the British Invasion. Their debut on his show on March 8, 1964, incited the same mania the teenage members of his studio audience showed for The Beatles the previous month, so Sullivan booked them for a return appearance. It was only then, in the face of the reception they received in America, that the band quit their day jobs and made the commitment to turn professional. The DC5 eventually racked up twelve appearances on *The Ed Sullivan Show*, more than any other rock band.

Realizing the expanse of the US market, Dave focused his energies on the States, organizing a tour that commenced May 25 at the Mosque Theater in Newark, New Jersey. The group commanded $10,000 per show. For touring the US, a Martin 404 propeller plane was leased from the Rockefellers. "DC5" was painted on the exterior, which would have been more appropriate if it had been a McDonnell Douglas aircraft, the DC initials for Douglas Commercial.

The band toured the States six times—to The Beatles' three. This resulted in the DC5 having more hits in America than in Britain. During 1964 they had seven Top 20 hits in America, all but one band-composed, and were second only to The Beatles in popularity. Because The Beatles style was described as Merseybeat (owing to Liverpool's River Mersey), the media described the music of The Dave Clark Five as the Tottenham Sound. Although there were a large number of bands from Liverpool, many of which also became successful, like Gerry & The Pacemakers and Billy J. Kramer with the Dakotas, there was no comparable scene in the north London suburb of Tottenham, and hence no other proponents of the sound.

On tour The Dave Clark Five mirrored the experiences of The Beatles: motorcades from the airport, sneaking into hotels through kitchens, fans chasing them and hiding in their hotel rooms. Among the hundreds of dolls and other gifts they received was a sheep. Dave didn't know what to do with it, so he left it in their hotel suite. Upon returning from the show, he discovered that the sheep had chewed every credit card and every piece of furniture. As he said, "We didn't trash hotel suites, but the sheep did."

Their live show was a different matter. It was the best production by a rock band for its day. It commenced with a dramatic, pounding cover of Henry Mancini's "Peter Gunn Theme." On "Five By Five," another instrumental—the band had primarily played instrumentals in its pre-hit years—Dave got up from his drum kit to stand at an array of large floor tom drums, to pound away as purple and red lights flashed from inside the drums. During such moments, black light made the band members seem to glow in the dark in their white shirts.

By 1965, THE DC5's popularity was exceeded by Herman's Hermits and The Rolling Stones. The band still produced good records, but they were no longer perceived as hip. Their lineup included a saxophone, an instrument more identified with the pre-Beatles era. Coming a year after the release of The Beatles' *A Hard Day's Night*, and only a week after their *Help!*, the group's feature film, *Having a Wild Weekend* (*Catch Us If You Can* in Britain), was pessimistic in tone, overly ambitious in its satire of consumerism and, ultimately, boring. It suffered from a lack of memorable songs comparable to those of The Beatles' Lennon and McCartney. The DC5's status fell further when they failed to progress as The Beatles had, whether embracing more ambitious concepts or psychedelic drugs.

The Beatles, The Rolling Stones, and other groups success with self-composed songs resulted in the confidence to depart from the rock 'n' roll covers that were part of their repertoires in their early years. After a very successful first year of Dave Clark and Mike Smith compositions, the DC5 fell back on covers of American rock 'n' roll hits "Over and Over" (Bobby Day), "I Like It Like That" (Chris Kenner), and "You Got What It Takes" (Marv Johnson), songs Americans at the air bases had turned them onto. Or maybe the change in repertoire owed to the group not having composed as many hits as they claimed? In a 2009 interview, Ron Ryan, once a friend of Dave's, claimed that he—not Dave—wrote "Bits and Pieces," "Because," and "Anyway You Want It." Because he was also a friend of the other band members, he agreed to a paltry settlement because he didn't want bad publicity to adversely affect the momentum of the band.

As fans became savvy, they realized how little value for money they were getting when they bought DC5 albums. The group's first two American albums averaged twenty-three minutes of music; their first *Greatest Hits* totaled twenty-three minutes, and *More Greatest Hits,* twenty-two minutes. The Beatles' and Herman's Hermits' first two American albums averaged twenty-seven minutes. (American albums had fewer tracks than the English ones owing to a different way of allocating publishing fees.) The Dave Clark Five had good album tracks, but not enough to make good value the seven albums they released in their first two years, making the listening experience less satisfying than albums by The Beatles, The Kinks, The Rolling Stones, and Herman's Hermits. All of these factors contributed to the group being dismissed as lightweight. Their popularity slid further, and after the summer of 1966, they had only one more Top 30 hit in America. When they tried to be progressive, with such singles as "Live in the Sky" and "Inside Out," they missed the mark. Dave gave up touring in 1967, and the band's activity slowed. He produced two records that made the Top 10 in England in 1970, before the band announced its dissolution in August of that year.

Being a fan of their music, one was often met with derision. It took so long for the group to be voted into the Rock and Roll Hall of Fame, it was almost an embarrassment when they were inducted in 2008. Joel Stein, writing in the *Los Angeles Times*, made a joke at their expense when they failed to get enough votes the previous year: "Monday, the Rock and Roll Hall of Fame turned down The Dave Clark Five for allegations of totally sucking. Even the sluttiest sixties groupie didn't want Dave Clark getting glad all over her."

Pop music fans had no concept that the exciting and charming rock bands that they saw and loved performing on TV and in concert may not have played on their records. Of course, it didn't matter. The records were judged and enjoyed on their own merit.

Mike Nesmith broke the code when, troubled that The Monkees were prevented from playing on their own records, he voiced his frustration in an interview with the *Saturday Evening Post*. As musicians were being perceived as artists, that session musicians might have been used in their stead knocked points off their credibility.

When, years later, I heard that noted session drummer Bobby Graham had played on most of The Dave Clark Five's hits, I felt betrayed. Through the years I had been defending the group's records, I promoted them when I was on the nominating committee of the Rock and Roll Hall of Fame, and I championed Dave as a skillful drummer.

No musician as part of a band wants to be replaced by a session man. It means that you're not good enough. When George Martin replaced Ringo Starr with Alan White for the recording of The Beatles' first single, "Love Me Do," because George was unsure of his ability, Ringo was devastated. Dave assessed that his drumming was only adequate, and wisely realized that hiring an accomplished drummer would help to make a better record. In listening to the recordings, Graham's superiority is evident. Graham also drummed on hits by other rock bands, including The Kinks, Herman's Hermits, Them, and even on Brian Poole's "Do You Love Me."

Despite their dull personalities, the DC5 were no cretins, and they distinguished themselves on many counts. In the first place, they were the only successful band of the time to be essentially self-managed, by Dave himself. In the category of drummer as composer, he's probably credited with more hits than anybody else from that era. The band's *Coast to Coast* album was the first by a British group to feature all original songs. And the identifiable sounds of the group's records, with uncommonly loud drums, were influenced by Phil Spector, and owed much to experimentation. "Anyway You Want It," "Can't You See that She's Mine," and "Catch Us If You Can" were the most chaotic hit records of their day.

I MET DAVE DURING a visit with Mike Chapman in the studio when Mike was producing Smokie. As it was during a session, we didn't talk much. Dave mentioned that he had been taking acting lessons with Sir Laurence Olivier, and explained that his arm was in a cast because of a skiing accident. Before the band happened, Dave had wanted to be an actor, but was relegated to stunt and extra work. He appeared in forty films and TV shows. His interest initiated TV projects for the band as well as their feature film. Given an opportunity to star in the band's own film, he realized his limitations when he saw the results. After his musical projects diminished in the early 1970s, he studied acting.

Dave channeled his aspirations into theatrical production. In 1986 he achieved the rare feat of cowriting and producing a hit West End production. *Time*, a science fiction musical, broke ground with its use of multi-media and special effects. It starred Cliff Richard, who was succeeded by David Cassidy.

By the mid-1980s, The Dave Clark Five hits had been unavailable in America for ten years. Dave refused offers to release the masters even after the proliferation of the CD format. He reasoned that, the more he kept them off the market, the more pent-up demand would become. Dave didn't need the money—he'd invested well in real estate—and could afford to wait for the huge advance he desired. Starting in 1984, I wrote him yearly for five years expressing our interest in releasing his catalogue. Only in the last year did he send a letter saying he wasn't interested. He didn't anticipate that, by keeping the records out of the stores, he would diminish their value. Oldies radio programmed fewer of the hits, as they were not available to the stations. Similarly, the records did not get exposed in other media such as feature films, TV shows, commercials. He also was insensitive to music fans who wanted to hear the records. Some wore out their vinyl copies; others replaced their turntables with CD players. Much of the band's great music faded from memory.

In 1989, the Disney Channel made a deal with Dave to program the 1960s English music show *Ready Steady Go!* during evenings, to attract adult viewers to the kids' cable channel. Dave had purchased the existing shows—only a small percentage of those produced—and reedited them, adding footage of the DC5. He taped new introductions that were shown before each show.

Although Disney's in-house record label was successful in the fifties and sixties, by the 1980s it was relegated to issuing soundtracks of Disney movies. The new regime, wanting to cultivate teen and adult record buyers, formed Hollywood Records to break new artists. This was similar to Disney establishing Touchstone in 1987 as a separate film division to attract more adult and mature teen movie patrons.

In the first two years of its existence, the label was a disaster. The president, Peter Paterno, acknowledged as much in a letter to Disney's chairman Michael Eisner and president Frank Wells, dated October 31, 1991. He referred to the perception of the label as "the Titanic captained by the Three Stooges," expecting losses in the coming year of between $20 and $30 million. Paterno understood that profits from catalogue sales could finance new artists until they become profitable. He signed Queen to release a new album, as well as their catalogue. In the letter, he refers to the Dave Clark "fiasco."

Five months earlier, Hollywood Record's Bob Reitman had sent a letter to Dave enticing him in many areas. He expressed interest in rereleasing Dave's catalogue, and referred to the "high priority" the company would have to get his songs in Disney, as well as other studios' feature films, and in TV shows and commercials. There were enticements relating to the theme parks, Disney stores, TV specials, and trailers plugging the product in movie theaters and Disney home videos. It was enough to make one's head spin, or in this case, for Dave to extract an agreement with Paterno for two million dollars. When Frank Wells heard about the deal, he blew a gasket, and nullified it. Paterno scrambled together a settlement, for a scaled-down deal paying Dave an advance of one million for two audio releases.

My partner Richard Foos and I had a good relationship with Wesley Hein, who, with his brother Bill, had started Enigma Records. Wes wanted to break out from the company, and in 1989 accepted a job as an executive vice president at Hollywood Records. Knowing Rhino's expertise with catalogue, he called Richard to see if we wanted to be part of the deal. It was smart of him. Between Gary Stewart, Bill Inglot, and me, we had three knowledgeable DC5 fans who could make suggestions on the repertoire. Comparatively, Hollywood had no DC5 fans. And Rhino's involvement and contribution to Hollywood's advance meant that their risk was diminished.

Richard made the deal with Wes. I was happy to be involved, happy that we might help create a package that would be much better than if we didn't participate. Our $300,000 advance seemed like a lot for the rights we were getting, made all the more questionable when Shelly Heber, the cohead of Image Marketing, predicted, quite presciently, that sales wouldn't be much more than one hundred thousand. Richard lessened our risk by making a deal with Warner Music Enterprises, one of Warner's two mail order divisions, guaranteeing an order of a certain amount of albums to be marketed through TV commercials.

Dave knew about Rhino's involvement. In the contract it stated that we had exclusive rights for direct sales to customers through a TV-advertised campaign, as well as non-exclusive rights to sell through mail-order companies. Hollywood retained the much larger retail market. Dave didn't know that we were directing the creative elements of the release. By mistake, Dave was sent a layout of the proposed package, created by a Rhino designer, that hadn't excluded Rhino's standard "manufactured and marketed by" credit. He caught it and had it changed, and quizzed Wes Hein on any larger Rhino participation. Wes mollified him. We were otherwise careful not to credit any Rhinos for their involvement.

It was a good package, but not up to Rhino standards. First, the package itself was cheap, two CDs in a jewel case (as the boxes are called) that normally included one. In order to scrimp on the number of pages of the booklet, small type was used, ignoring the diminishing eyesight of the original, now much older fans, who would most likely buy the album. It was Hollywood's call. They were trying to save money to recoup their advance. We provided track suggestions to Hollywood, who then relayed them to Dave, who had the ultimate decision. There were better tracks than some he included, but at least we got him to add "Try Too Hard," a number twelve hit in the States that he excluded. Bill Inglot also had problems with the mastering relating to a number of tracks, but, again, it was Dave's call.

The History of The Dave Clark Five only sold 110,000, which disappointed everybody. Even though the contract didn't terminate until 2002, Dave wanted to get the product off the store shelves early. He embarrassed Disney into deleting the album from their catalogue, but he failed to consider the rights that Hollywood had given Rhino. We had over thirty thousand pieces of inventory that we had paid for. Although sales were light, we had the rights to sell it to our own mail order customers and to other companies.

By 1997 none of the executives Dave had dealt with were still at Hollywood Records. I wrote him a letter expressing our desire to succeed Hollywood's deal—after all, Hollywood never issued a box set—or to make a new deal. Dave faxed us a curt reply that he was not interested. Given that we were highly respected in the industry, were enthusiastic Dave Clark Five fans, and willing to put a substantial amount of money into Dave's pocket—although not as much as he wanted—he could have at least been courteous.

When Dave became aware that Rhino was still selling product, it bothered him. He couldn't tie up loose ends and move on. It wasn't as if he wanted to make a deal with another company. In November 1998 he was in town and invited me to lunch at the Bel-Air Hotel to talk about it. I looked forward to spending more time with a man whose musical contributions I respected, but I was put in an uncomfortable situation. Rhino had not made a deal directly with Dave, and his desire put us in an adversarial position. It was a mostly pleasant lunch, sitting on the patio. Dave reeled off a few stories, but he was not an enthusiastic conversationalist. Or maybe he was focused on trying to alleviate the Rhino horn that suddenly poked his side. He kept reiterating his position, seemingly attempting to verbally bludgeon me into submission.

A year later Dave was in town, and I invited him to visit Rhino so he could see that we weren't a rinky-dink operation. In my office, I told Dave the extent that we had helped Hollywood with the album. He explained that Disney had all but promised him so much more than a label like Rhino could have delivered. From how things turned out, he admitted that he should have made the deal with Rhino instead.

I offered to sell him our inventory, at our cost, in order to get it off the market. His preference was that we destroy the albums, but then we would have lost that revenue. Whether or not the outstanding inventory was sold to customers—and even if it was destroyed—Dave had already been paid on both the artist royalty and the publishing. (Usually royalties are earned when a record is sold, but in this deal Dave was paid upon manufacture.) The bluff on my part was not stating the obvious, that we were never going to come close to selling our inventory. In most record deals, the company is able to salvage money on nonselling inventory by dumping it for a vastly reduced amount as cut-outs (product cut out or deleted from the catalogue). Because of our contract with Hollywood Records, we couldn't do that.

From the meetings and phone conversations, I felt good about Dave, but when he returned to London, he became nit-picky. I received faxed letters from him, his accountant, and his lawyer for minor infractions. He ordered a CD from Collectors' Choice, which proved that they were selling the album outside of the US, which they weren't supposed to do. Practically speaking, how many could they have sold of the more expensive double CD when a cheaper, single disc collection was available in England and other parts of the world? I notified Collectors' Choice that their sales were restricted only to the US, with which they complied. Next we received a letter from him complaining that Rhino mail order was discounting four dollars off the twenty-eight dollar list-price album. Forgetting that retailers had discounted the album, and even Amazon had sold it at 40 percent off list price, were Rhino's small sales a threat? I responded to Dave's letter, and had our mail order manager raise the price. The Dave Clark Five's music had brought me countless hours of happiness, but I couldn't please the man most responsible.

Prior to this scrutiny, I, on behalf of Rhino Video, offered Dave an advance of $250,000 to put his *Ready Steady Go!* shows on DVD. In 1989 he had released six VHS tapes—and laser discs—but they had never been on DVD. I assumed the amount wasn't enough, as I never received a response. As of this writing, he has yet to grant a license for the format. He never made a subsequent license for his DC5 masters in the US, except to make them available to download.

Everybody lost financially on the deal: Hollywood Records, Rhino, and Warner Music. Dave pocketed a large advance that wasn't close to recouping, but his catalogue was further devalued. The poor sales of the *History of* album made it appear a failure, and there was no subsequent product, which meant that his masters weren't available to the fans, and his copyrights weren't generating income. The group's original albums have never been issued on CD, nor has the band's oeuvre been appreciated in a significant box set, even though Hollywood Records had the rights to issue one.

Despite Dave's obdurate negotiating manner, and his low-key nature, I kind of liked him. In October 2001 I faxed him a letter that I was leaving Rhino. I was surprised when he called me from London, telling me I am "a gentleman," and wishing me "good luck." I'm glad we left our relationship on a positive note.

EMPEROR ROSKO AND THE PIRATES OF RADIO

IN THE MID-SIXTIES FEW Americans knew about Britain's pirate radio stations, so called because they were unlicensed and operated outside the country's three-mile limit. Their only exposure, had they recognized it, was on *The Who Sell Out*, the group's best album, which was released in December 1967. The idea was to format The Who's songs as though one were listening to Radio London, *sans* DJs. They initially wanted to sell commercials on the record, but as only Coca-Cola agreed, The Who wrote and recorded their own made-up ones.

When in London in the fall of 1979, I picked up a remainder copy of DJ Jimmy Saville's book *As It Happens* to read on the plane back to the States. I was curious about radio in the days before the BBC had its own pop music channel, primarily about Radio Luxembourg and England's radio pirates. Saville's book wasn't well written and there was much less information than I was expecting. It was soon in the discard stack. Other than digging through back copies of British newspapers, where would one find background on this colorful era of radio? I had asked Justin Hayward when I interviewed him, but he had scant knowledge.

With Rhino Films established, I thought a feature about the radio pirates would fill in a bit of history as well as provide a unique setting—a bunch of crazy DJs on a ship in the North Sea—and a sumptuous rock soundtrack.

One of the prominent DJs, Emperor Rosko, broadcasted from the pirate ship Radio Caroline. Unlike most of the pirate DJs, Rosko wasn't a Brit. Instead, he grew up in Beverly Hills, only a couple of miles from Rhino's offices. Peter Pasternak, head of Rhino's international department, was one of the three sons of noted film producer Joe Pasternak. Joe had produced one hundred movies, and was known mostly for guiding a number of MGM's musicals. Peter's eldest brother, Michael, is Emperor Rosko. I had him set up a meeting, in May 2000.

Michael, a rowdy underachiever, was sent to military school by his parents to straighten him out. He later joined the US Navy. As a young teen, he wanted to be a disc jockey, and became one on the aircraft carrier on which he was serving. To become a professional, he needed an FCC license, so he moved to San Francisco and enrolled in the only broadcasting school west of the Rockies. He helped to get his pal, Sylvester Stewart—later known as Sly Stone—also enrolled.

Having learned French in boarding school, he found himself in 1965 working as a compere and DJ in Paris for Barclay Records' Freddy Barclay. Most DJs created their own persona, usually with a DJ name. Michael called himself Emperor Rosko after two of his favorite Los Angeles personalities, KRLA's Emperor Hudson (Robert Howard Holmes) and KBLA's Rosko (William Roscoe Mercer).

The primary character in the pirate radio story is Irishman Ronan O'Rahilly. He managed a few rock acts, most notably Georgie Fame (whose only US Top 10 hit was "The Ballad of Bonnie and Clyde"), and was frustrated that he couldn't get airplay to build their popularity. At that time in the mid-sixties, the BBC played only three or four hours of pop music a week, preferring classical music and educational programs. Radio Luxembourg's programming for England and Ireland aired a few hours each night, but its signal was intermittent. The four major UK labels bought the available evening time to get exposure for their records, which meant that small companies were shut out.

Noting the success of ships outfitted with radio transmitters off the coasts of Scandinavia and Holland, O'Rahilly bought a Dutch passenger ferry and retro-fitted it into a sea-going radio station. O'Rahilly was inspired by the idealism and youthfulness of the recently assassinated John F. Kennedy—also of Irish lineage—and considered him a hero. He named his new endeavor Radio Caroline, after JFK's daughter. He exhibited a bust of JFK in his own office, and when incognito answered only to "Bobby Kennedy."

Radio Caroline launched on Easter Sunday, March 28, 1964, with The Rolling Stones' "Not Fade Away," which became the group's first big hit. A lot of music was played, from 6:00 a.m. to 6:00 p.m., but it wasn't all contemporary rock 'n' roll. There were segments for big bands, show tunes, and religious shows that bought blocks of time in the evenings. Labels also forked over payola to get play for their records. Later in the year, Georgie Fame had a hit with "Yeh, Yeh," his first of three number ones.

Henri Henroid, the European tour manager for Sam the Sham & The Pharaohs, was impressed with Rosko's panache when he emceed their show at the Olympia in Paris. He offered to get an audition tape to Ronan for him. As a result, Rosko became a DJ on Radio Caroline. Having spent four years in the US Navy, it was easier for Rosko to acclimate to the ship than for his fellow DJs. Rosko brought American radio know-how, a Top-40 style with a "have no fear, the emperor is here" rhythmic pattern. Also if he heard a French language record he liked, he included it in his show.

The schedule was two weeks on the boat, one week off. There were usually six or seven DJs who worked four-hour shifts. They slept in bunk beds, two to a cramped cabin. Rosko remembered far too many meals made with potatoes, including potato sandwiches. When not broadcasting, DJs played cards or chess, fished, oogled bikini babes who cruised by in warm weather, and tried to entice them on the boat for a sexual romp. Rosko also spent a lot of time honing his skills in the production studio.

Many listeners felt as though they were members of a secret club. As there were no audits done at the time, it's estimated that at least eight million people were listening to pirate radio at its peak hours. By far the most-listened to station was Radio London, followed by Caroline. The girlfriend of Caroline DJ Johnnie Walker (Peter Waters Dingley) gave him three spliffs—hash mixed with tobacco—on his return to the ship to alleviate his boredom. As he was a novice, she gave him a code phrase for him to say during his show so she would know that he enjoyed the experience and wanted her to send him more. Johnnie got high with his fellow DJs and found new popularity on the ship. During his broadcast he sent a "good evening" to this girlfriend, followed by "we've just run out of tea, love." Days later he received four more spliffs in the mail from her and, unexpectedly, sacks full of Ty-phoo and Tetley teas from listeners.

During their week off, the DJs stayed at the Bayswater Hotel or the Royal Garden Hotel, and genuine camaraderie developed. "We became like rock stars," Rosko said, "and in many cases we were making more money than them. We didn't think about anything except having fun and music." And when they spent time at the London clubs—Rosko favored the Ad Lib and Marquee—they rubbed shoulders with rock's elite. "They loved us. We played their records." Dusty Springfield became his girlfriend. (She later came out as a lesbian.)

Rosko had found the perfect job for himself, one that could accommodate his brash behavior and fondness for pranks. "I took on a pirate look, like Errol Flynn. I had my clothes custom-made." When new pirate ship Radio England was testing its transmitter by playing station identification jingles, Rosko recorded them off the air and altered them to plug Caroline. Incensed, Radio England threatened to sue until Rosko stopped playing them two days later. He also made a pet mynah bird part of his act and trained it to squawk "sounds fine, it's Caroline" and "long live rock 'n' roll" during his shift.

His wild behavior also got him fired. Phil Solomon, the Irish manager of The Bachelors, Them and other acts, invested a considerable amount in Radio Caroline with the expectation that he would get exposure on his acts. Rosko refused to play music he found inferior and thought nothing of sailing records on Solomon's Major Minor label out the porthole. Solomon fired him. O'Rahilly rehired him. This happened numerous times, almost monthly.

O'Rahilly had a consulting deal with French Radio Luxembourg, which was recently purchased by the owner of *Paris Match* magazine. The station wanted to create a pirate radio type of show to attract more listeners and needed a real pirate DJ. Rosko was perfect. He had previously been based in Paris, loved the city, and was bilingual. *Paris Match* raised his weekly salary from £70 to £250, and heavily promoted him. His popularity soared: he did emceeing, made personal appearances, and established one of the first—and best— mobile discothèques, the Rosko International Roadshow.

ONE REASON THE BRITISH government was lax in responding was that Prime Minister Harold Wilson's Labour government felt it would alienate younger voters in the March 1966 election. In 1964 the party had won with a small margin, but this time it gained a majority of seats. The catalyst for addressing the defiant pirates came from a near, real-life pirate adventure. A group of intimidating characters invaded Radio City and dismantled its transmitter, retaliating for a business deal gone bad between ex-military man Oliver Smedley and promoter Reg Calvert.

Calvert, an old-school manager well liked by his artists, had lowbrow taste and fondness for gimmick promotions. He took note of the surge in sales when a flop record by one of his artists, "Caroline" by The Fortunes, was adopted as a theme by Radio Caroline. One of his singers, lightweight talent Screaming Lord Sutch, shared Calvert's penchant for stunts and thought he would get press for himself by establishing his own pirate station.

Radio Sutch launched from a fishing boat equipped with a turntable and a weak transmitter powered by car batteries. The boat trawled for fish in the morning and from noon on was a radio station. Two weeks later, Sutch and Calvert reestablished Radio Sutch on a group of abandoned World War II forts in the Thames Estuary. Shivering Sands and other marine forts had been erected to shoot down German planes and guard against submarines and small boats. A writer for the *Daily Telegraph* described the signal as so weak, it was "broadcasting to an audience of seagulls." After a few months, Sutch became bored with it, but Calvert saw the possibilities and bought him out. Calvert upgraded the weak transmitter so the station had a fifty-mile radius and renamed it Radio City.

Major Oliver Smedley, sensing that the pirate stations would lead the British government to accept commercial radio, was one of the backers of Radio Atlanta, which followed Caroline into the market. A few months later Atlanta entered into a merger type of arrangement with O'Rahilly to become Caroline North. Smedley never made any money from Atlanta and thought that involvement in Radio City— which didn't have the vast expense of maintaining a ship—had real possibilities.

Smedley promised Calvert a new transmitter and then cheaped-out on a used one that barely functioned. This soured their relationship, and when Calvert was in talks with Radio London about a sale, Smedley sent a group of seventeen men to Shivering Sands to protect his property, namely the antiquated transmitter that Calvert hadn't paid for. Calvert went to the police, who, flummoxed, said it was out of their jurisdiction. A very agitated Calvert learned that the elusive Smedley was at home, and visited him on the evening of June

21, 1966. During a heated exchange with Smedley's secretary/mistress, he threatened her with a statuette. Was Calvert's anger genuine, or was he acting out for effect? No one will ever know. Smedley stepped out from hiding and blasted Calvert with his shotgun.

Smedley was arrested and charged with murder, then revised to manslaughter. He testified that he feared for his life, though Calvert's only weapon had been a tear gas pen in his pocket. Smedley was acquitted on grounds of self-defense. (Calvert's wife recommenced operations, and ran the station until February 1967. Smedley, who died in 1989, never did claim his "valuable" transmitter, which rusts on the abandoned fort.) It was this nefarious act that led the government to realize that the pirates—at this point there were ten stations— had gotten out of hand and needed to be shut down. In addition, a number of European countries complained to the British government that the frequencies used by the errant pirates were interfering with their broadcasting.

Parliament passed the Marine Broadcasting Offenses Act, which decreed "prohibition of broadcasting from ships and aircraft … marine structures." All but one of the pirate ships went off the air at midnight August 14, 1967. Radio Caroline restructured, relocated, and attempted to cultivate international advertising—British ads were prohibited—but the new business model didn't work.

Seeing an obvious need, the BBC created its own pop music channel, Radio 1. A majority of the initial DJs came from the pirate ships but few lasted because they lacked polish. John Peel, Kenny Everett, and Tony Blackburn, all from Radio London, were among the more popular. Blackburn kicked off the channel on September 30, 1967, with The Move's "Flowers in the Rain."

The BBC wanted to hire Rosko, but he was making too much money—$5,000 a week, according to him—in France. He made an arrangement where he produced his show and sent them the tapes. In May 1968, when the violent student riots and labor strikes gravely affected his business, Rosko drove his mobile DJ truck to London to physically join Radio 1. Throughout the 1970s, Rosko was the most popular DJ throughout Europe.

When I heard that Richard Curtis—the writer of *Bridget Jones's Diary, Four Weddings and a Funeral,* and *Love Actually*—planned to write and direct a movie about pirate radio, I was delighted because I felt that Rhino Films lacked the clout to get such a movie made. In the publicity leading up to the release, I became concerned. Curtis grew up listening to the pirate stations on a transistor radio hidden under his pillow. He wrote his script in a burst of inspiration, making a totally fictional story. Only later did he introduce some factual references.

The UK release of *The Boat That Rocked* garnered poor reviews. In an effort to shore it up for the US, it was shortened and retitled *Pirate Radio,* but it didn't help. When I saw the movie, I was dismayed that there was little plot, dramatic structure, or reality. Among the many things wrong with this movie was the use of music outside the 1966–67 timeframe, and actors much older than the young-twenties DJs they were portraying. Philip Seymour Hoffman, at forty, played "The Count," a character loosely based on Emperor Rosko, who was then twenty-four. Nick Frost, at thirty-six, also played a DJ. The movie's climax comes when a boat sinks, which happened much later, in 1980.

The true story was so rich, I felt Curtis squandered an opportunity. There wasn't going to be another pirate radio movie—especially as this one lost around $40 million (my estimate).

A lot of the wonderful—and not so wonderful—obscurities that the pirate radio stations programmed in the sixties can be heard on http://www.radiolondon.co.uk and the associated http://www.oldiesproject.com. Weekly playlists for Radio London have been reconstructed, interspersed with station jingles. I've found scores of worthwhile records that I had never heard before. But like anything that involves personal taste, one has to separate the wheat from the chaff.

AN HOUR WITH MARC BOLAN

O N THURSDAY, DECEMBER 16, 1971, I was killing time in the lobby of the Continental Hyatt House, waiting to be called upstairs to interview English rock star Marc Bolan for *Phonograph Record Magazine*. Marc fronted T. Rex, the most popular group in England with four big hits in the past year, two number ones and two number twos. The group's latest album, *Electric Warrior*, had been released the previous month and I liked everything about it: the songs, the musical performances, and the sparse, resonant sound. Howard Kaylan and Mark Volman, then members of The Mothers of Invention, provided exquisite backup vocals.

Bolan described his previous duo, Tyrannosaurus Rex, as "acoustic rock and roll." In 1969, two years after the original group's formation, percussionist Steve Took became too aggressive and radical for compatibility and left. He was replaced by Mickey Finn, primarily a painter, and "the world's best conga player," according to Bolan. Tyrannosaurus Rex was later shortened to T. Rex, reflecting the high-energy rock and roll and Bolan's reimagined vocal delivery: subtle, sensual, direct, and snarlingly animalistic.

When the call came for me to take the elevator upstairs, it was past 5:00 p.m., two hours after we were scheduled to begin. Bolan still hadn't arrived. Next was a wait in his room, chatting idly with his wife,

June. An *Electric Warrior* sticker was planted on the side of the color television as Fred Flintstone "yabadabadooed" from the screen. An H. P. Lovecraft paperback sat on the dresser and we casually discussed things like the cost of albums in England. "Domestic albums go for around five or six dollars," June remarked, "with American imports usually three dollars more. [In 1971 the US list price on LPs was $4.98.] Even bootlegs are expensive. There's only one discount store, but a few used record stands sitting in places like vegetable markets exist. It is suspected that a large portion of these used records were stolen." Taking advantage of being in LA, Marc and June had raided nearby Tower Records, picking up *Eddie Cochran's Greatest Hits*, among other delights. June mentioned that when Marc was young, he once carried Eddie Cochran's guitar for him.

Marc arrived in a flurry of apologies, enthusiastically spouting, "I did the news," which he sang on a local radio station accompanying himself with hand claps and percussion from a brandy bottle. "It's a sure number one," he said throughout the night.

Marc reminded me of Ray Davies. He was very English and neat and a dedicated follower of fashion, modeling a magnetic gold-threaded coat, black satin pants, and girls orange Mary Jane shoes. Marc's soft features, direct stare, and his flashy, colorful clothes reminded me of female movie stars of the 1930s. Although Marc was a fan of *The Lord of the Rings* and *The Hobbit*, his song titles—"Mambo Sun," "Lean Woman Blues," "Monolith," "Planet Queen," "Cosmic Dancer," and "Bang a Gong"—seem lifted from 1930s science fiction movie serials.

Meeting Marc in person was an unforgettable experience. Because he was so behind schedule, I was asked to share my time with Jim Bickhart, which I didn't mind doing. Marc alleviated whatever discomfort I felt from my long wait with his charm and energy. I had never experienced anyone greeting me with an effusive "so nice to meet you." He was so up and so responsive, it was almost like being on a ride that I didn't want to end. He was so engaging, I didn't mind his arrogance or tendency to exaggerate. Our interview:

MARC: It's so nice to meet you, man. You blow my mind. I can't apologize enough, I'm sounding like an American, all of this apologizing bullshit.

JIM: So don't.

MARC: I do because I feel it, man. If I didn't, I wouldn't say it. So let's rock.

HAROLD: That's what I wanted to ask you about. Can you explain the transition from folk to rock?

MARC: The transition comes from the need to communicate with more people than I'd done in the past. I feel I only have five years I want to devote to rock and roll. I want to be a moviemaker and write books. My time is limited and I love human beings. I don't feel I have the stamina to continue for the next forty years as some people have. I just don't want to do it. There are many things I haven't gotten into that I wanna do now. I want to do them fast, for no material gain, only to make people's hearts feel good. You follow that, man?

JIM: Does that five years start with "Ride a White Swan"?

MARC: That five years starts with "Ride a White Swan," although I don't disown the earlier stuff. It was my apprenticeship. I'm mainstream now. I wanna be hip AM [Top 40 radio]. To me, The Who, Hendrix, and Cream were. That's my bag. I don't wanna be a cultist group. I have more to offer than that. I don't wanna be put into a bag. I'd rather be a lion tamer. [Pause] I'm feeling good.

re's The Kinks' first official photo session, with whips hinting at the sexual perversity in their name. Ray *ivies: "I never really liked the name. It was Larry Page's idea." Left to right: Mick Avory, Pete Quaife,* *ive Davies, Ray Davies. January 1964.*

In America, The Spencer Davis Group had only two Top 10 records, but in the UK they had five big hits and three Top 10 LPs, in just fifteen months. Left to right: Pete York, Muff Winwood, Steve Winwood, Spencer Davis.

The Dave Clark Five were the best looking and most stylishly dressed of all the bands, and second to T̲ Beatles in popularity in 1964. Left to right: Mike Smith, Lenny Davidson, Denis Payton, Rick Huxl̲ Dave Clark.

In a remarkable run of little more than a year—from March 1965 to April 1966—Herman's Hermits had nine Top 10 US hits, more than The Beatles, The Dave Clark Five, or The Rolling Stones. Clockwise: Derek Leckenby, Peter Noone, Karl Green, Keith Hopwood, Barry Whitwam. September 1965.

The Yardbirds most formidable lineup lip-synchs "Shapes of Things" on The Lloyd Thaxton Show. Left t
right: Paul Samwell-Smith, Chris Dreja, Jim McCarty, Keith Relf, Jeff Beck. January 11, 1966.

Ian Whitcomb, in a deerstalker hat and herringbone suit, fashioned a distinctive look more associated with Sherlock Holmes. On the strength of his spring 1965 hit "You Turn Me On," this honor history student at Trinity College, Dublin, took a break from his studies to tour America.

...he Hollies excelled with a great singer in Allan Clarke, exquisite group harmonies, and a substantial ...ongwriting unit. Left to right: Allan Clarke, Bobby Elliott, Graham Nash, Bernie Calvert, Tony Hicks. ...ote Allan's psychedelic Granny Takes a Trip jacket.

In November 1969 Hugh Grundy, then working for CBS Records in London, responded to my request to the US company for a Zombies photo. He sent me this still and a nice letter. Clockwise from top left: Colin Blunstone, Chris White, Hugh Grundy, Rod Argent, Paul Atkinson.

Manfred Mann may well have been the most musically adept among the bands of the British Invasion. Left to right: Tom McGuinness, Mike Hugg, Manfred Mann, Paul Jones, Mike Vickers.

Privilege *wasn't a great movie, but how could you not be entranced by such a great looking couple? Jean Shrimpton and Paul Jones. September 1966.*

*e second chapter of Manfred Mann. Left to right: Klaus Voormann, Manfred Mann, Mike d'Abo, *n McGuinness, Mike Hugg. Voormann was better known as The Beatles' friend who designed their *volver LP cover. He also did Bee Gees' 1st.*

*e Take Six clothing boutique responded to the challenge in creating a distinctive look for The Troggs. *e group wore these gaudy striped suits early in their career. Clockwise from top left: Ronnie Bond, *g Presley, Chris Britton, Pete Staples.*

The most popular disc jockey in Europe throughout the seventies, Emperor Rosko built a following as pirate broadcasting from Radio Caroline in the sixties.

Granny Takes a Trip was the hippest boutique in Swinging London. Partner Nigel Waymouth was eas bored and changed the facade six times in three years. 1930s actress Jean Harlow inspired this one.

anging backstage with Procol Harum at the Santa Monica Civic Auditorium. Left to right: B. J. Wilson, eith Reid, Harold, Alan Cartwright, Gary Brooker, and his wife. July 2, 1972.

This is how Marc Bolan was dressed when I interviewed him, taken an hour before at a Los Angeles radio station. He was the most charismatic person I've met. December 16, 1971.

Performing at an end-of-the-school-year Daily Bruin *party. Left to right: Jonathan Kellerman, Je Weber, Martin Rips, Harold. Out of frame: Jim Bickhart and Joseph Hymson (aka Staretski). Kellermo became a* New York Times *bestselling novelist. Rips and Staretski had a nice run as writers/producers network TV shows. May 30, 1970.*

I hung mostly with Michael Ochs at CBS Records' regional sales meetings. We're flanked by Rod, the re from USC, at left, and Frank Shargo of the label's campus department, at right. Century Plaza Hote January 22, 1972.

gan David and his Winos rehearse after-hours at the Daily Bruin *office prior to our debut at the* ᵉr's *school-year-end party. Left to right: Bill Pique, Mark Leviton (in back), Harold, Paul Rappaport, ᵇ Lampl (in front). I wonder what time it is? April 25, 1972.*

I created these two ads that ran in UCLA publications, inspired by those generated by Stan Cornyn's te at Warner Bros. I'm pictured in the top; Mark Leviton in the bottom. (Note: I'm wearing B. J. Wilson's shi

Heather Harris posed me with a few of her friends in front of the Whisky a Go-Go for a photo spread to accompany an article in the Daily Bruin. *I bought these shoes after seeing Todd Rundgren wearing a similar pair on the third Nazz LP. March 1972.*

Heather Harris

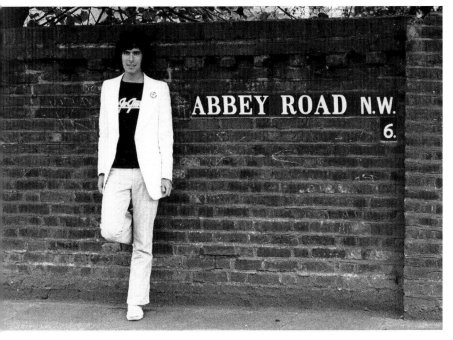

* made postcards to send to the States, standing in front of a brick wall with the street sign that most ...sely resembled the one on the back cover of The Beatles'* Abbey Road. *Oct. 2, 1973.*

I toured Disneyland with Status Quo. Top, Alan Lancaster, Francis Rossi in Tomorrowland. Bottom, left to right: road manager/songwriter Bob Young, Rick Parfitt, Alan Lancaster, Francis Rossi in Fantasyland. April 30, 1973.

The Sex Pistols last performance, at Winterland in San Francisco. Left to right: Sid Vicious, John Lyd Steve Jones; Paul Cook out of frame at left. January 14, 1978.

Here's how Peter Noone looked when I met him in 1973.

...e Noones and the Bronsons enjoying a rare evening together. Left to right: Peter and Mireille Noone; ...arold and Stephanie Bronson. March 9, 1996.

Attending a Yardbirds reunion rehearsal, the original rhythm section (left to right: Chris Dreja, Jim McCarty, Paul Samwell-Smith) sounded just like it did on their records in the sixties. Also pictured vocalist Mark Feltham and music journalist John Tobler; guitarist John Knightsbridge is out of frame South London's Terminal Studios, June 11, 1983.

Dave Clark visits Rhino. My good friend Mark Singer is at left. November 18, 1999.

HAROLD: Before you made the transition, did you think what you had to offer in the new rock style would be commercial AM?

MARC: It's weird when I talk to people. I always sound like a cunt. I'm good at what I do because I don't do it until I've spent a long time learning how to do it. Do you understand? I don't rush into anything. The only album I'm not happy with is *A Beard of Stars*, and that's because I ventured into electric guitar before I should have. I didn't play it well enough for what I was attempting to do. I love the songs, though, but there are some moments when I just cringe. I had my Marshall amp full up like everyone does and I shouldn't have done it. Which is why I hardly do any guitar solos even though I think I'm a fucking good guitar player.

HAROLD: Why don't you do solos?

MARC: I do, live. Live in England, "Get It On" is twenty minutes long. It's filled with guitar solos. I blow my head off, but I play to the audience. There are certain points where one likes to play. At that point I was playing to prove that I was no longer a heavy Donovan. Look out, man, I'm really Marc Hendrix! I got over that one. And now I'm just a guitar player and a songwriter. To get back to your original question, I was never a folkie. I started with an electric rock band, which was John's Children. I started with a 1962 Les Paul and a 400-watt stack [amplifier].

HAROLD: Were you on "Smashed! Blocked!"? That was a hit in Los Angeles.

MARC: No.

JIM: That's the only one we know in the US.

HAROLD: How did you join the band?

MARC: The guitar player they had was pathetic. Track Records was just formed and they wanted a folk-poet, good-looking superstar, boogie-woogie Pete Townshend guitar player, and I was around. I wrote "Desdemona," which was a dynamite song. Was that released here?

HAROLD: The only one we know is the other one.

MARC: It was a number one in Australia, Germany, and places like that. In England, it commands a great deal of respect, as does "My White Bicycle" by Tomorrow—the guitarist [Steve Howe] is the guy in Yes. [Responding to our quizzical looks] You dudes are out of touch.

JIM & HAROLD: We know Yes.

MARC: Yes is, like, last week.

JIM: Didn't Tomorrow have Keith West?

MARC: They were the best group in fucking England, for a week.

JIM: "Excerpt From a Teenage Opera."

MARC: He sold out with that. That was the rip-off.

JIM: That's the only thing we heard here.

MARC: Let me fill you in. There were four bands happening in the underground in England: Fairport Convention, who were totally different than they are now; Arthur Brown, who had his flash hit for a week; there was Tyrannosaurus Rex; and there was Tomorrow, who were trying to be The Byrds, but were better. They were hot for three weeks. Do you ever get that over here? A band that is so hot you can't believe it.

JIM: Maybe in certain areas, but the US is too big.

MARC: There were three records: "My White Bicycle" by Tomorrow, "Granny Takes a Trip" by The Purple Gang, and "Desdemona" by John's Children. Dynamite records. Dynamite! Those three records are what you would call turntable hits. They got mass airplay—mass—but they didn't sell a fucking record because they were three years too soon. Each one now would be a number one, no doubt about it.

You see, the underground in England was slow to establish itself. It was too early. I did a show with Van Morrison when I was seventeen. My first record was "The Wizard" and he had "Mystic Eyes" with Them. [For his first record, Mark Feld changed his name professionally to Marc Bolan, the surname a contraction of Bob Dylan.] He'll hate me for saying it. We did a children's TV show called *5 O'Clock Club*. If he thought about it now it'd really blow his mind, all those little kids. There was no underground then. It was too early. I used to play with Cat Stevens, man. There was nowhere to play. I used to play at his old man's restaurant. He would play at my house and I would play at his house and we also played on the streets.

JIM: That was even before the UFO club?

MARC: Yeah, two years before. Cat got involved with "I Love My Dog" and he was bullshitted with commercial rock and roll, then he backed off when he got very sick with TB. I never made it. But when I did make it, it was much bigger in my field. Fortunately, Cat made it again. We both know the mistakes we didn't make. In those days to make a record was a big deal. Now I avoid signing anything.

HAROLD: So, how did you get signed?

MARC: I had four singles that did nothing, three years before John's Children. I met someone who knew someone. It just happened like that. I met a cat, Jim Economides, an American dude who produced the first Beach Boys album. He did "Little Deuce Coupe." He met me and said, "Hey man, you're going to be a big star." I said, "Of course I am." He was a good man, but he got fucked. The things that were happening in those early times are just incredible, the crooked people who were running around. It took me three years to get out of that recording contract. I spent five years getting out of contracts from everyone.

Let's talk about something exciting. There are things which you wouldn't believe. The first demo I made has John Paul Jones on bass, Jimmy Page on guitar, and Nicky Hopkins on piano. This was about 1964. We weren't very good. I guess Jimmy was. He was in a group called Neil Christian & The Crusaders. America doesn't know what went down. To become what people consider an accomplished musician takes about ten years. When you get there you are undeniable, you are a craftsman, end of story.

HAROLD: From a rock 'n' roller, how did you get into Tyrannosaurus Rex?

MARC: Lack of money. I left John's Children because they wanted to make me into a Monkee. It was one of those, "Hey kid, with your face you're gonna be a star!" When I left John's Children, they took my guitar away. They took my Les Paul and sold it. They took my stack and sold it. All I had left was a twenty-four dollar acoustic. I played in the park for nothing. I would never ask for money. People used to take me home and feed me. Legally, it put me out of action for three years. For two years I slept on people's floors. I wrote the first Tyrannosaurus

Rex album on people's floors. I met Steve on someone's floor. He had bongos and T. Rex was formed.

HAROLD: What are your vocal influences?

MARC: I don't have any. Ford cars, Greta Garbo. I don't know. You tell me who you think.

JIM: The only time I got an idea of who you might sound like was on "Elemental Child." I thought it sounded like Ray Davies. The first time I heard that song I thought it was The Kinks.

MARC: On "Victoria" he said that he was trying to sound like me.

JIM: Yeah, I read an interview where he said that.

MARC: I never listened much to The Kinks. I love Ray's writing but I think the band let him down. Live I think they're terrible and I can't understand it. [Tony Secunda, Marc's manager, enters] Tony, can you check on the dude next door from *Cash Box*? Where's the champagne we ordered over an hour ago?

TONY Maybe it went next door.

MARC: I wouldn't like that at all. Someone spaced out. [To us] You want some champagne? Of course you do. Get on that, Tony. Can we get our main man together as well? [Tony leaves]

MARC: You know The Move?

JIM & HAROLD: We know The Move.

MARC: He formed them. Procol Harum? The Moody Blues? He did it all. He's living history. I haven't had a manager for two years. He went to New York with me and did more in two weeks than people had done in three years, and didn't even want a penny. I rang him up and asked him to manage me, and he said he didn't know if he could do it. In England we go for $30,000 a night. Don't print all my bullshit. It would embarrass him. I'm too loose. I assume, and you're people to me. In England it's weird. I tend to talk too much and people print it all. I've got into so much trouble. I look upon people as people. And they print it like an animal. That's what's been freaking me out. That's when I realized how big we really are.

HAROLD: What are your musical likes?

MARC: The only thing I live for is music. I have a list that would fill up your whole fucking magazine. You want some: Robert Johnson, Eric Clapton, Jimi Hendrix, John Lennon, Jeff Lynne, Roy Wood, Pete Townshend, Howard and Mark from The Mothers, Jimmy Burton, Scotty Moore.

HAROLD: How did you hook up with Mark and Howie?

MARC: We played in Detroit with their last gig as The Turtles. We did four gigs in America. One was here.

JIM: At The Experience, right? That was the last tour you did with Steve?

MARC: That was the only tour I did with Steve. What a bummer that was. Who managed that place?

JIM: Marshall Brevitz

MARC: A lovely man. Give him a bullet. [On *Cash Box* magazine's chart, a "bullet" indicates a record that's rapidly ascending.]

JIM: He was a lovely man who was too nice to everybody and that's why the club went down the tubes.

MARC: Elmer at the Whisky was dynamite, a very nice man. He told me, "Kid, you are going to have the biggest group in America." We filled it for four days and got paid nothing.

HAROLD: I want to know more about your lyrics. They're more like poetry. And the imagery, like "mambo sun" and "alligator rain." Is there meaning, or do they just sound good?

MARC: They do sound good. For me to explain it, I would have to transpose you and put you inside my brain. There are certain things an artist can't talk about. Let me get an album. *You're slim and you're weak you've got the teeth of the hydra upon you.* Do you know what a hydra is? Is that weird? You're putting Greek mythology in a number one record for eight weeks. *You ride like a car, you've got a hubcap diamond star halo.* C'mon.

JIM: I'm talking about the consistency. It's not like "The Children of Rarn."

MARC: You haven't heard "The Children of Rarn."

JIM: Not the whole thing, just the song.

MARC: It's the beginning of a giant epic. It's a taste, like a blowjob, man. Ezra Pound did some straight poetry. He did one or two line poems. He was razzed off. In English it means hacked off. *You slide so good with bones so fair, you've got the universe reclining in your hair.* I don't know if you've met a woman that has in your estimation every piece of knowledge that you know, floating in the top of her head. I've met many people like that. I'm very fortunate. There's no better poetry than that. If Ray Bradbury were here, he would agree with me. I said his name because he lives down the road. I haven't met him and I'd like to. As a poet, I've never written such good shit, man.

The throne of time is a kingly thing, from whence you all know we all do begin. The beginning of time. *And dressed as you are, girl, in your fashions of fate.* Which is your boogaloo kaftan, whatever you want to get into. How many ladies do you know that hang onto last week's patched jeans thinking they're funky? *Shallow are the actions of the children of men.* That's us, baby. *Fogged was their vision since the ages began.* Caine and Abel. *And lost like a lion in the canyons of smoke.* Pollution. *Girl, it's no joke.* And if that's not poetry, man, there ain't no poetry. It makes me cry, because I can't go to every single person who bought an album and explain to millions of people what the stuff means. I don't write nonsense. A lot of people in the press in England wrote that it's a dynamite album, it's going to go to number one, but it's all nonsense. And I cry. Top it, Dylan. I want to hear him top it because I love him.

HAROLD: What is "Jeepster" about?

MARC: Ask Bob Dylan. I got that from him.

HAROLD: Is there a certain amount of pressure to remain at the top of the charts?

MARC: In England we topped The Stones' "Brown Sugar," McCartney's "Another Day," and Lennon's "Power to the People." We got to number one and they couldn't top us and they love it. 'Cause it's not bullshit. They know we're no Herman's Hermits. The Stones' new stuff I heard the other day is really hot, of course, not as hot as my new stuff. Because what you do is good, they have respect for you instead of if you were at the top of the charts with some artless commercial stuff.

McCartney told me, "Marc, you're gonna dig it now, but in two years' time they're gonna rip your pants off and you're gonna hate it." Three months later I was tired. He knows and he's seven years in. What was important is to accept someone who is total competition and not be worried about it. I am totally paranoid of everyone, unless it's people who I think are as good as me, and all I want to do is watch them.

HAROLD: Established artists like John Lennon or The Rolling Stones aren't all that paranoid or neurotic about their...

MARC: Bollocks! You are so off beam, baby! Everyone is paranoid, from the day they're born to the day they die. Every number one you get you have to top it or else you're not hot. To anyone else, a number two is a ginormous record, but to you it's a flop. I've got a room full of silver discs, but if I put a record out and it only gets to number five—which is a big record—to me it hasn't made it. In the end you don't listen to radio, you don't look at charts. You back off—everybody, The Stones, The Beatles, Dylan. You slowly back off which is what I'm doing, which is why I'm here and not in England. We're so hot there, it's burning me. I had to get away. The phone never stopped ringing. We had four TV shows on this week. Everyone's scared. The mania never stops. How many number one records do you need when there's no security? We're born to die. You're getting older every day. You get forty years if you're lucky, end of story. Where's security? Where's the champagne? Don't believe there's security in being a star. Why do you think Bob Hope does that yearly show? How old is he? When I'm sixty-nine don't get me on TV. In two years' time I expect to be conducting the Royal Philharmonic Orchestra because that's what I hear in my head. If not, I'll retreat into my country Welsh island and disappear. I'll send bootlegs out.

HAROLD: How does Tony Visconti as producer work with you on the albums?

MARC: [to Jim] Can you go next door and ask for the champagne?

As an American producer, very little. He's an American, from the Bronx. He's my friend. He does what Jimmy Miller does for The Stones. He's in the control room when I'm out front.

JIM: [reenters the room] They have coffee and Coca-Cola, but no champagne.

[Marc goes next door, and returns after a couple of minutes.]

MARC: They said the Dom Perignon costs twenty-four dollars a bottle. I said OK. Warners is playing for it. Tony's a gas. Tony to me is what every record producer should be. He's your main man. You're out there doing it, you can't judge what you're doing until you go back and listen to it. If I do something I think is amazing, Tony lets me know if it's good. If a garbage collector comes in and says, "Hey, man, that tambourine is too loud." I'll say, "Hey, get out." After he shuts the door and leaves, I'll say, "Hey, the tambourine is too loud." I'll pull the tambourine down and go out and give him one hundred dollars. I've done that. I judge by my heart. Forgive me, we're supposed to do this other man.

Afterward, Tony Secunda and Marc's next interviewer, *Cash Box* magazine's Todd Everett, joined us for a glass of champagne. It seemed only fitting and proper that we would toast "to rock and roll, may it live forever" before we were sent back into the real world.

MARC HAD A REMARKABLE run. Over a three-year period, every single he released in England—all eleven—went Top 10. Even though he only had one hit in the US—the retitled "Bang a Gong (Get it On)" barely made the Top 10—one occasionally hears a T. Rex song in a commercial or film in the US. One of T. Rex's big hits from 1972, "Children of the Revolution" (not even released in the States) was used in a 2013 commercial for the Fiat 500.

From Marc's comments, he seemed concerned with his own mortality. From an early age, not only did Marc believe he would become a star, but he also thought he would die young, like his hero James Dean.

Marc perished in a car crash with his second wife behind the wheel, in September 1977, two weeks shy of his thirtieth birthday.

LONDON 1972

B
Y THE SUMMER OF 1972, I was well aware that I'd missed the zenith of British rock culture. It was years past the creativity of The Beatles' *Sgt. Pepper's*, The Rolling Stones' *Between the Buttons*, The Kinks' *Something Else*, The Who *Sell Out*; photographer David Bailey shooting pop stars, The Beatles hanging out at Apple Corps, and designers filling King's Road's and Carnaby Street's boutique windows with colorful clothing. Yet, as a rock music fan whose taste in rock culture was shaped by those Brits in the sixties, I had to make the pilgrimage.

I had the time. I had graduated from UCLA a couple of months before and had no job. I booked a flight for $124 on a charter that advertised in the *Daily Bruin*, and found myself in a cramped seat next to an elderly Eastern European couple who didn't smell very good. They were like the Romanian peasants in the Dracula movie who wore garlic around their necks to protect themselves from vampires. We made a stop to clear customs in Bangor, Maine, where they made a big deal of pushing their duty-free lobsters, including having a tank of them in the lounge.

In taking the train from Gatwick Airport to London, my first impressions were, oddly, American ones. The rows of old residential buildings and street configurations reminded me of Disney, not Disneyland, which has no themed Old Londonland, but of the quaintness found in a movie such as *Mary Poppins*. Having grown up in arid Los Angeles, the extensive green foliage reminded me of an east coast clime, like suburban New York or New Jersey.

Arthur Frommer's book *London on Six Dollars a Day* recommended the Russell Square area, home to a large number of small hotels. Mark Leviton was spending his junior year at the University of Birmingham, and in advance of joining me for a few days in London before reporting to school, he asked me to take his guitar so it would be one less piece of baggage for him.

My first day in London, Wednesday, September 6, was unusually warm. I was jet-lagged, hot and weary, as I walked down the street lugging my suitcase and Mark's guitar. All the hotels in my two-pounds-a-night price range were full. I noticed a long-haired, would-be pop star of Indian extraction dressed in a trendy black coat, pushing a huge amplifier, with his traditionally attired mother looking on. I felt sorry for him as I trudged on, as Indians were unknown in English rock bands. I was thirsty, but unlike in Los Angeles, I discovered there were no public drinking fountains.

Running out of energy, I sprang for a more expensive, three-pounds-a-night hotel. It didn't have a bath or toilet in the room, but it did include an English breakfast—whatever that was. I changed into my Humble Pie "Smokin'" T-shirt, and as it was still afternoon, I had time to visit one record company. I had packed a stack of American record company promotional T-shirts thinking these unseen-in-the-UK items would cause a minor sensation, but no one batted an eyelash.

"Do you have any coke?" Sure, I was fatigued, but did he really ask me for cocaine, a drug of which I was only vaguely aware? It was an odd introduction to Derek Taylor. Among Beatles fans, Taylor is revered for having been an early supporter of the band when he was a journalist, stepping into the role as The Beatles' charming and ingratiating publicist for most of the latter half of the sixties. He was now Director of Special Projects at Warner's UK label. Warner Brothers, Elektra, and Atlantic were significant record labels in the States. With fewer hit artists in the UK, the three labels were combined into one umbrella company. The sign on the building indicated WEA

Records—from the first initial of each label. Here the individual letters were articulated compared to the name of the stateside distribution company which was pronounced as one word, "We-Uh." It took me a while to accept that there were no separate offices for Warner, Atlantic, or Elektra Records.

I had met David Berson at UCLA, and we became good friends. He looked like a hippie Groucho Marx with his bottlebrush mustache, wild, unkempt hair, and a bent-over walk. He was researching the aging of potato tissue at a molecular level. I knew him as one-half of Crazy Horse, who contributed editorials to the *Daily Bruin*. After graduation he was hired by Warner Brothers Records in Burbank as the assistant to Mo Ostin, president of the label. As a primarily classical music fan with eccentric taste in rock music, his only qualification seemed to me that, as Ostin's neighbor, he had babysat Ostin's kids. David's claim to fame was having made the deals to release the two worst-selling albums at the label, Richard Thompson's *Henry the Human Fly* and Vivian Stanshall's *Men Opening Umbrellas Ahead*. He told me to see Derek, and sent advance word of my arrival.

Although I used Derek's office as a base, mostly to rest between appointments and to make calls, I saw little of him. One afternoon he introduced me to Legs Larry Smith, the colorful drummer of the Bonzo Dog Band, who would come out from behind his drums at least once a performance to tap dance. It was a small thrill for me, as the Bonzos were among my favorite bands. Larry told me he had a new group.

Mostly I would visit with Derek's hospitable assistant, Mandi Newall. One afternoon she expressed her excitement over Alice Cooper's forthcoming single, "Elected," and played it for me. I liked it too. It sounded familiar, and I recognized it as the same song as "Reflected," from the group's *Pretties For You* album released three years earlier, with different lyrics.

The highlight of my first night in London was checking out the nearby Safeway. Supermarkets were a novelty in Britain, and I wanted to compare it to those in Los Angeles. It was similar, but the products were different, of course. Being on Los Angeles time, I didn't get much rest my first night.

The next morning for breakfast, my eggs swimming in grease didn't seem so sunny-side up to me. I'd never experienced that before, or the grilled tomato sitting on the plate. I was hungry, so I ate, and was ready to face my first full day in sunny London.

I walked down Goodge Street, singing Donovan's "Sunny Goodge Street" on my way to Mortimer Street, home of United Artists Records. Displayed throughout the city were government-sponsored posters of T. Rex's Marc Bolan reminding citizens to "Keep Britain Tidy." This truly was a rock 'n' roll city.

The publicists based in Hollywood had sent advance word for me to see Andrew Lauder, head of A&R for UA in London. He was a devotee of the San Francisco psychedelic scene of the 1960s, which was not in vogue at the time, and the hallway leading to his office was lined with framed posters of the era. Although soft-spoken, bald, and British, Andrew dressed like an American cowboy: boots, jeans, and bolo ties. At the label's former location he even installed swinging saloon doors. A lot of this came from his fondness for The Charlatans, among the first and least successful of the San Francisco bands, who had a residency at the Red Dog Saloon in Virginia City, Nevada, where they had dressed like Wild West gunslingers.

He didn't use a desk, but a wooden dining room table. He entered his appointments and other notes into a large ledger. He was welcoming, and I used his office as a second base. I had to get used to some unfamiliar phrases: "Give me a bell," *phone me*; "Call at half-twelve," *come by at 12:30*. He introduced me to Richard Ogden, head of their press office. I learned that in the UK it was the "press office;" in the US the comparable department was "publicity."

Andrew was excited about a local power trio, the Groundhogs. Over the course of my stay, Andrew gave me the Groundhogs album with the foldout cover, *Nervous on the Road*, the new album by Brinsley Schwarz, and *Rebel Trouser*, an EP (for *extended play*, shorter than an LP) by ex-Bonzo Dog Band member Roger Ruskin Spear. Andrew signed the Flamin' Groovies, a San Francisco band whose previous three albums had failed to chart. He gave me a copy of their impressive "Slow Death" EP.

I had lunch and a beer at the Speakeasy Club. It was a press party for the release of Linda Lewis' second album, *Lark*. Linda gave me a big, welcoming smile, but I was too shy to approach her. That night I took in my first West End play, Tom Stoppard's *Jumpers*. I never saw plays in Los Angeles, but here the theaters were old, elegant, and accessible. Admission was cheap, too. A seat in the upper circle went for two or three pounds. I briefly nodded off, but enjoyed that portion of the play for which I remained awake.

I had envisioned an extended stay, and thought about renting a furnished apartment, something I had done with friends my junior year at UCLA. I discovered that "flats" in London were hard to come by, and expensive. As three pounds (about eight dollars) a day was beyond my long-term budget, I knew I was not going to be staying in the hotel long. I lessened my burden by checking Mark's guitar at the train station. I inquired about living accommodations at the nearby University of London, thinking that there would be availability in dormitories during the summer, and got a referral.

I took the London Underground, the world's first underground railway, commonly referred to as "the Tube," to the Elephant & Castle stop, which was south of the Thames River, and then a bus two miles down the Old Kent Road. Half a block down Rowcross Street was a collection of impermanent bungalows that passed for student housing. It was less than two pounds a night. I would have expected a school dorm to be on campus, or close by, but this wasn't. It was a long way from where I wanted to be in the city, but I was relieved to have a place in my budget. I moved in the next day, a rainy Friday. My room didn't have a radio or TV, but it did have an electric coil heater that had melted the ceiling.

On Saturday, I took up Badfinger on their offer and visited them at their house at 7 Park Avenue, a large mock Tudor in Golders Green, an upscale suburb in north London known for its large Jewish population. Tom Evans and Joey Molland were watching the Olympics on TV, broadcast live from Munich. The picture was outstanding, and that's when I learned that the British broadcasting standard was different from and superior to that in the States. The games that year were marred by the trauma of eleven Israeli athletes kidnapped and then killed by Palestinian terrorists.

We then left for Apple Records in Tom's two-seat Porsche. Joey squeezed in the back. Tom had purchased it used with the money he made as the cowriter (with Pete Ham) of "Without You." Harry Nilsson covered it after hearing it on the group's *No Dice* album, and had topped the charts earlier in the year in both Britain and the US.

We arrived at Apple, at 3 Saville Row, but it wasn't the familiar site shown in the *Let It Be* movie. Because of neglect, the building had deteriorated and was being renovated, and Apple's business offices had moved elsewhere. We walked through the basement, past the recording studio, in disarray. Tom and Joey were there to rehearse with Geoff Swettenham, a new drummer for Badfinger. Publicly, there was no word that their long-term drummer Mike Gibbins had been sacked. Pete Ham showed up later, in a good mood and wearing a white suit, as he had attended the wedding of a friend. I watched the rehearsal for a while, and then left.

That night I took the train thirty miles southwest to see Colin Blunstone perform at the Guildford Civic Hall. He was among my favorite singers from when he was a member of The Zombies, and that night he performed their two biggest hits, "She's Not There" and

"Time of the Season." His voice—melodic, crystalline, aching—was in fine form. Considering it was only the third public performance of his new band, I thought they did well.

An unexpected surprise was the opening act, Good Habit, a delightful, humorous sextet garbed in green monk tunics. They were patterned after other horn bands of the day, like Blood, Sweat & Tears and Chicago, but with better arrangements. The bill drew a small audience—about 150—for the size of the auditorium. I went backstage to tell Colin how much I liked the show. I didn't stay long, but when I got back to the train station, I was surprised that the next train to arrive was the last one for the night to London. I had no idea what I would have done had I not caught it. I was freezing, and my nose dripped all the way into the big city.

On Sunday I rested most of the day. My complimentary breakfasts at the dorm weren't substantial: hot tea and three or four cinnamon rolls to fill me up. Most evenings I would buy what passed for dinner at a small market across Old Kent Road that was run by a Middle Eastern family. I sliced the small block of cheese with the metal nail file from my grooming kit, and placed it on a Ry-Krisp cracker. Dessert was a banana. With no radio or TV in my room, my main source of entertainment was two cassettes. Mike Warner had made me one of unreleased Rolling Stones songs, and Jim Bickhart one which included selections from James Taylor's and Rod Stewart's first LPs.

WEA's press officer Moira Bellas invited me to a party on Monday night for the English band Family at the Revolution Club to announce the release of their new album, *Bandstand*. Family was big in Britain, but not in America. I wanted to like them, but couldn't get past the vocals of their lead singer, Roger Chapman, who sounded like a bleating sheep. Family played like they were soused. Nobody from Warners introduced me to any of the other writers, or anybody else.

The only person I spoke to was the one who asked my name for the guest list. I sat by myself and felt lonely.

BEFORE I LEFT LOS Angeles, Rodney Bingenheimer gave me the phone numbers of a few of the people he had spent time with on his recent trip to London. The highlight of his visit had been filling in for bassist Ronnie Lane when the Faces mimed their latest hit on the *Top of the Pops* TV show. He gave me Rod Stewart's phone number, but I didn't feel comfortable calling such a big star out of the blue. More my speed was Speedy Keane. When he served as Pete Townshend's chauffeur, The Who recorded his "Armenia City in the Sky" on *The Who Sell Out*. As the lead singer of Thunderclap Newman, his composition "Something in the Air" had topped the British charts three summers previously. It was to be his only hit. During our phone conversation, he expressed his general frustration with life, which made me hesitant to meet him.

Much more welcoming was Ian Whitcomb, who invited me to visit him in Putney, in the south of London. He even picked me up from the train station. It was cold and rainy, Wednesday, September 13. Although Ian was considered a one-hit wonder, I found his music interesting, and had three of his albums. We sat in the dining room of the flat he shared with his mum, who served us tea sandwiches. This was my first encounter with the thin, buttered, triangle-cut item that could hardly qualify as a sandwich in the States. I was impressed when Ian told me that Ray Davies had recently been over to return the ukulele he had borrowed.

In the summer of 1964, in the year The Beatles conquered America and turned every young man with long hair and an English accent into an instant sex symbol, Ian Whitcomb was on vacation in Seattle when a local girl whispered in his ear, "Ian, your accent is really turning me on." It was such a unique, American phrase, that it stayed with him. He turned it into a song, borrowing heavily from the boogie shuffle rhythm of a hit earlier that year, "Hi-Heel Sneakers."

In March 1965, while recording the song with his band, Bluesville, in Dublin, he knocked an ashtray off his piano. Thinking the noise would disqualify the take, he camped up his vocal with a Supremes-like falsetto. George Sherlock, a radio promotion man, heard the tape at Capitol Records in Hollywood and labeled it "a smash!" Ian was into protest music—"I felt sure I was going to be the next Joan Baez"—but to his dismay, "You Turn Me On" was released. The American public responded in kind, buying enough singles in the summer of 1965 to take it to number eight in the charts. A cuter version of Mick Jagger, Ian was launched as a teen idol and semi-regular on *Shindig!*, all on the strength of a fluke record, a mistake that he never dreamed would be released.

Ian's embarrassment had more impact than anybody imagined at the time. He learned that his song was all the rage in gay clubs, "apparently because of the high-pitched ambisexual nature of my singing." Bruce Springsteen's first band, the Castiles, included it in their repertoire. In his autobiography, *Born to Run*, he describes "You Turn Me On" as "wheezingly lecherous." Steven Tyler, in his memoir *Does the Noise in My Head Bother You?*, discusses for an extended paragraph how the song contributed to his sexual awareness: "By singing it in that crazy falsetto voice he was able to convey unspeakable emotions that made girls blush and turned heads everywhere. And he nailed it, it was a huge hit."

In the fall of 1966, The New Vaudeville Band scored a big hit with "Winchester Cathedral," which recalled the music of the 1920s. Other artists, including The Beatles and The Rolling Stones, thought they could have fun adapting the style for a song or two. But Ian made it a way of life. He was the first to follow "Winchester Cathedral," with "Where Did Robinson Crusoe Go With Friday On Saturday Night?"

a song made famous in 1916 by Al Jolson. Ian's version was played in Los Angeles and other cities, but failed to become a national hit.

It was unusual to find a college graduate among rock 'n' rollers. With a history degree from Dublin's Trinity College, Ian qualified as an intellectual among his musical peers. His history degree worked in tandem with his love of the older musical styles of Ragtime and Tin Pan Alley, which dominated his subsequent recordings. My visit was timely as Ian was awaiting the publication of his book on the history of pop music, *After the Ball*, and his latest album, for United Artists, *Under the Ragtime Moon*.

He thought I was very polite, and was impressed that I knew so much about his music. I brought over a few of the singles I had pressed up with my band, Mogan David and his Winos. When I gave Ian a copy of "Nose Job," he seemed perplexed in how to respond.

My first tourist attraction, the Tower of London, was also the best. I was enthralled with the history of the place and the tales, as told by the Yeoman Warder, and the exhibit of the Crown Jewels. I was curious about the "Old Bailey," actually the Central Criminal Court, named after the street on which it is located. I wandered into the upstairs gallery and got lucky. It was a good case, a skinhead stabbing. The judge, who was addressed as "My Lord," and the barristers (lawyers) wore the customary white wigs and dark robes. It was just like in the movies. I was there for about an hour. I saw *Sleuth*, an excellent play, at St. Martin's Theatre.

Mike Ledgerwood, whose name was familiar to me when he was a writer for *Disc and Music Echo*, took me to a fine lunch in his capacity as press officer for A&M Records. We didn't have much of a conversation. As much as I enjoyed the food, I felt he was using me so he could have a good meal at his company's expense. A few days later, I thought I should eat a healthy lunch and ordered a salad at a modest restaurant. When it arrived, I was dismayed to find that it was mostly tomatoes and onions—no lettuce. I asked the waiter who explained that lettuce was in short supply that time of year. I learned that a "salad" in England wasn't the same as in the States.

Record albums and record shops were different from those in the States. The cardboard used for the jackets was flimsy, in part because they didn't need to stand up to shrink-wrap. The images on the better covers were more striking owing to a plastic film on the front called Clarifoil. To prevent theft, the vinyl usually wasn't stored in the jacket. A customer would bring the cover to the clerk who would then fetch the matching record housed in a paper inner sleeve from a shelf behind the counter.

I was curious to see Roy Wood's Wizzard, who were performing in the East End at Sundown Mile End. The club, converted from an Odeon Theatre, had opened the previous week. Wood had recently left the Electric Light Orchestra, but on this night it looked like a bad move as his new group was terrible. Not many people were there, about 135.

Even though I had a cheap place to stay, the location was too far from the happening areas of the city. This was most apparent when I checked out the Speakeasy. The club opened in December 1966, and was for many years the preeminent club for rock's royalty. On the night The Turtles first visited in 1967, Howard Kaylan told me he saw The Beatles, Jimi Hendrix, Eric Clapton, Brian Jones, and members of The Moody Blues. It was a late-night club and private, which meant that I had to purchase a membership. Fortunately they had one that was temporary, and it didn't cost much.

On the night I arrived, little was happening, and there was no live entertainment. I don't think I stayed even an hour. Jeff Beck showed up and hung out at the bar, but I was too shy to approach him. When I made it to the nearby tube station, I saw that one side was chained up. I went to the other entrance and noticed that it was chained as well. It was probably between 12:30 and 1:00 a.m. I didn't know what to do, and started walking. Then I saw a cab, and had no choice but to splurge for the ride. I learned that the London Underground closed around 12:30 a.m.

The weather improved, so I thought it would be a good day to check out what Mandi told me was the hippest shopping area in London. Exiting the Sloane Square tube station, I crossed the street and entered the King's Road. I stopped at a newsstand and contemplated updating my foldout street map for a *London A-Z* book, when I noticed an attractive girl I had chatted with months earlier at an end of the school year *Daily Bruin* party. I reintroduced myself. She said she was off to Canterbury to spend her junior year. I flashed a thought about visiting her, but it was a long way from London, and as I was heading back to the States, I wouldn't see her again for a year. A lot could happen in a year, I reasoned, so I didn't pursue a friendship.

As I continued walking, I heard them before I saw them: bells jangling and voices chanting. I wondered if they were the same Hare Krishnas who regularly accosted passengers at the Los Angeles airport. Here they only added to the street ambiance. At the corner of Royal Avenue stood the modern façade of the Chelsea Drug Store, known to me from The Rolling Stones' song "You Can't Always Get What You Want." At this point, three years later, there is no intrigue, just a plethora of concessioners.

Here in the King's Road, shopping had a soundtrack, as pop music spilled out of the clothing stores: "Metal Guru" by T. Rex, "Mama Weer All Crazee Now" by Slade, "School's Out" by Alice Cooper, "Standing in the Road" by Blackfoot Sue, "You Wear It Well" by Rod Stewart. Sometimes a nearby shop was playing the same record as one I'd just passed. It made walking down the street fun.

The flashy clothes of the sixties were out of fashion. I couldn't even find the short, tight jackets with the puffy shoulders favored by Rod Stewart and the Faces. I bought a blue velvet suit, just like the one Bee Gee Barry Gibb wore in a promotional photo. The salesman at Take 6 was Indian, but spoke like a native Brit. He inquired if I were related to Charles Bronson, a question nobody had ever asked me before. And it happened twice more during my stay. Bronson, whose real surname was Buchinski, was a much bigger movie star in Europe than in the States. The salesman also asked me if I wanted "turnips" with my suit. Turnips? "Turn-ups" were trouser cuffs, and I declined. The trousers were fashionably wide, but not to the ludicrous extent of the "loon pants" popularized by David Bowie.

Let It Rock catered to English rockers, or Teddy Boys, as they were called. It was not an authentic 1950s look (at least not an American fifties look), because it was also influenced by Edwardian fashion (hence the Teddy nickname). The style included long "drape" jackets, "drainpipe" trousers or tight jeans, thick crepe-soled shoes (called *brothel creepers*), swept-back hairstyles and long sideburns (called *sideboards*). A few times during my stay I saw older guys dressed in this manner. Elements of fifties style were apparent in a number of those glitter rock stars of the day, like T. Rex and Gary Glitter, who catered to a young teen audience.

On Saturday the sixteenth, I went to an all-day rock festival at the Oval Cricket Ground. The opening acts weren't that impressive: Biggles and Sam Apple Pie, who had opened for Wizzard days before. Man, Wales' answer to the Grateful Dead, played well, but like the Dead, they lacked strong material and vocals. My main reason for going was to see Jeff Beck's new group, billed as Beck, Bogart & Appice. Beck was my favorite guitarist. I had seen him perform the previous October, but he now had a different group. Years before, Beck had fallen in love with Tim Bogart's bass playing and Carmine Appice's drumming when they were in Vanilla Fudge, but it had taken him until 1972 to form a band with them. This was their first public performance. There weren't that many people in attendance, about fifteen thousand, so I was able to stand close to the stage. Beck played great, but Bogart was bombastic.

Frank Zappa's new group, the Grand Wazoo, was up next. I waited a while, but I could see that it was going to take them much longer to complete their setup. It was damp and so bitterly cold that, much as I would have liked to have stayed—Linda Lewis and Hawkwind were following Zappa—I had to leave.

On Sunday, it rained. At that time in London, owing to the Sunday Trading Restriction Act of 1936, all the stores were closed on Sundays. Museums opened at noon. What could I do? I took a tube to the St. John's Wood station. Mick Jagger referenced the area in "Play With Fire," so I was curious. I walked a rectangle in the rain and noted that it was an upscale neighborhood. London was so gloomy, I thought of the government launching an artificial sun to cheer everybody up. That, and what would happen when the real sun appeared, infused the lyrics of "Artificial Sun," the song I wrote that afternoon.

More rain. On Monday morning the eighteenth, I walked a mile from the Tube station to the Imperial War Museum. Manfred Mann's excellent cover of Bob Dylan's anti-war-themed "With God On Our Side" played in my head. In a few hours I was scheduled to interview Paul Jones, the original lead singer of the group. None of the museums in Los Angeles had World War I or II artifacts. This one was chock full of them. As much as I was impressed with the collection, the reminder of the brutality of war combined with the rain outside cast a pallor over my spirits. (In rock history, the museum is where Jeff Beck asked Rod Stewart to join his band in January 1967.)

I met Paul at the office of Noel Gay Artists, his theatrical agent, and felt excited to be in his presence. Although Paul's face was marred from the acne he had as a teenager, he was still handsome. Most of our discussion was about his starring role in *Privilege,* a prescient film about the manipulation of a pop idol. A film buff, Paul was a scintillating conversationalist who came across more as a graduate film student than a rock 'n' roller. His last album had been released about a year before, and hadn't made much of an impression. To his dismay, his record company declined to issue the one he had just finished recording, claiming the jazz influence made it uncommercial.

Paul had written "The One in the Middle," among his favorite Manfred Mann songs, about being the singer in the band. He didn't know that the Leaves—a Los Angeles based band best known for the definitive rock version of "Hey Joe"—had recorded it. When I got back home, I mailed him my copy of their second album.

"Hey, Joey, it's that guy again." Joey Molland's American girlfriend Kathie turned away from the phone and handed him the receiver. It was the second time I had called the Badfinger house to get the cassette they had offered me, a copy of the original recordings George Harrison had produced for the *Straight Up* album, songs that producer Todd Rundgren had rerecorded with them. They thought Harrison's were better. Joey was cagey. I figured I'd cut my losses and not waste any more money on the payphone.

I'd been forewarned about the low quality of food at the Wimpy Bar chain of restaurants. In an issue of *Melody Maker* Pete Townshend talked about the group's frequent patronage: "The food is atrocious and the chefs are carefully trained in the art of self-defense." But the lure of a budget price, and a fondness for the *Popeye* comic strip proved too great. Unlike whatever the name promised, the interior was simple and charmless. There was one item on the menu, a Bender, which was like a hamburger except the meat was a sliced frankfurter sausage. I had the regular burger, but it wasn't even up to McDonald's standard.

I was a big fan of The Hollies, but they'd never performed publicly in Los Angeles. I tracked down their recently departed lead singer, Allan Clarke, and met him as he was recording his second solo album at AIR Studios, located in London's busiest shopping district, at 214 Oxford Street. As the better-known recording studios in Los Angeles were on the ground floors, it felt odd taking the elevator ("lift") to the fourth floor in an office building. His first album, *My Real Name Is 'arold* (because he was born Harold Allan Clarke) had been released earlier in the year, and failed to make the charts.

Clarke and the other musicians shared a smoke, but it wasn't a marijuana cigarette, which was prevalent among rock musicians in the States. He explained that in Britain marijuana was uncommon. The counterpart, hashish, was also from the cannabis plant, but more potent. It was smuggled in from North Africa. The Brits usually smoked it mixed with tobacco.

We adjourned to a nearby pub's billiard room, where a game was in progress. As we ate sandwiches and drank pints of beer, Clarke was candid about the recent state of The Hollies, why he left, and his feelings about Graham Nash. I was surprised that on our walk to and from the pub, and lunching in a public place, nobody approached the lead singer of The Hollies. When we returned to the studio, I asked him about an album that was propped up in the control room window. He said the 1966 Hollies' LP, *For Certain Because …* was displayed for inspiration. As it hadn't been released in the States I wasn't familiar with it. He gave it to me upon my departure.

On Wednesday, September 20, I took in a set by Rab Noakes at the Marquee. A Scottish folksinger, his name was familiar to me from his credit on Gerry Rafferty's *Can I Have My Money Back?* I had reviewed the album in *Rolling Stone*. I quite liked him and picked up his album on A&M.

I had had a couple of articles published in *Melody Maker*, "the world's best selling weekly music paper," so the editor, Ray Coleman, invited me to meet with him at the publication's offices. I thought he was a nice man. He was curious about my impressions of London, but wasn't interested in any of the subjects on my radar. He assigned me to track down Hilton Valentine, The Animals' original guitarist, when I returned to Los Angeles, as "House of the Rising Sun" was creeping its way back up the charts.

For the next few days Mark Leviton occupied the even smaller room adjacent to mine, and we were able to explore London together. We went to a United Artists–sponsored night in North London, in Chalk Farm, as a showcase for Brinsley Schwarz to perform songs from their new album, *Nervous On the Road.* Brinsley Schwarz and support act Help Yourself were influenced by country & western, and were part of the new "pub rock" movement of groups that built followings playing in pubs. The venue, the Roundhouse, had historical significance to us as most of the top rock groups of the sixties had played there. The building was made circular so train engines could be redirected on a large, circular turntable, before the increased size of train engines made that purpose obsolete. It wasn't that noteworthy inside, except for the novelty of curved walls.

For Mark and me, meeting The Troggs gave us a thrill similar to an archaeologist uncovering a hidden treasure. As The Troggs had never played in Los Angeles, I tracked them down and set up an interview. Sitting in their management office, it felt almost surreal: the three original members, Reg Presley, Ronnie Bond and Chris Britton; and Tony Murray, their bass player of four years. They were friendly, and offered cigarettes all around. Neither Mark nor I smoked. They were managed by Peter Walsh, an old-school manager. His representative, Barry Perkins, greeted us when we arrived. His name was familiar to us. A copy of a letter he wrote in 1965 as a talent agent was among the reject notices in The Who's *Live at Leeds* album.

The Troggs were best known for "Wild Thing" and "Love is All Around," two of their eight Top 20 British hits, but hadn't had a hit in almost five years. That didn't mean that they weren't still releasing new records, or that they weren't good, as we soon found out. Although the group dressed fashionably in the sixties, they were never good-looking, and were showing their age on this late-summer day. As they had never been musically proficient, they weren't well considered. But for us, it was like meeting legends. Lead singer Reg Presley looked, spoke, and laughed more like a lumpy leprechaun than a rock singer. They recalled with glee the thick sandwiches served in New York. Having experienced the poor excuse for a sandwich in Britain, I had to laugh.

In the States, we hadn't heard their most recent records. They played us the B-side of their latest single, "Feels Like a Woman." It was a revelation: the same, simple Troggs' sound, but a couple of steps toward the heaviness of Led Zeppelin, courtesy of Black Sabbath's ex-producer Roger Bain. They recounted the band's history, and the success they'd had despite the parsimony of their manager Larry Page.

Although they performed mostly on the cabaret circuit, they made a point that they played the same way they had in the sixties. As I expressed a strong desire to see them live, they invited me to ride with them in the van on Friday to their next engagement, in Liverpool.

Thursday night we went to see Status Quo at Sundown Mile End. The group had had a hit in May 1968 with the psychedelic "Pictures of Matchstick Men." Four years later, we didn't know what to expect. Their sound was now that of a boogie blues band. The chugging rhythm section was tight, but their vocals were lacking, and they played much too loud. Mark and I preferred the support band, Stray, who were more melodic. Adding to our bewilderment was the enthusiastic response for both acts from the mostly male crowd, around two thousand by my estimate.

Mid-morning on Friday, I interviewed Mickie Most, Britain's most successful record producer. Early on, I mentioned that he was the producer of records I bought, primarily by Herman's Hermits, The Animals, and Donovan. In 1969 Most had formed his own record company, RAK Records, and continued having hits in Britain. I met him at his office, at 2 Charles Street in Mayfair. With a baby face crowned by wavy, orange-tinted hair, Mickie looked much younger than a man of his accomplishments and age (thirty-four years).

As rock groups progressed musically and sales of LPs increased, those who looked upon themselves as "artists" were indulged, wasting hours of expensive studio time until they found inspiration. Record producers like Mickie Most, who preferred more disciplined approaches, were considered passé by many rock groups. After Jeff Beck left The Yardbirds, Mickie established him as a solo artist by producing a handful of hit singles and his first two albums. Still, Beck criticized him for his regimented way of recording. Until I spoke with Mickie, I would have taken Beck's side.

Maybe Mickie hadn't given an in-depth interview in a while because it was slightly intense, almost like a therapy session. I was caught off guard at his candor about how unappreciative his artists had been.

"All that work with Jeff Beck and Led Zeppelin, all that work with Donovan and him saying, 'I can do it better without you,' working my balls off making Lulu the number one international female vocalist, and reading in the papers how she's looking for a new producer—I just went, 'I've had enough of these people.' Most of the artists are slags: they use you, vacation on your yacht, borrow money and never give it back, and then don't have the decency to tell you to your face."

When Mickie told me that family was the most important thing to him, and that his goal was to finish in the studio in time to have dinner with them, I had a renewed respect for his approach to recording. That's one of the reasons he had turned down producing The Rolling Stones, because they were undisciplined and liked to start recording at midnight.

He readily admitted his strength, finding and/or picking material to be released as singles. Unlike others in his position, he had the confidence to reveal his shortcomings. He said that he wasn't interested in getting the sounds of the instruments, leaving that to his recording engineer, nor in arranging the songs, preferring to hire an arranger such as John Paul Jones, whom he used extensively before Jones joined Led Zeppelin.

In the two years since Most started RAK, allowing others to helm the productions, he'd accumulated twenty-seven hit records, a good many of which earned sales awards that lined the walls of his office. For someone who didn't reveal a sense of humor, I liked him because he was frank and responsive.

I returned to The Troggs' management office Friday afternoon. They weren't quite ready, so I sat and waited. Over the next hour I learned that the door to their van had come loose, and they were trying to find someone who could fix it. When that proved an impossibility that afternoon, I overheard a discussion about getting a doctor's note to indicate that Reg had a sore throat, and couldn't sing than night, so they wouldn't be penalized for cancelling the appearance for non-medical reasons. I was obviously disappointed. Only later did I think about the discomfort I would have experienced riding four hours in the back of a windowless van two hundred miles to Liverpool.

Had I been knowledgeable enough to have sought a more centralized living accommodation, I would have never experienced the two jewels I discovered nearby. Goldie Oldies was a record collector's dream. The selection was excellent, but the prices were high for my budget. I bought an early Manfred Mann single, "5-4-3-2-1," two latter Herman's Hermits' singles, "Lady Barbara" and "Bet Yer Life I Do," The New Vaudeville Band's "Green Street Green," and Small Faces' "My Mind's Eye," a French release with a colorful cover. I bought these records without having heard them. They had all been hits in England, but hadn't been released in the States. Unit 4 + 2 had had a hit in England and the US with "Concrete and Clay," and I had their album. I didn't know that they had recorded a second one, and when I saw that in the bin, I snatched it up. I also bought a series of *Teen Beat Annual* books that had fabulous photos of the pop stars of the sixties.

The Thomas A Becket pub at 320 Old Kent Road had historical significance in boxing, but I didn't care about that because Blunderbuss was the weekend entertainment—and the best overall unsigned band I've ever seen. They were decent musically and vocally, but projected a rare sense of humor, and their repertoire was excellent. I saw them play three nights.

The lead singer, with long, flat hair and wire-rim glasses over an aquiline nose, looked like a cross between John Lennon and The Lovin' Spoonful's John Sebastian, and acted like The Spoonful's Zal Yanovsky with his swaying and mugging. Their set included recent English hits: Elton John's "Rocket Man," Roxy Music's "Virginia Plain," Mott the Hoople's "All the Young Dudes," David Bowie's "Starman," and The Move's "California Man." There was one song that Mark and I had never heard before, a picaresque bolero titled "Jackie." When I asked the singer, Laurie Beazley, about it, he told me that it had been a hit by Scott Walker in the sixties.

We were also introduced to the drinking customs of the English public house. In the States we might order "a beer," here it would be "a pint of ale," or just "a pint." We also drank a shandy, which is a beer mixed with a lemonade soda. Sweet.

On Saturday I took Mark down the King's Road. The Hare Krishnas were still there. I bought a cheap, unlined, purple satin jacket with large lapels in the style of Marc Bolan. When we returned, we walked a few blocks down the Old Kent Road and knocked on the door to Manfred Mann's studio. No one answered. If I had realized that it was so close to our rooms, I would have called him earlier in the week.

That evening we took in a screening of *Performance* at the Odeon Elephant & Castle. It starred Mick Jagger in an offbeat gangster story, and had only had a limited run in the States. The film had been made in 1968, but not released until two years later. Normally we would have seen the film in Los Angeles, but viewing it in London gave us a strange feeling. The London we saw in the movie theater looked just like the London when we exited the theater. It had rained and the cobblestones were wet.

On our last Sunday in town, September 24, Mark and I went to Abbey Road to see where The Beatles had taken the photos used on the last album they recorded together, three years earlier. The front of the album cover showed them walking in a crosswalk, or "zebra crossing," as the locals referred to it. The back cover featured a close-up of a tiled Abbey Road sign with "The Beatles" spelled out in similar tile above on a brick wall. Riding the Tube to St. John's Wood, we joked that there would be lines of Beatles' fans waiting to take their pictures in front of these landmarks. When we arrived on the street, we were surprised that there was no one else there. The zebra crossing didn't look quite right. Maybe the lines had been reconfigured. We walked a few blocks along the road and noticed that there were few of the regular, tin Abbey Road signs. We learned that fans had stolen them. We never found the tiled one depicted on the back cover.

We visited the Tate Gallery, which I loved, particularly the peerless pop art collection. Stimulated by an afternoon of enthralling art, we almost floated to the Tube when a skinhead spat "cunts!" in our direction as he marched passed. I didn't feel threatened, but was mildly shocked as I hadn't experienced anything like that on the trip. At the same time, it was so outlandish it seemed almost humorous.

That evening we saw The Everly Brothers, who were headlining the Palladium, the most prestigious theater in London. Although there was tension between the brothers, and they were soon to dissolve the act for a number of years, they were very professional. They looked great, their harmonies were spot on, and they performed a crowd-pleasing set of their hits.

Equally thrilling were the second-billed Searchers, who had never played in Los Angeles. Unfortunately, their newish drummer showcased his hair in a natural, hippie fro, rather than conforming to the more restrained look of his bandmates. Their act was more cabaret, similar to a slick Las Vegas lounge act catering to adults, rather than a rock band, but they still performed their hits in a fine fashion.

It was time to leave London. Mark was going off to the University of Birmingham. Incoming students would soon be occupying the bungalows. And I'd had enough of the cold weather. I took a commercial flight back to the States, to New York, to join my mother, who was visiting her brothers in Elizabeth, New Jersey. There weren't that many passengers, so I had three seats to myself toward the back. As I transcribed the interview with The Troggs for my *Phonograph Record Magazine* article, I thought of how open and candid my interview subjects had been. Afterward, I read *Apple to the Core*, a revealing book about the difficulties The Beatles experienced in bringing utopian values to running their record company.

STATUS QUO GO TO DISNEYLAND

"What's Fantasyland like? Is it young girls showing their knickers and stockings?"

—Francis Rossi

THE WHISKEY A GO-GO. February 6, 1974. The British rock quartet Status Quo take the stage and kick their set off with a cover of B. B. King's "Rock Me Baby." The guys look so skinny, and so young. Guitarist Francis Rossi, singing at the mic, has the same sophomoric quality of Ozzy Osbourne. Rick Parfitt crouches intensely, playing guitar in the corner like a high school kid doing his homework. Bassist Alan Lancaster's heavy guttural vocals, evocative of Steppenwolf's John Kay, are twisted from his skimpy, studded-black-leather frame. Straight-faced drummer John Coghlan hides in the back, content to bash out a noisy rhythm.

Together they bob up and down, shake their hair out to dry, and chase each other around the stage, momentarily grouping in various spots before dispersing. All the while the incessant, infectious, 4/4-rhythm machine boogies on. Rossi plays note-bending leads, and he and Parfitt join for some impressive parallel runs, and during "Roll Over Lay Down," Parfitt channels Arab-flavored melodies. Emerson, Lake & Palmer, Rory Gallagher, and Manfred Mann's Earthband have all graced the Whisky this opening night. It was devastating, unremitting boogie all the way.

In America, Status Quo were known for "Pictures of Matchstick Men," which climbed to number twelve on the *Billboard* chart. Replete with whooshing phasing effects and a catchy, stinging guitar pattern, the record's psychedelic arrangement was passé for the summer of 1968, but the record was too good not to become a hit. Their subsequent singles failed to make the Top 40, but I bought their album anyway.

On my first visit to England in the summer of 1972, checking out concerts for the coming week in *Time Out* magazine, I noticed that Status Quo were performing on Thursday, September 21, at Sundown Mile End. I wondered if it were the same group whose album I had. As they had yet to set foot in America, I was curious. I couldn't have expected them to sound the same as on their psychedelic album of four years before, but I hadn't heard any of their newer records. Considering the imagination they had displayed previously, I wasn't prepared for their assault of chugging rhythms as throughout the previous year "boogie blues bands" had been made fun of throughout Los Angeles.

It all started with Canned Heat. Inspired by John Lee Hooker, whose most known song after "Boom Boom" is "Boogie Chillen," they popularized the boogie blues style. Boogie-woogie was a piano style that first gained popularity in the twenties. Rock groups adapted the groove to guitar, but many played with few chord changes making the songs monotonous to some ears. In 1968, Canned Heat made the Top 20 with an album titled *Boogie With Canned Heat*. This limited and repetitive style was so nearly omnipresent in the early seventies that it was derided from the concert stages in LA. Flo & Eddie satirized the form in an overlong and repetitive encore in which they inveighed, "You wanna boogie? We'll give you boogie!"

On that night in London, the band was tight but much too loud, and the singing lacked dynamics. I was bewildered by the enthusiastic response from the mostly male crowd.

Seven months later I was visiting with Lee Cadorette, a publicist at A&M Records, Status Quo's US label. The group was coming to town for a weeklong engagement at the Whisky. She said they planned on spending a day at Disneyland, and suggested I go with them to conduct my interview for *Rock Magazine.*

On Monday, April 30, I met them at their motel, at the corner of Sunset Boulevard and La Brea Avenue, a stone's throw from the offices of A&M Records. Compared to the small rooms found in English hotels, this modest American one was roomy. When I entered, band members Alan Lancaster and Francis Rossi were engaged in a jocular wrestling match, tugging each other's stomachs, with the bed standing in for the ring. Rossi then took a quick shower. He emerged with his limp hair tucked under a plastic shower cap, a small, gold earring gleaming from his left ear lobe, long fuzzy sideburns and a smooth leering grin, reminding me of a scheming pirate. "Bring on the dancing girls!" he hooted, as he bumped and grinded with hotel bath towel in front of the TV obscuring an old Robert Mitchum movie.

Rick Parfitt, whose healthy looks recalled those of a seventeen-year-old high school surfer, bounced on his bed in his silky-red underwear, like Tarzan, or better still, like one of the castaways in *Lord of the Flies.* Later he was aghast on discovering he'd mistakenly brushed his teeth with Clearasil. "At least your teeth won't get spots," someone shouted. The deceptively handsome (because the facial hair hid his features) John Coghlan was sedate, but made his presence known nonetheless. Elsewhere, in various combinations, they swung badminton rackets through the air, or related cheerful jokes. Here's one from Francis: "This geezer goes into a bake shop and says, 'I'd like a loaf of bread.' The shop keeper asks, 'Will that be white or dark?' He says, 'It don't matter, I've got my bike outside.' Ahahahah…"

Before departing for Disneyland, Francis gave me a quick history of the band's early years: "The Status Quo have existed since 1962. I was twelve then and our staple was 1950s tunes. We were signed to a recording contract late in 1965 and made four singles the next two years as the Spectres and Traffic Jam. We dropped Traffic Jam when Steve Winwood started his band, and became the Status Quo. Our managers made me change my name from Francis to Mike because they thought Francis was a bit poofish. Our sound was a product of the time and our producer John Schroeder, who felt it necessary to contribute a third of the material, along with the publishers who had us do a third of their songs. If John didn't like one of *our* songs, we couldn't do it.

"It just got to be a very unhealthy scene with the business. We were playing gigs, getting screamed at for the fifteeen minutes we were on. Amen Corner was hitting the top of the charts selling only eighty thousand singles. It was a time when the music business started to change."

When the hits dried up, they found themselves booked in clubs for seventy pounds a night. The band's psychedelic style was jettisoned after hearing The Doors' "Roadhouse Blues"—which they covered on their January 1973 album *Piledriver*—and Fleetwood Mac's blues rock when they opened for them on a UK tour. To coincide with the transformation, they changed their name from The Status Quo to Status Quo. The new direction clicked, and the band was on its way. *Piledriver* rose to number five in the UK.

The members of Status Quo were jovial the morning we departed for Disneyland, the Magic Kingdom. Rick rode with me in my 1967 red Firebird convertible, the others in a station wagon. "Groucho Marx has got a pink Cadillac outside his house, and Hugh Hefner's got this unbelievably huge estate with tennis courts, and outside of Elvis' house all these girls have signed their names," Rick highlighted his previous day's excursion through the opulent homes of Beverly Hills as we cruised down the Santa Ana Freeway. Traffic was light on this Wednesday morning as we passed a billboard that read: "Thank the Lord for our Nation and our President." "Is that a piss-take [a put-on]?" Rick asked. It wasn't. "We'd never have anything like that in England."

As we neared the park, we saw the Matterhorn ride from the freeway. Rick leaned back and puffed on his Picadilly cigarette. "I'm into futuristic things," he said. "I saw *Fantastic Planet* [sci-fi film], but it wasn't any good. You know that spaceship to the moon they've got at Disneyland? I've gotta go on that."

We arrived and the members were fascinated with the cars in the vast parking lot. They were most impressed with the Porsches. Rick met a stumbling block when an official suggested he cover his exposed chest by buttoning his blue Levi's jacket before entering the park. Rick must have been shook up, because he kept falling down after entering the Magic Kingdom. But he was OK, hopping about and racing around. For the most part it was all mouths agape, and shouts of "it's amazing!" They didn't have much to say, being too transfixed for speech. Even jester Rossi was silent. It was as though they were eight years old again.

"Whooaaaaaaaaahh," everyone roared as our boat descended into the murky depths of Pirates of the Caribbean, a glimpse of the pillaging, raping, looting pirates of old. It's Disneyland's most progressively animated, and best-realized attraction. Everyone loved it. "I could knock around here the rest of my life," said Rick.

It was a perfect day, the temperature in the mid-sixties. To top things off, as it was a weekday during the spring, most rides that would otherwise involve a forty-to-fifty minute wait required only ten. It was a relaxing afternoon. Everybody was busy snapping photos. I took ones of the band on the deck of Captain Hook's Pirate Ship.

To be sure, a good deal of Status Quo's humor is engagingly bawdry, whistling slyly like a pack of high school punks at the beach. "Look at her jumpers!" exclaims manager Colin. "Look at 'er box, ah ya missed a good one," observed someone from the back. "What's

Fantasyland like?" queried Francis. "Is it young girls showing their knickers and stockings?"

While munching sandwiches in Bear Country's Mile Long Bar—it's done with facing mirrors—Rick poured a fourth packet of sugar into his tea and talked about the group's new LP. "It will be a progression from our last one. We recorded tracks at A&M, but we couldn't do more because of hassles with the musicians union. We'll finish it at our regular studio at IBC on Portland Place. It's a cellar and we feel comfortable there, but we record at full volume with all our stacks of amps, and there have been complaints from the people in nearby homes. We can record from ten a.m. to eleven p.m." A listen later on at the motel to four cuts on a cassette revealed a natural progression from the standard boogie format, utilizing catchy riffs and a heavier and harder-edge sound, approaching Black Sabbath by half a step.

The gift store offered many tantalizing items: John bought a Disneyland photo book, Alan gobbled up three View Master film packets, and Chas, the lovably dumpy roadie, bought a cowboy hat in which he recalled the character Hoss from the *Bonanza* TV show. Chas reeked of an indescribably moldy odor—like he's worn the same clothes over a year, which he claims he has, "to break them in." He, and the others, discovered that a root beer was not really beer with alcohol. All bemoaned that there was no place to secure a pint of ale in the park.

The crowd was composed of mostly old ladies who slowly strolled the streets with sloppy lipstick smiles and impenetrable sunglasses. The rest consisted of families, a few scattered teens, and tourists. Rick seemed puzzled why so many American women were obese. He speculated that it must be over-consumption because the food was so plentiful and cheap. "Yeah, you sure get more food here, but in England I bet you get more vitamins." Status Quo, gaily strolling about in a public place, would have been mobbed back home, but here they received only casual glances. As we exited the Swiss Family Tree House, a couple asked if they were in a rock group. "Led Zeppelin," Francis told them.

"I've never been to the moon before. I want to drive," said Rick, as our space rocket proceeded to countdown. From there it was an afternoon of viewing the lost city of Atlantis in a nuclear submarine, cruising down the headhunter-infested waters of the Zambezi, and excessively shrinking to view the nucleus of the atom. "This would be a great place to take the wife on vacation," John smacked, only to be disappointed later when the last raft to Tom Sawyer's Island had left only seconds before we arrived at the dock.

It was a tiring day for all. Rick's energy dissipated as his consumption of champagne and other alcoholic treats the night before took their toll. Driving back to Hollywood, we listened to and sang along with The Who's hits from *Meaty Beaty Big and Bouncy*.

And, as the early evening faded into night, Rick, Francis, Alan, and John were sprawled out on beds, trying to summon enough energy to trek off to dinner. John had the last word: "I'd like to go on the Universal Movie Studios tour tomorrow."

LONDON 1973

FLUSH WITH THE MONEY I'd saved from a four-month appointment as a US Passport Agent—to handle the seasonal influx of applications—I flew to London on September 21 for another bite at Big Ben. To ensure that I made a good start, Barbara DeWitt, a United Artists Records' publicist, convinced Andrew Lauder at the UK company to spring for two nights at the chic Portobello Hotel.

Converted from a mansion, the hotel was only two years old. It was located in Notting Hill, close to many antique shops, but as they didn't specialize in 1960s, I wasn't interested. I had a well-appointed room—it even included a shower and toilet—but it was the smallest I'd ever seen. It recalled the joke that the room was so small, I had to step into the hall to change my mind. There wasn't enough room to stretch out on the floor and perform a push up. For such a posh hotel, the complimentary breakfast was a disappointment. I learned then that a Continental breakfast was merely a fancy name for nothing more than a roll, juice, and tea or coffee.

I liked being there, but didn't feel comfortable enough to test my jet lag and budget to hang out at the bar waiting to see if any rock stars would show up that I would be too shy to approach anyway. I did see somebody whom I knew, John Mendelsohn, my first editor at the UCLA *Daily Bruin*. As I walked down a hallway, there he was, sitting next to his girlfriend, publicist Patti Wright. Neither John nor Patti looked in my direction as I approached, or I would have said, "Hello." They weren't chatting, just sitting, looking down. I didn't know where I stood with John. He could be warm and gracious, but also cold and alienating. I believe I was on the outs with him because I gave his band, Christopher Milk, a bad review two summers ago when they played an impromptu set at a UCLA dormitory recreation room. I found out later the couple was waiting to be picked up by David Bowie.

Mendelsohn was a champion of The Move, and so was Jim Bickhart who turned me onto their *Shazam* LP in Februaray 1970. It became one of my most-played albums throughout the year. Imagine discovering that there was a British group making records almost as good as The Beatles or The Who. The Move, who were from Birmingham in the Midlands, had had nine big hits. None of the eight singles A&M released on their behalf made the *Billboard* Hot 100. None even skirted the Bubbling Under category, which extended to number 135. Or as Bev Bevan put it in respect of *Shazam*, it "brought us from total obscurity in America to merely relative obscurity."

Roy Wood, their guitarist and sometime lead vocalist, wrote all of the group's hits. He became enamored by how The Beatles incorporated classical backing during their psychedelic phase, most appealingly in "I Am the Walrus." He took The Move in that direction as the Electric Light Orchestra (aka ELO), but with the members of the band playing the classical instruments rather than a hired orchestra. Curiously, the group's debut album had different titles in the UK and US, respectively, *The Electric Light Orchestra* and *No Answer*. Roy explained that when the US company called the band's UK management office to get the title, no one answered the phone, so the executive assistant wrote "No Answer" on the message.

Problems soon arose. The expanded band didn't sound cohesive live, and their repertoire favored newer member Jeff Lynne. After their first album had been released, Wood left and formed a new group, Wizzard. He retained the classical instrument augmentation, but went more in a 1950s-influenced rock direction, similar to that of The Move's last hit, "California Man."

I met Wood in the lounge of the Sandringham Hotel. His yellow-tinted glasses matched the yellow wisp in his brown hair. We had just gotten started when who should come by for a quick hello but Jeff Lynne, who was also staying at the hotel. Roy claimed that he and Jeff were on good terms. If they weren't, Jeff wouldn't have come over. Roy said that one of the reasons he left was so that Jeff would get more recognition, rather than being in his shadow.

Roy wasn't a great conversationalist. He gave short, conventional answers with little insight. Compared to ELO, he wanted Wizzard to have a more dynamic sound, similar to that of the John Barry Seven. John Barry was best known for scoring the James Bond films. Roy said that he had been listening to Led Zeppelin, the Carpenters, and lots of classical music.

When I interviewed Bev last May in LA, he told me that Roy had forged his plans for Wizzard in secret: "We didn't know it at the time, but he was rehearsing Wizzard behind our backs. Everyone but we knew about it in Birmingham, and when we got a call from our manager saying that he and two other members left to play in Wizzard, it was pretty embarrassing. Here we were all buddies, all good friends, and he doesn't even give us the courtesy of saying, 'I'm leaving the band; it just isn't working out.'" Over the subsequent year, Roy had three hits with Wizzard in the UK, including two number ones, and a hit as a solo artist. So, it appeared that he'd made the right decision.

I'd met Nancy Retchin through Harvey Kubernik, and used to chat with her at concerts in Los Angeles. She had recently moved to London, sharing a flat with others. I wanted to make a postcard to mail back to friends and relatives in the States, a photo of me standing next to the Abbey Road sign depicted on the back cover of The Beatles' album of the same name. Four years after the release of the album, I was surprised to find how few of the street signs remained. We found a suitable one mounted on a brick wall. I don't think the one used on the album cover was still in place. Nancy took the photo of me modeling the white suit jacket I just purchased from Take 6 on the King's Road, over the English-only Jo Jo Gunne promotional T-shirt that I got from WEA.

Knowing I was going to London, A&M Records had asked me to write a two-page biography of Stealers Wheel to accompany the US release of their second album, *Ferguslie Park*, produced by Jerry Leiber and Mike Stoller. I interviewed Gerry Rafferty at Island Records' Basing Street Studios in Notting Hill during the final mixing. Before Stealers Wheel, Rafferty had partnered with fellow Scot Billy Connolly in The Humblebums. I liked their two American-released albums. After they split, he teamed up with an old school friend, Joe Egan, who sang background on seven songs on his solo album, before they formed Stealers Wheel.

I saw Mike Stoller in the control room, but not Jerry Leiber. I also saw stacked cases of Newcastle Brown Ale and Scotch whiskey. Rafferty was introverted and shy, but I was able to get what I needed from him as he inhaled a Picadilly cigarette. He told me that he left the band for a time, but rejoined when "Stuck in the Middle With You" became a big hit earlier in the year. About the song he said: "Shortly after the group was signed, we all went to a big, very crowded party. I was a little drunk, and I was stuck next to this guy whom I had very little in common with. The conversation was forced. I was stuck in the middle with him."

Man—Wales' answer to the Grateful Dead—had recorded a handful of albums, but none had sold well enough to make the charts. Andrew Lauder had signed them and invited me to join a train trip United Artists organized to see Man perform in their hometown of Swansea. On Thursday, September 27, we departed from Paddington Station. On the way I chatted with English writers Geoff Brown

(*Melody Maker*) and Charles Shaar Murray (*New Musical Express*), whose writings I admired.

That evening Man headlined Brangwyn Hall, and played well for the hometown crowd. Deke Leonard's Iceberg opened. Leonard had been Man's guitarist, but had been fired. I loved his song "A Hard Way to Live." He performed it as part of his set, and then reprised it, joining Man for their encore. During the break I chatted with Mike Gibbins, Badfinger's drummer, who was in town visiting his family.

After the concert our party went to Pandora's, a local disco that had few patrons. We drank, but mostly stood around, and were bothered by the constantly changing colored lights coming from the dance floor. None of the English writers seemed interested in me, or where I came from. No one was friendly. Unlike most in our party, getting drunk on the record company tab didn't appeal to me. I was so bored I didn't feel like waiting around until the band arrived so I took a taxi back to my hotel. My impression of Swansea was that it rained all the time, not just from our two days there, but also from the moss growing on the roofs of the houses.

I saw a listing that ELO were appearing the next night in the Refectory at Brunel University. I took the Metropolitan Line on the Underground all the way to Uxbridge, the last stop, then walked a mile until I got to the university. Beside me most of the way was a young student, who asked me if America were as violent as what he saw in the movies and on TV. It made me realize the impressions that those in other countries get solely from our media.

When I arrived, I was disappointed to see that ELO had cancelled. Suzi Quatro was the replacement. Suzi was a cute, short blonde from Detroit. She and her band of Englishmen dressed in black leather, and she cultivated the image of a tough, aggressive male rocker. Her two recent British hits made me curious, and as I'd come all that way, I bought a ticket to check her out. I loved her personality and energy, but the overall sound wasn't that tight or powerful. She needed better songs, too.

I TOOK A "COACH" (bus) northwest to Stratford-on-Avon, birthplace of William Shakespeare. The Avon struck me as the perfect width for a river. I walked around the quaint town and saw Shakespeare's first home. That evening I took in the Royal Shakespeare Company's performance of *Romeo and Juliet* at the Royal Shakespeare Theatre. It was a pleasure to see such an accomplished cast.

After spending the night in a bed and breakfast hotel, I took a bus to Warwick Castle in Warwickshire. Located in a bend on the River Avon, it was everything I imagined a medieval castle to be. It satisfied a childhood curiosity from viewing movies and TV shows about knights in shining armor. Built primarily in the twelfth century, it was unlike anything we had in America.

I took a bus to the University of Birmingham to meet one of the friends Mark Leviton had made while attending the school the previous year. John Clark made arrangements for me to sleep on the floor in a dorm room. We didn't do much that night, spending most of the time at a pub for the students on the ground floor of the dorm, something you would never see at an American university.

Bev Bevan picked me up the next morning in his luxurious Aston Martin DB6. It was like having a longhaired James Bond as a tour guide. He pointed out a few of the sights, and then we stopped by his modest record store, Heavyhead Records—with his mum manning the counter. Originally a toy store, he converted it to records two years ago. When Bev was in town and he wasn't playing soccer, he regularly manned the counter. Roy Wood, replete with makeup, had joined him on occasional Saturdays. At his house, his wife served us lunch, and he showed me his scrapbooks from his previous group, The Move.

Of particular interest to me was the postcard that had caused the group a lot of trouble. Trying to get publicity for their single "Flowers in the Rain," manager Tony Secunda, unbeknownst to the band, had circulated a caricature-illustrated postcard depicting Prime Minister Harold Wilson in bed, nude, with his secretary. Wilson sued the band for libel. Secunda settled, with all the money earned from the record—a considerable sum, as it soared all the way to number two—given to charities chosen by Wilson. As the record climbed the chart, The Move were upset about the money they were losing because they had nothing to do with the stunt or the settlement. I enjoyed the day, and Bev's hospitality. He dropped me off at the railway station so I could take the train one hundred miles back to London.

I still popped in at United Artists and WEA, but based myself more out of *Rolling Stone*'s London office, located at 25 Newman Street. Andrew Bailey, handsome and nattily dressed, was head of the bureau. I became friendly with writers Chris Hodenfield and Paul Gambaccini. The office received an advance copy of David Bowie's new album, *Pin Ups*. We grouped around the office record player for a preview. I liked the concept, a collection of his interpretations of the mid-sixties songs he loved, but preferred the originals.

With a lot of construction in the area, I walked through the cold and soot under scaffolding down to Oxford Street to have lunch. I visited the newly opened Biba department store on Kensington High Street. From the gloom and rain outside, I stepped into an Art Deco paradise. It was the most beautiful store I'd ever visited, but also the dimmest lit. It was as though there had been a power failure and the auxiliary generators had kicked in. I was struck by the amount of glass—mirrors, black-glass counters—splashes of plumed feathers and Egyptian motifs throughout. The women's clothes on view, reflecting the prevailing glam style, looked like they had been appropriated from an early-thirties Hollywood musical. For all anyone took notice of me, I could have been the Invisible Man. Yet, sweating in my unfashionable lined trench coat, I felt too intimidated to explore the upper floors, and left.

Andrew Lauder recommended me to Andrew Bailey to write an article for *Rolling Stone* on Hawkwind. Although I liked some of their songs, I wasn't a fan of the band. But as it was an opportunity to get another piece in the magazine, I agreed. On Saturday, October 6, I took a Lufthansa flight to Düsseldorf to join the band while they were on tour in Germany. I was the only longhair on the flight. Most of the passengers were, I presumed, German businessmen in suits reading *Die Zeit*. That night Hawkwind were playing in a neighboring town. I was told I would be met at the airport.

My flight arrived, and there was no one to meet me. All the passengers had dispersed. I inquired at an information booth, but there was no message. I had no contact information, and didn't know where the band was staying or playing. As it was Saturday, I couldn't phone United Artists in London, as it was closed. I was admiring the construction of the brand new terminal, when I heard my name paged on the public address system.

Stacia, who was sincerely apologetic, met me. She was one of the reasons I wanted to see the band. I did not find her attractive, a six-foot-two-inch overweight woman with large breasts. She got so carried away as a fan of the band's music that she would get up on stage, dance interpretively, and take off her clothes. She soon became a fixture of the live show. And here she was in the flesh—well, actually with clothes on. The handsome, blond German roadie drove a two-seat sports car. Stacia sat on his lap; I in the passenger seat. The Black Forest's tall green trees lined the highway as a light rain fell. I was overcome by sadness, thinking of the millions of people who had died at the hands of the Germans during World War II.

At the club, before the evening's performance, I spoke with a few members of the band, but couldn't get much out of them. They did reveal that the band's name was derived from sci-fi writer Michael

Moorcock's Dorian Hawkmoon character. Lemmy Kilmister, the bass player who sang lead on their "Silver Machine" hit, was amiable despite his intimidating 1950s rocker look—which seemed out of place as a member of a psychedelic band—and spaced-out eyes. As befitting his looks, Lemmy was a big rock 'n' roll fan. He liked Little Richard most of all; also Eddie Cochran, Jerry Lee Lewis, Buddy Holly, and (Britain's) Billy Fury.

That night a guy in the audience asked me, in German, if I had a light for his cigarette. I replied, "Nein." It was the extent of the German I was able to muster. I wish I had remembered more from my high school classes, but "Wo ist die Bibliothek?" *Where is the library?* wasn't going to put me in the right direction.

Hawkwind's sound was similar to Black Sabbath's, mostly based around riffs, except when they revealed their hippie folk roots. Most of the themes were science fiction, augmented by a synthesizer. Writers had slapped the description of "space rock" on them. Robert Calvert, their resident poet and lead singer, had recently departed the band. Andrew Lauder played me the new single, "Ejection," that Calvert, with members of Hawkwind, had recorded as Captain Lockheed and the Starfighters. I preferred it to anything by Hawkwind, which I felt had been diminished by Calvert's departure.

The band performed a number of selections from their recently released Top 10-charting album *Space Ritual*, which was about the dreams of a group of astronauts who are in suspended animation. The music was loud and hard, and the vocals were difficult to hear. The droning rhythm almost intended to put one in a trance. The show included DJ Andy Dunkley, who played records before the set and introduced the band; dancer Stacia, displaying little more than iridescent paint; and psychedelic liquid-light affects projected on the band.

Back at the hotel, we all shared a large dormitory room. It was low-key: no rambunctious drinking, no drug taking, no groupies brought back to the room. Stacia had her own room, which she shared that night with the German roadie.

The breakfast spread at the hotel was sumptuous: lots of sliced meats and cheeses, and dark breads. We ate together at a large table in the breakfast room. There were no discussions I could spruce up my piece with: no frustrations aired, no discourse on German culture, no bantering. Despite the drama of the music, as people, they were approachable, just not interesting.

Dropped back at the airport, I wandered around and came upon a gift store that stocked a few records. On the counter were extra, empty picture sleeves for Wizzard's new single, "Angel Fingers," on the EMI Electrola label. I took one.

On Sunday I arrived from Germany, checked back into my hotel, and then met Nancy at Fairfield Hall in Croydon to see The Kinks on the last date of their tour. It was a difficult time for The Kinks' lead singer Ray Davies. In June his wife walked out with their two children. A week later he overdosed on drugs and was admitted to the hospital. Two weeks later, on July 15, playing a rock festival at White City Stadium, he announced his retirement from the stage. Later that day, having overdosed on amphetamines, he was admitted to the hospital and had his stomach pumped.

The audience was charged, since many, me included, felt that it could be the last Kinks appearance. The band was charged, too, but that didn't mean that they were able to play well. Still, it was an effective and entertaining concert.

I typed up my article on Hawkwind at *Rolling Stone*, and gave the copy to Andrew Bailey. I wasn't happy with it, because I didn't get much of a story. Doug Smith, Hawkwind's manager, asked to see a copy. Normally, a journalist would never show his article to an artist, manager, or record label employee prior to publication. But

Doug seemed nice, and I was compromised, so I did. Doug used his standing to have the story pulled from consideration in favor of having somebody else write about the band the following year to promote the US tour. My disappointment in not getting paid was slightly lessened because I didn't get a good story.

I met Peter Noone at Marquee Studios, located around the corner from the Marquee Club, at 10 Richmond Mews. He was working on a song, "I'm a Gambler," that I thought was catchy, but it needed another part, like a bridge, to keep it from being so repetitive. He took a lunch break and we walked to a nearby restaurant.

After all the hits he'd had with Herman's Hermits, Peter had had only one as a solo artist, with the David Bowie composition "Oh You Pretty Things." Bowie had had a fluke hit in 1969 with "Space Oddity," but had been unable to follow it up as a singer or songwriter until Noone's hit returned him to the charts in 1971.

Peter told me that, because it was a hit, he had given Bowie a shot at the subsequent single. "Right On Mother" aired a contemporary social topic of a boy making the transition into manhood by moving in with his girlfriend, and getting his mother's approval. As on the previous single, Bowie played piano, but this one failed to hit. As we walked back to the studio, I was surprised no one came up to Peter, who in my mind was a very recognizable star.

Later in the day, Peter and his wife Mireille picked me up at Trafalgar Square—where I had gone to say hello to Bev who was taping a segment with ELO for *The Midnight Special*—and we had dinner at the Westbury Hotel. His hospitality made a big impression on me, and he even invited me to spend the night at their home in Buckinghamshire, fifty miles away. I wanted to go, but as I'd gotten a ticket from *Rolling Stone* to see Steeleye Span at Royal Albert Hall, I thought I should attend the show on the chance that they wanted a review. Peter drove a luxurious Jaguar Vanden Plas. He dropped me off across from the concert arena.

The next evening I listened to the radio in my room. It had been installed in the wall, and had two knobs: one for on/off/volume and one that turned to two channels, BBC and Light. It was an old setup as Light was now known as BBC 2. The channel programmed what was referred to as "housewives' choice," which meant a good amount of radio soap operas and easy listening music. The other channel, now called BBC 1, played mostly rock. Hits that I liked included: "Angel Fingers" by Wizzard, "Ballroom Blitz" by Sweet, and "Nutbush City Limits" by Ike and Tina Turner. There were a couple of records by a talented new group, 10cc, that hadn't made an impression yet in the States. The songs were more like miniature plays riddled with theatrical sound effects and voiced by different characters. The settings were American, as were the accents of the British singers. "The Dean and I" described an unusual high school romance, and "Rubber Bullets" a dance-cum-riot at the local county jail.

Given that basketball wasn't that well known in Britain, I couldn't fathom why Cheech and Chong's comedic "Basketball Jones" was receiving airplay. And then I heard a song that was familiar to me, "I'm a Gambler." It sounded like a rough demo compared to Peter's new version. The announcer said it was by Red Herring. I thought it was probably the original version as it, too, could have benefitted from a bridge.

In Andrew Lauder's office, he had artwork for an upcoming new Man album pinned to his wall. As a fan of psychedelic posters that advertised sixties rock concerts, Andrew commissioned one of those artists, Rick Griffin, to paint a cover featuring *Mad* magazine's Alfred E. Newman, splashed by water, holding a large fish. United Artists' lawyers objected to using the art because it infringed the magazine's trademark.

On October 11, the Thursday before I was to fly home, I was fortunate to be able to see 10cc who were performing their fourth concert at Greenwich Borough Hall. I took the train to Greenwich in southeast London. It's best known for providing the standard for setting time, as in Greenwich Mean Time. As I arrived at night, I wasn't able to partake of the tourist attractions. Before the show, I met the members of the band backstage, actually one floor below the stage.

The members of 10cc were from Manchester, and three of the four were Jewish. In the mid-sixties, guitarist Eric Stewart had had two big hits as a member of The Mindbenders, and bassist Graham Gouldman, as a songwriter, scored more than a handful of hits for The Yardbirds, The Hollies and Herman's Hermits. With fellow musicians drummer Kevin Godley and guitarist Lol Creme, they built a recording studio in Manchester as a new business venture. A recording to test the acoustics of the new studio became a fluke hit in the summer of 1970. "Neanderthal Man" by Hotlegs hit number two in the UK and advanced into the Top 20 in the US. In 1972 Neil Sedaka, hoping to revive his career, hired them to record his *Solitaire* album. Creme, Godley, and Gouldman provided the backing; Stewart engineered. Sedaka was so impressed with them that he suggested they form a band, a thought that hadn't occurred to them.

Gouldman confirmed the band's fascination with American culture and the sound of American phrases, and even admitted the band's preference for Schlitz over English beer. Unlike most English rockers of their age—they were all twenty-eight—who profess to have been inspired by 1950s rockers or bluesmen, they cited American records of the early sixties, particularly those of The Beach Boys, as prime influences. The band's current hit, "The Dean and I," was sparked by a love of Hollywood musicals.

Both Godley and Creme had been trained in graphic design, quite atypical for rock musicians. The band's visual sense was obvious on record. Kevin referenced cartoons as an influence for their songs, and Eric mentioned comic books.

Live, they were enjoyable, but not as dynamic as on record. As a hit singles act, their audience was rather young, and responded with enthusiastic shrieks. Blackfoot Sue, whose English hit from the previous summer, "Standing in the Road," was a favorite of mine, preceded them onstage. They played well, and a highlight was "1812," which made use of drum-like canon explosions. Teenybopper Ricky Wilde opened.

The next night I was invited to have dinner with a Jewish family in the north of London. A month earlier, a girl Mark had met in England was in Los Angeles with a girlfriend of hers and we took them out for an evening. I took a shine to the girlfriend and got her phone number in London. She was supposed to arrive that evening from the States, and I was looking forward to seeing her again, at dinner.

I was well appointed in my new white suit, but being unfamiliar with the area, arrived almost an hour late. They welcomed me, but the girl's flight had been delayed, and wouldn't arrive until much later that evening. My disappointment transitioned into extreme discomfort. I was flustered from my effort to get to the house. They served a Shabbat dinner, which including reading prayers in Hebrew, which I hadn't retained since my bar mitzvah. They were all reading aloud, and I could barely join in. In the course of the evening, they had me confused with somebody else. They were expecting the son of a rabbi. The meal was good, but it was an evening I could have done without. I left a note for the girl, but never heard from her.

The records I bought included the first albums by Love Affair and Los Bravos. I picked up a *Top of the Pops* album, mostly for its curiosity value. The producers of the series of albums recorded the hits of the day with studio musicians and singers trying to come as close as they could to sounding like the recent hit record. The budget price was an enticement. I bought Volume 31, which included covers of "You Are the Sunshine of My Life," "Walk On the Wild Side," and "Rubber Bullets." Like all the other albums in the series, it featured an attractive model on the cover.

Andrew Lauder gave me ex–Bonzo Dog Band member Neil Innes' *How Sweet to Be an Idiot*. From CBS Records I got two singles, both on the Epic label. Steve Ellis had been the lead singer of Love Affair, which had had a few hits in Britain in the sixties, but were unknown in America. I liked "El Doomo," from his new band Ellis. "Much Too Young" was a heavy pop record performed by Vulcan, a German band—or studio group—that tried to sound like Sweet. They succeeded, in a good way.

LONDON 1976

I HAD MET TODD Schneider when we both worked as sackers at Fedco, a discount department store, in the summer of 1969. We both loved rock music, and became fast friends. On the last day we worked together, when I changed my nametag to read "Pete Townshend," he was the only one who noticed.

Since I'd last visited London, I'd worked for two solid years at the Rhino store without a vacation break. As Todd had never been to London, I thought it would be fun for us to go together. I had enjoyed my two previous trips, but as music styles had changed, I had less desire to go on my own. I also thought I could do business for the store that I now managed.

I made a reservation at the Sandringham Hotel, solely because The Move booked rooms there when they came down from Birmingham. Even after The Move, in the early seventies, Roy Wood and Jeff Lynne stayed there.

We arrived on Wednesday, September 1, to find that England was in the midst of a drought. As it had been three years since I was last in London, my familiarity with the city had diminished. We took a train from Gatwick Airport, and then a taxi to the hotel, but the trip seemed much longer than I thought it would be. When the taxi driver left us at the hotel, it didn't appear familiar, nor did the woman who received us have our reservation. After a few minutes, she offered that there was another Sandringham hotel, not affiliated with hers, closer to the West End. That was the one we wanted.

In that part of northwest London, as we walked down the high street, we didn't see a taxi, so we schlepped our luggage down the steps into the Underground Station and onto a train. Being jetlagged, I was far from my sharpest, and angry that I had wasted money on an expensive taxi trip, and that the driver did not ask me which of the two hotels I wanted. I also felt I had let Todd down, as I was his guide to the city. Todd, as usual, was unruffled.

We checked in at the proper hotel, and they did have a room with a shower reserved for us. The lobby was more modest than I remembered. Our room was acceptable, but I thought a hit group of the stature of The Move would have lodged at a better place. Still, it was a step up from the fleabags in the Paddington area where I had boarded on my previous trip.

I made an effort to stay awake to try to adjust to the new time. Todd fell asleep, and later, when he awoke, thought he was dreaming because he heard me speaking with a French accent. Peter Noone was living with his French wife in the south of France. Thinking of flying over to visit, I'd called his house, and spoken with his mother-in-law, who didn't understand much English. I didn't speak French, but thought speaking English with a French accent might make me more understandable. She said that Peter and Mireille were in Paris, but she didn't know at which hotel.

That night we didn't want to stray too far from our own hotel, so we dined at the nearby McDonald's, which had opened in London less than two years ago. The experience of going to a McDonald's, seeing what menu items were different from those in the States, paying in English currency, and being asked for our order in English accents appealed to our jetlagged sensibilities. Afterward, we watched TV in the lounge. I'd heard good things about *Fawlty Towers*, which starred Monty Python's John Cleese, but it was never shown in the States. We found it hysterical.

The next day we were up and running. Jeff Gold, from the Rhino store, had set me up with Larry Debay, whose Bizarre Records was the primary distributor for the burgeoning punk scene. Larry, flaunting long ginger-hennaed hair and a dyed-green beard, greeted us in his Praed Street office in the Paddington area. He raved about the Ramones, the New York punk band that had toured England earlier that summer. Larry gave me their English pressing of "Blitzkrieg Bop," which came with a picture sleeve. Maybe because the cover of the album I produced of my band, Mogan David and his Winos, featured us all wearing leather jackets—just like Ramones—Larry ordered a box. I was there to deliver it, and pick up extra spending money for our visit.

I had an appointment to see Colin Walkdon, a buyer for the Virgin Records retail chain. I met him at Virgin's warehouse, and we rode in the van to S. P. & S. Distributors, which sold records that were deleted from their respective catalogues. I bought a couple of hundred records for the Rhino store. I loved getting English imports for a low price, but the shipping to the States was still expensive.

On his recommendation, Todd and I saw Chas and Dave that evening at the Bishop Bonner, a boxing-themed pub in the East End. Colin met us. I was familiar with Chas Hodges, as I had seen him play as a member of Heads, Hands and Feet. They displayed a fondness for pre-Beatles rock 'n' roll and music hall humor. Afterward, we went to a small fish 'n' chips shop. The fried food was handed to us in pages from a newspaper folded into a cone to absorb the grease. Colin encouraged me to try the jellied eel, which wasn't to my liking.

On Friday, September 3, we checked in at a few of the record companies to see what was happening. I always looked forward to visiting Andrew Lauder, the head of A&R for United Artists. While we were in his office, he introduced us to Jake Riviera (real name: Andrew Jakeman). Jake had been a manager of pub rock acts, and he and fellow manager Dave Robinson had recently started a new label,

Stiff Records. I loved the name and the sense of humor behind it. In record business parlance, "a stiff" was a record that failed to become a hit. I related to the name, knowing the difficulty an independent label has competing against the majors in trying to get a hit record—regardless of how good the music is.

Andrew Lauder played us their first single, by Nick Lowe, which had been released three weeks earlier. Lowe's band, Brinsley Schwarz, had broken up the previous year. Robinson had managed them, and Andrew had released their records on UA. I thought the two sides, "The Heart of the City" and "So It Goes," were terrific. I told Jake I wanted to buy a quantity to sell at the Rhino store.

The hottest new group in town was Eddie and the Hot Rods, who were at the vanguard of the developing punk rock scene. In the evening we saw them perform at the Marquee Club. The capacity was five hundred, but it seemed that there were twice as many fans, predominantly guys, squeezed in. The Hot Rods' engaging sound, with its fast, throbbing rhythms and choppy guitars, was similar to Dr. Feelgood's. (Guitarist Dave Higgs had roadied for the Feelgoods.) Barrie Masters, the band's capable, boyish, good-looking singer, led the band through a set of promising, teen-angst originals mixed with 1960s hits "The Kids Are Alright" (The Who), "Gloria" (Them), and "Wooly Bully" (Sam the Sham & The Pharaohs). We went backstage—a narrow room directly behind the stage—to say hello before the set. It looked like they were popping amyl nitrate. I guess that explained why they played so fast.

On Saturday, we went to the King's Road to see the latest in hip British fashion, which, unlike in my previous visits, was nowhere to be seen. The flashy velvet suits, the quintessence of male pop fashion, had given way to American styles. The popular movie *Bugsy Malone* had sparked a revival of American 1930s-cut gangster suits, double-breasted with wide lapels and pinstripes. Tweed and checkered patterns were also on view. There was a much higher percentage of jeans and leather worn than in the States, and even an occasional rocker walking down the street flaunting a long, felt-trimmed coat and ducktail haircut. Let It Rock, a clothing store I had visited before, was now named Sex and sold bondage gear in addition to leather jackets. In the window of one of the boutiques, we were amused to see a male mannequin that looked a lot like Fee Waybill, the singer of the Tubes.

Bugsy Malone was indeed the hot new movie. Produced in England, it was a Prohibition-themed musical, with kid actors assuming the adult parts. We enjoyed it, and thought Paul Williams' songs were wonderful. Todd was surprised that the tickets indicated specific seats to occupy, and that there was no open seating, as in the States. Stimulated by the kids shooting custard from sub-machine guns in the movie, Todd bought a cup of ice cream. He loved the taste and the smooth texture until he read the label and discovered that it contained lard.

I HAD MET JEFFREY Levinson through David Berson in Los Angeles. Levinson, originally from New York, made a living in England contracting musicians for recording sessions. He lived in the village of Jordans, a train ride north of London in Buckinghamshire. I looked upon the opportunity to get out of town and experience a night in the country, so I accepted his invitation to visit on Sunday.

It was a low-key visit. Not much was happening, and the village didn't have much charm. Not far from his house was an appealing little forest that seemed typical of England to me. Walking through it reminded me of the woodsy area The Rolling Stones were photographed in on their *High Tide and Green Grass* album. That night we drove to the neighborhood pub for dinner. Because of restrictions on water use, Jeff hadn't washed his car in a couple of months.

Back at the house, he played records. I was most taken with "Hi! It's Herbie Flowers," one of the most joyful records I'd ever heard. Flowers was an in-demand session musician, having most notably played bass on Lou Reed's "Walk On the Wild Side" and David Bowie's "Space Oddity." I liked the song so much that Jeff gave me the single.

Todd had a more rewarding Sunday. He saw Kursaal Flyers headline at the Roundhouse, but was also impressed by the support band, The Clash. He reported that they were like a "Cockney Ramones," true punks with good songs, but with one too many guitars causing them to sound cluttered. They had yet to record, but elicited an impressive response from the audience. Second-billed Crazy Cavan and his Rhythm Rockers were a 1950s revival band that channeled songs by Eddie Cochrane, Buddy Holly, and others from the era, and inspired their fans to dress as those stars had.

We visited Stiff Records in a storefront at 32 Alexander Street in Notting Hill. As we had issued a handful of singles at Rhino, I identified with and took interest in what Stiff was doing. Jake introduced us to his partner, Dave Robinson. We also met two friendly guys from Clover, a band from the San Francisco area that had relocated to London: Alex Call, the lead singer, and Huey Lewis, the harmonica player. While I talked to Jake and Dave, Alex expressed his frustration to Todd, of the difficulty he had in meeting reserved English girls. We heard the other Stiff releases, by Pink Fairies, Roogalator, and Sean Tyler. I wasn't impressed. I bought a box of twenty-five Nick Lowe singles, and three copies each of the others.

We were hipped to the Hard Rock Café, which we soon found served the best hamburgers in London. Unlike those offered by the Wimpy restaurant chain, these were thick, like those in the States. The cafe had a 1950s American rock 'n' roll theme as hits from the era—by Elvis, Jerry Lee Lewis, Buddy Holly, and others—played on the sound system. The inside had a rustic look, like somebody's garage. Concert posters, sports pennants, cigarette advertisements, and license plates were mounted on the dark brown walls. The waitresses dressed like carhops from American drive-in restaurants. We had to wait in line before a table opened up, but it was worth it. We went back a couple more times and observed that we could circumvent the line by either arriving well before the lunch crowd, or taking a seat at the counter.

We loved Tom Stoppard's new play, *Dirty Linen* and *New-Found-Land*, which we took in at the Arts Theatre, a small venue near Leicester Square. *Dirty Linen* was a pun-filled sexual farce involving Members of Parliament and predatory newspaper writers looking to boost their circulations. It bookended *New-Found-Land*, during which one Member of Parliament delivered an appreciation of America in a clever monologue as a means of justifying an American's application for British citizenship.

On Tuesday, we took the train to tour Windsor Castle. Queen Elizabeth II wasn't in residence when we were there, but we were impressed nonetheless. On another day we saw the Tower of London and the Crown Jewels, my favorite historical site in the country.

AC/DC, a new band from Australia, were on tour in England, with a number of dates scheduled for the Marquee. They were highly recommended, but when we arrived at the club, a posted sign indicated that they had cancelled, much to our disappointment. We couldn't return the next night because we were going to see The Count Bishops.

The next day we ate lunch at a mediocre Chinese restaurant, and then went shopping at the nearby Soho Open Air Market. We each bought leather jackets, which were considerably cheaper than those sold at Sex. From another vendor, I bought an embroidered, velvet Indian tunic. We ran into Huey Lewis, and showed him our purchases.

That evening we went to the Speakeasy and saw another band newly emerged from the pub scene, The Count Bishops. Their tightly arranged, hard rock sound was influenced by American blues rockers like Howlin' Wolf and Chuck Berry. They even took an American name, that of a New York street gang. Similar to Eddie and the Hot

Rods, they performed covers of sixties rock bands: Them's "Don't Start Cryin' Now" and The Yardbirds' "I'm Not Talkin.'" They were the first band signed to the local Chiswick label headed by Ted Carroll and Roger Armstrong of the Rock On record store in Camden Town.

We saw Stonehenge on Thursday. It wasn't easy to get to. We took a train from Waterloo Station to Salisbury, and then a twenty-five-minute bus ride to the formation. There weren't many people there, and we were able to walk among the large stones. When we learned that the arrangement was over four thousand years old, it was quite moving. We were appalled to see graffiti etched into the stones. On the way back, we stopped for a meal in Salisbury. Todd was baffled that they didn't have Salisbury steak on the menu.

That evening before going out, we watched *Top of the Pops* on TV. I was familiar with the show, but it was my first opportunity to see it. I would have enjoyed it more if the contemporary artists lip-synching their records had been more to my liking.

I was looking forward to seeing Kursaal Flyers, who were playing in the grubby, smoked-filled basement at the Hope and Anchor pub in Islington. Where most clubs located the stage at the long end of a room, here the audience was squeezed into an elongated, shallow area in front of the stage. The Kursaals were a pub band that incorporated humor into their melodic repertoire. I was disappointed that the band delivered a set of largely country and western material rather than the clever rock songs more familiar to their fans.

London's West End theatre had premiered a number of rock-themed musicals, such as *The Rocky Horror Show* and *John, Paul, George, Ringo...and Bert*. We took in this year's entry, *Leave Him to Heaven* at the New London Theatre, which was little more than a spirited, Sha Na Na–like review of fifties/early-sixties hits. The leading actor, Brian Protheroe, sang well, as did the other soloists. Although lacking in substance, it was still enjoyable, especially the two Shangri-Las–like, tough-girls-in-leather numbers, and Stan Freeberg's "The

Old Payola Roll Blues" performed by a pimply rock star in a squeaky voice singing about high school.

On Saturday we went to Camden Town. We didn't spend much time at Rock On. They sold mostly collectors' records, and they were expensive. Much more rewarding was Compendium Books, on Camden High Street, near Camden Lock on the Regent's Canal. Although the store had a plethora of political books and small press publications—mostly leftist—I was more impressed by the mind-blowing selection of music books. I bought two volumes of Charlie Gillette's *Rock File,* David Dalton's *The Rolling Stones,* and ZigZag magazine's *The Road to Rock.*

With nothing else better to do, and with no other enticing theatrical productions, we went to St. Martin's Theatre to see what *The Mousetrap* was all about. An Agatha Christie murder mystery, it was London's longest running play, with continuous performances going back to 1952. With that longevity, how could it not be good? It wasn't. We both thought it was mediocre.

On Sunday the twelfth, our last full day in town, we went to the Petticoat Lane Market in the East End. Not intended for tourists, it catered to locals who could better understand the colorful characters hawking merchandise in Cockney accents. There were a large number of poor American knockoffs, like football jerseys with inappropriate team names on them, such as the "76ers," which is a basketball team. We saw a "Los Angeles Dodgers" basketball shirt—the Dodgers are a baseball team—various uses of the "Los Angeles Police Department" on shirt backs or pockets, and university sweatshirts with wrong colors and insignias. By far the most in-vogue were Boy Scout- and Girl Scout–styled shirts with random phrases on the pockets, and meaningless numbers on the sleeves.

That evening we saw Ted Nugent fronting his band in concert at the Hammersmith Odeon. The set was almost the same as the one we had seen that April at the Santa Monica Civic Auditorium.

Ted's heavy metal was appealingly over-the-top, intense, but prone to excess. Some guitar players stood in one place, their face grimacing in emotional pain. With an excess of energy, Ted ran all over the stage and even climbed atop his amplifiers. We went to the after-show party at the Speakeasy. Ted drank what appeared to be ale directly out of a punch bowl. When we exited, it was late, and we couldn't find an available cab so we made the long walk back to our hotel.

Unlike the exciting music I heard on my previous trips, the Top 20 was composed of the same hits by major artists popular in the States: Rod Stewart, Wings, and ABBA, and disco artists The Stylistics and The Ritchie Family. Still, I was able to come home with a number of records: Eddie and the Hot Rods' *Live at the Marquee* EP, the Count Bishop's "Train Train," and Flamin' Groovies' "Don't Lie to Me." I found a used copy of Herbie Flowers' *Plant Life* album. Andrew Lauder gave me a copy of *Mersey Beat '62 / '64*, a double album he'd compiled of the earliest beat groups, *Captain Lockheed and the Starfighters*, and Dr. Feelgood's first two LPs, *Down By the Jetty* and *Malpractice*. I couldn't have imagined a better trip.

MIKE CHAPMAN

*C*LANG! *CLANG! CLANG!* MIKE Chapman banged the ceramic ashtray with his cigarette holder. The keys from his leased Mercedes-Benz jumped on the console. "Chris, step back a cunt hair," he commanded into the control room's microphone, getting the attention of the singers through the large glass window.

The singers grouped around the microphone in the adjacent studio were members of an English band named Smokie—originally Smokey, until Smokey Robinson, the lead singer of the Motown vocal group The Miracles, threatened to sue. Chapman and his partner Nicky Chinn had signed the band to their production company. Chapman produced them in the studio, and the pair had written two Top 10 hits for the group in England. In this summer of 1975, the band was recording their third album at Whitney Studios in Glendale, California.

The first I heard of Mike Chapman was in the summer of 1973, when Sweet's eponymous debut LP was released in America. Nicky Chinn and Mike Chapman were credited with writing the group's "Little Willie" hit as well as the album's four best songs. Chinn and Chapman (who were often referred to as Chinnichap, the name of their company) were an extremely successful songwriting team during England's glitter rock trend in the 1970s.

Glitter rock, also referred to as glam rock, was a return to the simple, melodic elements in a rock 'n' roll arrangement. The trend was a reaction to a period during which rock had developed pretensions to "heaviness," had demanded to be perceived as serious art and had overindulged in psychedelic, heavy metal, and progressive (jazz and classical) influences. Glitter contained catchy riffs, 1950s rock 'n' roll influences, and a fun spirit.

The term was initiated in 1971 after T. Rex's Marc Bolan had silver glitter dabbed under his eyes to match his satin jacket for a performance on *Top of the Pops*. Singer Paul Gadd adopted the name Gary Glitter, had hits, and further popularized the trend. The glam description was short for the glamour in dress, as worn by female Hollywood stars from decades past. The look included satin jackets, feather boas, and women's clothes purchased at thrift stores—all worn by cross-dressing men, who were the hit artists of the period. Campy behavior and a suggestion of androgyny—most effectively carried off by David Bowie—were par for the course. Platform shoes that came in vogue for women in the 1930s manifested themselves in exaggerated platform boots worn by members of Slade, David Bowie's band, and others.

Even artists whose music had nothing to do with glitter appropriated the fashion. When The Rolling Stones toured to promote their *Exile On Main Street* album in 1972, Mick Jagger and Mick Taylor sported facial glitter and eye shadow as well as satin jackets. Suzi Quatro, the biggest female star, despite her feminine good looks, felt more comfortable dressing like a guy, in jeans and leather jacket.

Glitter was big in England and throughout much of Europe. I wanted to write an overview for *Rolling Stone*, but because the style was slow to catch on in America, my request was turned down. I felt that the magazine should be in the vanguard covering music trends, but that component was diminished as the publisher redirected the magazine to appeal to supermarket shoppers.

Ultimately, the style's impact in the US was slight. The biggest artist, T. Rex, had ten Top 10 hits in the UK, but only one in the US. Gary Glitter had eleven in the UK, but only one, "Rock 'n' Roll, Part II," in the US. Everyone who attends stateside-sporting events recognizes the song, but few know the title or the artist. It's the instrumental that contains a chorus of "hey!" that's been played for decades. Mud, Showaddywaddy, Cockney Rebel, Slade, and Wizzard combined for forty-three Top 10 hits in England, but had none in America.

David Bowie was the one star to have emerged from this scene who became big in America, but during this period none of his seven glitter-era Top 10s hit in the US. Sweet had the best ratio of three US Top 10s to nine in Britain.

I first met Nicky Chinn in the summer of 1974. As Nicky was associated with London's trendy rock scene, I was surprised to meet a rich kid staying in a rich man's hotel. He was tanned, had permed hair, and spoke in a cultured clip. He was sporting tennis whites and had a gold medallion around his neck. There was nothing about him that was rock 'n' roll as he swirled an early afternoon scotch and Coke in his room at the Beverly Hills Hotel. Even though he was only twenty-nine, he reminded me more of a veteran movie actor, like David Niven. In the previous three years, Chinn and Chapman had seventeen Top 10 hits in England as songwriters, but only one, "Little Willy" by Sweet, in America.

Chinn's family was affluent, Jewish, and owned a number of service stations and car dealerships in England, in one of which Nicky had been employed. As a rich kid, he frequented the members-only, posh nightclub Tramp, where he became friendly with one of the few waiters who wasn't Italian, Australian Mike Chapman.

Chapman had aspirations of being an actor, and had exercised his vocal chops at an early age. In 1969, he joined London band Tangerine Peel, which recorded for RCA. During one performance, when Mike was groveling on his back as he sang, he was set upon by growling skinheads. As a result, in 1970 he retired his rock 'n' roll microphone and leopard skin pants in favor of the more sedate (and safe) world behind the scene. Mike and Nicky discovered a mutual interest in songwriting, and started writing on a daily basis.

They had a hit with only the fourth song they had written. Sweet's "Funny Funny" entered the charts in March 1971, nine months after they started writing together. "I knew Sweet would be stars," Nicky said. "They were performing a directionless set of The Who and Tamla-Motown covers, and a lot of Deep Purple. We took them into the studio to record 'Funny Funny' [produced by Phil Wainman], and made a deal with RCA."

Mickie Most, the successful English producer, nurtured the duo, recorded their songs with acts on his own RAK Records, and gave Mike opportunities in the studio producing Suzi Quatro and Mud.

Rather than being repelled by Chinn's rich kid, non-rock-n-roll manner, I was drawn to his warmth and engaging demeanor. He gave me copies of their recent hits in England, two singles by Mud and one by Suzi Quatro. On that summer day, although exuding the confidence that only a string of hits can provide, Nicky was flummoxed as to why British rock wasn't popular in America, too.

Most people who listened to radio stations that played contemporary hits thought that a record became a hit because fans bought the record, or requested it on the station's phone line. Payola was rampant in the seventies and eighties. It was a practice that started in the 1950s, whereby radio programmers and DJs were illegally paid to play records on their stations. In many cases a program director kept a good record off the playlist if the money, or other favors, was not forthcoming from the label or its designated independent promotion man. Most of Chinnichap's records that were proven hits in England, Germany, and other countries were neglected by radio in the States.

Toby Mamis called me and told me that Mike Chapman had moved to town, and was recording a new group, Smokie, that he thought I would like. He invited me to the studio to meet Mike and the group.

Similar to Sweet and Mud, Smokie—then called Kindness—were playing a lot of Top 40, "Bee Gees and Leo Sayer covers" as Nicky recalled. So Chinn and Chapman felt they had a blank canvas to work with. Chapman was all too aware of how popular the soft-rock style was in the States, and fashioned them in the mode of The Eagles and Crosby, Stills & Nash. To complement this country direction, Chinn had them photographed in front of a barn. Chris Norman was an excellent lead singer, the group's harmonies were tight, and the ensemble playing was solid. I liked the group, and I liked Mike. He invited me to subsequent sessions with them, as well as other acts he was producing.

Whitney Studios was an odd place for Mike to use as a base. Located on Glenoaks Boulevard in Glendale, it was not convenient to his Beverly Hills home. With a large pipe organ in a studio that could accommodate a sizeable choir, it was used primarily for religious recording. It was also the preferred studio for Barry White and his Love Unlimited Orchestra. Mike worked mostly in the smaller Studio B. I often closed the Rhino store around 6:30 p.m., grabbed a sandwich at Olympus Burger, and then drove the twenty-three miles to the studio.

With a cigarette holder cocked at the side of his mouth, wearing tinted glasses, Mike Chapman looked like the commander on the bridge of a ship as he sat behind the expansive control room console. He guided the members of Smokie through multi-tracking their vocal harmonies (thickening the sound as they sang along with their previously recorded take). Mike was exacting. Even when the group was recording an instrumental backing for a song, he made sure that the performance was tight, or it was recorded again. Some producers and artists look for a musical feel or groove, and are more tolerant of the occasional mistake. Mike strived for perfection.

Mike was focused, worked well with the musicians, and progressed in a timely manner. But he also saw the value of having fun. He could drop his nice-guy facade for the cloak of super-ham: clutching his heart, waving his arms, and dropping to his knees during final playbacks.

On more than one Smokie session I attended, after the vocal harmonies were finished, he encouraged the group to release the tension by getting silly, announcing it was time for the members to do "the Bill Hurley." As the music played, they exaggerated their manager's dancing technique by flopping around as though on quaaludes. To celebrate a well-executed recording, he encouraged the artist to redo the lead vocals, substituting lewd lyrics. The tapes to such an example as Sweet's "Dirty Big Tits" (from "Ballroom Blitz") are in Mike's tape vault.

Mike had been a big fan of The Easybeats, who were thought of as Australia's Beatles. The ex-lead singer, Stevie Wright, had released a solo album produced by his former bandmates, Harry Vanda and George Young—who also produced AC/DC. Even though *Hard Road* had been out a few years, Mike wasn't familiar with it, so I grabbed a copy from the store's bargain bin and headed over to his house. Rod Stewart had recorded the title track on his *Smiler* album, but I wanted to turn Mike onto "Evie."

During our discussion Mike revealed that the guitar intro to Sweet's "Hellraiser" was appropriated from The Easybeats' "She's So Fine." Mike couldn't play me the example because he didn't have a copy of "Hellraiser." Mike made good records. I was surprised he didn't have copies of all of them. I then realized how much he was focused on his current projects.

The artistic philosophy was strong on immediate, dispensable hits; danceable records with teen lyrics that satisfied only until the artist's next hit arrived. "I need to keep a finger in the pop pie." Mike explained at the time. "Teenagers matter to us all, and in a sense, I feel like I'm eighteen all over again. I've got to keep a pulse there because it's so volatile."

In writing together, Mike and Nicky started with a title, like "Hellraiser," "Daytona Demon," or "Teenage Rampage." The melody came next, and then the words. The song was a mere frame for a production that added musical hooks, sound effects, and enthusiastic vocals more suitable to a theatrical play. They admitted that Sweet's "Blockbuster" was copped from The Yardbirds' "I'm a Man," that "Funny Funny" was inspired by "Sugar Sugar" (one of Mike's favorite songs), and "Wig Wam Bam" a copy of their own "Little Willy."

Mike and Nicky's first big US hit, "Little Willie" by Sweet, was written around the seven-note musical riff commonly referred to as Shave and a Haircut—Two Bits. "I just thought of it while walking down the street," Mike said. "It's a riff everyone knows so they won't forget it: 'Little Willie Willy won't, go home.' It was funny, slightly suggestive and sold three million worldwide." In Britain "willie" is slang for penis.

Often the initial idea came from another song before the composition evolved its own identity. The guitar pattern in "Little Willie" was similar to what Pete Townshend played on The Who's "I Can't Explain." For Exile's "Kiss You All Over," Mike recreated the feel and atmosphere of Barry White's "Ecstasy." Smokie's "Living Next Door to Alice" clambered to number twenty-five in the US in 1977 and sold four hundred thousand copies, according to Mike. The song's models were, more obviously, Dr. Hook's "Sylvia's Mother" and Billy Joe Royal's "Down in the Boondocks."

Many of the song titles have an instantly recognizable dramatic feel, conjuring recollections of intense Marlon Brando or James Dean movies. Some titles are the same as classic films: "The Wild One," "In the Heat of the Night," "For a Few Dollars More," "Wild Wild Angels." Much of the imagery is complementary: nights perforated by howling winds and tormenting rains with strangers lurking in the shadows; midnight rendezvous, the man with eyes as red as the sun;

and mysterious settings like Devil Gate Drive. In 1987 Dolly Parton recorded Mike's "Red Hot Screaming Love."

It's important to note that many recordings in the early days of rock 'n' roll embraced a considerable amount of fun. The personalities of many of the original rock 'n' rollers made them seem more like cartoon characters than professional musicians. Think of the outrageousness of Little Richard and Jerry Lee Lewis, or the duck walk of Chuck Berry. Mike Chapman, through his records with Sweet, Mud, and Suzi Quatro, championed this fun spirit. It largely dissipated from Mike's stateside productions as he focused on competing with serious records in the soft rock and disco genres.

As Richard Foos and I were partners in our new Rhino Records label, I was curious how other partners worked together. Mike was the real creative talent, but he couldn't do it on his own. He needed a collaborator. Nicky's role was a lesser, but still necessary one. Mike called him "the carpenter" because he helped shape the songs. Nicky came up with ideas and suggestions, but mostly he was a sounding board for Mike. As Mike could often be opinionated and tactless, the arrangement worked best with him sequestered in the studio. Nicky interacted with the record companies, negotiated the deals and made sure the records were promoted. He acquired an interest in business from discussions around the family dinner table.

Mike's first two years in the US had been a tough slog. His English hits had afforded him the luxury of living in Beverly Hills, in a Paul Williams-designed estate on 1.3 acres. But he still felt "like a nobody." Mike thought the key to making it in America was to amp up his workload. In the first six months of 1978, he had finished albums with Rick Derringer, Smokie, Suzi Quatro, Exile, and Blondie, and produced three songs for Nick Gilder. He was in town only two weeks. I felt sorry for his wife, who surely was neglected. In social settings at their house, she was always nice to me. There was an additional connection: her parents had rented the space next to the Rhino store in Claremont to sell antiques.

In July Mike called and invited me to the studio. He had just returned from New York, where he was producing Blondie's third LP. Toby Mamis was Blondie's publicist, and he brought Mike to see them perform at the Whisky in February 1977. He loved them, and wrote on the club's napkin "I must produce this band." Chrysalis Records' cofounder Terry Ellis, with whom Mike had a good relationship, bought the group out of their contract with Private Stock Records for $500,000. It was a hefty sum considering neither of their first two albums sold as many as fifty thousand copies.

In Whitney's mastering studio, Mike played me an acetate (test record) of "Heart of Glass." He enthused that it sounded like a number one hit. I could tell it was Deborah Harry singing, but it didn't sound like Blondie to me. It was disco. I had him play it for me a second time. It was a new style for Blondie, one I wasn't expecting. The group's original sound was fun, energetic, rough. This was polished and sonically superior.

I heard more songs as they were mixed, and thought Mike had done a wonderful job on the whole album. The group retained its frantic energy, but Chapman improved their sound. The band's playing was tight and Deborah sang well. Chapman's help with the arrangements, the placement of the instruments, and the overall dynamic sound was superb. It was quite an achievement, and began a fruitful relationship for both Mike and the band, but it almost didn't happen. During his initial meeting with Deborah and Chris Stein, the band's guitarist and her songwriting collaborator, Mike was unnerved by Deborah's intimidating stare. "She didn't say a word," he said. "She was the most frightening person I'd ever met."

"Once I Had a Love" was a song Stein and Harry wrote that Mike thought had promise, but he didn't like the title or the reggae arrangement. He asked Deborah what artists she liked, and when she responded with Donna Summer, Mike cast the song, retitled "Heart of Glass," in a disco arrangement. He felt secure in this new direction for the band knowing The Rolling Stones had scored a number one with their disco arrangement of "Miss You."

One of the reasons I spent time with Mike in the studio was to pick up ideas I might use when I produced. During the mix for "Living in the Real World" for Blondie's 1979 album *Eat to the Beat*, Mike dropped a reverb (echo) unit at 1:47 into the song to create a small explosion that propelled the arrangement. I would have liked to have attended a Blondie session, but those first two albums with Mike were recorded in New York and my budget didn't permit an excursion.

Mike finally exploded in the US with a remarkable twelve-month run, starting with Exile's "Kiss You All Over," written by Mike and Nicky, which topped the charts at the end of September for a four-week run. During this period, he also produced number ones with Nick Gilder's "Hot Child In the City," Blondie's "Heart of Glass," and The Knack's "My Sharona." He even managed to get a US hit for Suzi Quatro, whose popularity was bolstered by her recurring role as Leather Tuscadero on *Happy Days*. He had Suzi duet with Smokie's Chris Norman on "Stumblin' In," a song he had written with Nicky, resulting in a number four hit. (Smokie became so successful in Europe, they outsold ABBA in their native Scandinavia.) He also scored two number one albums, with Blondie and The Knack. A few months later, Pat Benatar's debut album climbed to twelve.

Lou Naktin and I met the stunning Benatar during the recording at Whitney. Terry Ellis had signed her to Chrysalis Records. The band was working on a John Cougar Mellencamp song, "I Need a Lover." Mike and rhythm guitarist Scott St. Clair Sheets were in a heated exchange because Sheets wanted to leave in a guitar phrase at the beginning of the song that Mike thought was extraneous. Mike's authoritarian tone came out: "I didn't sell tens of millions of records by arguing with a guitar player!"

Sitting in Studio A's control room, our senses were assaulted. The air conditioning was cranked up high, and the playback speakers were set to ear-splitting levels. We were like the guy in the Maxell tape ad whose hair was blown back by the volume. Mike had a reputation for blowing out speakers. His ace engineer, Peter Coleman—who produced most of Benatar's *In the Heat of the Night* album—wore a pair of unplugged headphones to protect his ears.

Mike preferred that I visit him when he was working on a potential single or prominent track, usually when background vocals were recorded or during the mixdown, so I could hear a close-to-complete version of the song. Hearing these wonderful songs many times made it easy for me to like them. These Chapman productions may not have hit the Top 10, but they're on my playlist: Exile's "Try It On," Smokie's "Wild Wild Angels" and "I'll Meet You at Midnight," Suzi Quatro's "She's In Love With You" and "Lipstick" (in which Mike had Suzi sing a vocal phrase I suggested), Thieves' "400 Dragons," and Bow Wow Wow's "Aphrodisiac."

With Mike's success as a producer, and Mike and Nicky as songwriters, Al Coury, the head of RSO Records, gave them their own label deal. RSO—the initials stood for the Robert Stigwood Organization—was the most successful record company in the world. In 1977 and 1978, with the soundtracks for *Saturday Night Fever* and *Grease*, and The Bee Gees' *Spirits Having Flown*, RSO had sold tens of millions of albums and was overflowing with cash. It made sense for Coury to invest in the industry's top creative team.

Well into 1979, I was not sure that our fledging Rhino label would be able to survive. I asked Mike and Nicky, separately, for a job as their A&R person. It wasn't as if Mike didn't take note of my recommendations. He first heard about The Knack from me, but didn't approach them about producing until they were signed to Capitol Records months later. I also recommended that he sign The Heaters and The Rubinoos. He didn't sign either, but with Suzi he recorded

The Heaters' "Never Been In Love," as well as Stevie Wright's "Evie." I made these suggestions out of friendship, not because I expected to get anything out of it.

I got $500 from United Artists Records to record demos of two songs, which turned out really well, but not to the extent that UA offered me a contract. Mike liked one of the songs Mark Leviton and I had written, "1977 Sunset Strip," and played it for amused visitors to the studio. I was pleased that he liked the song, but noted that he wasn't more encouraging. In response to my query, Mike and Nicky told me that they would be jointly handling the A&R function at their new Dreamland Records label.

When I went to London in the fall of 1979, Mike offered the use of a spare office at Chinnichap. I took lunch breaks at the Hard Rock Café, a third-of-a-mile away. I called Terry Uttley, the bass player in Smokie, with the intention of visiting him. I didn't know that Bradford, Yorkshire, was 175 miles to the north, but he was busy anyway. One afternoon I went to RAK and visited with David Most, Mickie Most's ace promotion man brother. Suzi Quatro was there and I chatted with her. David gave me a RAK single from the previous year, "While I'm Still Young" by Autographs. It didn't make the charts, but I loved the record. Later that day, flipping through the used record bins at a record store, I bought the Tangerine Peel album for four pounds. It wasn't good. When I next saw Mike, as a joke, I had him autograph it. He wrote, "Don't ever play this record for anybody!!! Please, Harold!!!"

By 1980, Mike had run out of gas. When he arrived in LA, he was anti-drug. Bernie Taupin, Elton John's long-time lyricist, introduced him to cocaine and Mike acquired a drug habit and a bloated ego, evidenced by his photo on the cover of *BAM* magazine outfitted like General George Patton, referring to himself as Commander Chapman. His momentum carried him through 1980 with a number one album and single with Blondie and a number fifteen LP with The

Knack, and in 1981 with a number one album with Blondie. But by then his life had cratered. Dreamland, hitless in a little more than a year of releases, had failed. His obsessive workload resulted in his wife divorcing him for neglect. And his partnership with Nicky Chinn was over.

His last number one was a fluke, a 1970s castoff he wrote with Nicky that languished until Mickie Most recorded it for an album he produced with English band Racey. Choreographer Toni Basil changed the title from "Kitty" to "Mickey," added a football cheer to the intro, and produced a video that was a mainstay of MTV in its early years. "Heart and Soul," an unsuccessful Chinn-Chapman song when first recorded by Exile, became a Top 10 hit for Huey Lewis and the News in 1983.

Mike still produced good records, but none were a hit in America. He forged a successful songwriting collaboration with Holly Knight, the keyboardist from Dreamland signing Spider, which resulted in three Top 10 hits in the eighties: Tina Turner's "Better Be Good to Me," Pat Benatar's "Love Is a Battlefield," and Rod Stewart's "Love Touch." Nicky fared less well. Kim Wilde's "Dancing in the Dark," written with Paul Gurvitz (of Baker Gurvitz Army) became a modest European hit in 1983.

Mike's goal was to make hits. It didn't seem to occur to him that a record could be of value decades later. The albums Mike produced weren't well reviewed, and only Blondie's *Parallel Lines* made it into *Rolling Stone*'s "500 Greatest Albums of All Time." But I loved his records. On my playlist I have over fifty songs that he wrote or produced. There are no songs by Tangerine Peel.

ROTTEN

HINO FILMS WAS IN post-production on our first three features when I got a call from Eric Gardner, an artist's manager who represented Todd Rundgren. I had made a deal for Rhino to license the Bearsville Records masters, which included Rundgren's catalogue, and I had developed a good relationship with Eric the past ten years.

Now he was representing John Lydon, better known as Johnny Rotten, the lead singer of the 1970s band the Sex Pistols. He'd called to inquire if Rhino Films would be interested in making a movie from Lydon's 1994 autobiography *Rotten: No Irish, No Blacks, No Dogs.* I was surprised when he told me that no one had previously optioned the property.

"Punk rock" was coined in the early 1970s to refer to American rock bands of the 1960s that sounded like they got started practicing in their garages. More specifically, it meant edgy bands with attitude that derived their sound from The Rolling Stones, bands like The Standells, The Seeds, The Shadows of Knight, and ? and the Mysterians. In 1976 the Sex Pistols emerged, spearheading a movement in Britain composed of angry, ragged musicians and singers who railed against the class system, the bleak economy, and the unresponsive government. The press called the music "punk rock." The better known performers included The Clash, The Jam, The Damned, and Siouxsie and the Banshees.

I loved the Sex Pistols' debut single "Anarchy in the UK" as soon as I heard it. I was curious to know more about the group, and Robert

Hilburn, the pop music editor of the *Los Angeles Times*, assigned me to interview their manager, Malcolm McLaren, by phone. This may have been the first interview article to be published in the US, and ran many months prior to *Rolling Stone* covering the group. At this point it might be apt for an overview of the band, and my March 1977 *Los Angeles Times* piece is a good place to start.

England's Sex Pistols are already being called The Rolling Stones of the seventies. But The Stones' legendary outrageousness pales in comparison to the Pistols' antics, which have caused them to be banned from English radio and TV. Municipal governments have banded together, forbidding them from performing anywhere in the UK. It seems as if America is the only market open to them. "Right now we're making arrangements to come to the States," manager Malcolm McLaren said by phone from London. "But instead of just tour there, we may move there completely."

McLaren is part-owner/designer of London's SEX shop (now called Seditionaries), which deals in avant-garde clothes, often with a bondage motif. Johnny Rotten, 21-year-old lead vocalist of the Pistols, used to come into the store and steal items. McLaren decided to get back some of the lost money by managing the band.

The Pistols' music is loud and aggressive. On stage Rotten flaunts a ripped wardrobe barely held together by safety pins, which also pierce his ear lobes, inspiring a whole new fashion in Britain. With a ghostly pallor, he looks as if he'll keel over any moment, which contrasts sharply with his shockingly dyed-orange hair. After he's through smoking cigarettes, he puts them out on his arms. He's got the marks and a stay in the hospital fighting the incurred infection to show for it. When the Pistols find themselves in an extremely good mood, it's not uncommon for them to abandon their instruments on stage and join their audience in brawls.

Soon after their first release, "Anarchy in the UK" (on the EMI label), late last year, the Pistols made a much-publicized appearance on a British TV show. The group's use of obscenities led to headlines in all five national papers, lots of indignant letter writing, and organized protests. One irate viewer kicked in his picture tube.

A week later the band was waiting in a smoky airport departure lounge for a flight to Amsterdam. Guitarist Steve Jones, reportedly nauseated from a night of heavy drinking, threw up, unable to make it to the toilet. Photographers swarmed on the scene, and it was blown out of proportion.

Amid mounting protests, EMI cancelled the band's contract. Groups of mothers planted themselves outside the home of the general manager of EMI with petitions and banners that read: "Pop Profiteers Stop Ruining Our Kids Ears!" Others as well, including McLaren, were confronted with complaints and hecklers. In England the record went from 46 to 32 on the charts before it was withdrawn.

"The Sex Pistols are totally committed, and honestly don't care," said Rory Johnston, their representative in the United States. "They're real anarchists, they're not paper-outrageous like The

Damned or the other punk groups around. Now that they're successful, they're still out there on the street. Johnny Rotten, for instance, doesn't ride around in a car now that he's made money. He still takes the buses and subways. People know who he is and he gets abused. The Sex Pistols are a national institution; they're the most talked-about group since The Rolling Stones."

With all of this interest, England A&M's Derek Green convinced Jerry Moss (the M of A&M) to sign the group. Contracts were inked March 10 outside Buckingham Palace, and a new single, "God Save the Queen," was announced. The record was never issued and they were off the label in six days. No explanation was given publicly, and local A&M spokespeople were tight-lipped, leaking only a "no comment."

McLaren is just as puzzled. "A&M is a good company. They wanted us, and looked to us to open up the label to a wider spectrum of music that they were not usually associated with. Immediately there was dissent from other artists on the label. Lots of people at the BBC, as well as people in publishing and promotion at A&M, expressed their negativeness toward A&M signing the Sex Pistols. Initially A&M thought they could handle things but they quite clearly bit off more than they could chew. There's a whole degree of mystery surrounding their actions; it's kind of an industrial blacklist. The reason, if you want to call it that, we were given was that the Sex Pistols would tarnish the kind of quality MOR label image A&M has."

With a studio already booked, the Pistols proceeded to record an album with producer Chris Thomas (whose credits include Procol Harum, Roxy Music and the Climax Blues Band). The titles confirm the whole negative image: "No Feelings," "No Love," "There Is No Future," "Problems," "Liar," and "Pretty Vacant."

Mulling over how to expose his group under the enforced restrictions, a light bulb over Malcolm's head flashed "a film." "It will be a way for people to see the group and hear their music, without the theater owners risking an unpredictable live show." Written by English comedian Peter Cook, in some ways it will be a fantasy/factual melding à la *A Hard Day's Night*. Malcolm also feels the film will aid the group in attracting record companies.

Understandably shaken, McLaren is negotiating with other labels, but even with a sizeable cash settlement he's feeling the effects of the turmoil. "The image I've got now is almost like a contagious disease. When I walk into record company offices people really scatter and lose themselves very fast."

I think it's interesting that McLaren had contacted Peter Cook about writing the Sex Pistols' movie. Sexploitation director Russ Meyer was hired to direct a script written by American film critic Roger Ebert. Meyer lasted only four days before he abandoned the film. An ex-military man who normally ran a tight ship, he couldn't deal with the Pistols' lack of discipline and commitment. A documentary of sorts was admirably cobbled together by director Julien Temple and released in 1980. John Lydon did not participate in the newly filmed segments.

I was a fan of the group's music, initially from the UK singles, which we sold in the Rhino store. I loved *Never Mind the Bollocks, Here's the Sex Pistols* when the album was released in October 1977. I thought it was an exceptional album, now as well as then. It's remarkable how a group of street urchins could deliver such a confident collection of performances. The music was simple, but powerful—Steve Jones' grinding guitar, Glen Matlock's throbbing bass, and Paul Cook's solid drumming—providing the perfect pocket for Lydon's raging vocals. (Jones also played bass on a number of tracks.) One has to give a lot of credit for the result to producer Chris Thomas. He created the band's dynamic sound by having Jones quadruple his rhythm guitar while ensuring that Lydon's vocals could be heard, and provided subtleties like ghostly background vocals on "Bodies." The album did not sell well in the United States. It got only to 106 on *Billboard*'s LP chart, dropping off after twelve weeks. But it sold steadily though the years, and by the late-eighties had totaled over a million.

In the early days of Rhino, to enhance the appeal of one of our new bands compilations—1978's *Saturday Night Pogo*—I produced a cover of the Sex Pistols' "Belsen Was a Gas." The group hadn't released their version. I learned the song from a tape a friend had of the group's Winterland concert from earlier in the year. I think on the strength of my approximating Lydon's scabrous vocals, months following the death of Sid Vicious, Rory Johnston asked me if I would audition to be the group's new bass player. I didn't play bass, but neither had Sid. I thought about it only for a few seconds, and declined. The music was too angry, the scene too negative, and I couldn't relate to the fashion.

I loved Lydon's book, though. His memory was intact and he had a cynical sense of humor and an entertaining way of telling his story. Lydon's cowriters complemented his reminiscences with those of others on the scene, including his ex-bandmates.

JOHN WAS BORN INTO an Irish family and survived a tough childhood. His family had an odd bathing regimen: "I used to get scrubbed with Dettol, a toilet cleaner solvent we also used for the sinks to kill off the bugs." When he was seven, he spent a year in the hospital battling spinal meningitis, frequently in a comatose state. When cured, he couldn't recognize his parents when they came to take him home. He attended an Irish Catholic school "with wicked and violent nuns." He described himself as a "shy, nervous kid."

His mother was often sick and he was responsible for getting his brothers dressed for school. This later led him to feel comfortable working with troubled kids. He described his mother as "a thinker," and he was, too. He loved reading and treasured Shakespeare's *Macbeth* and the writings of Oscar Wilde. His favorite musical acts were Alice Cooper, Hawkwind, and T. Rex. Seeing the gangster Kray Brothers on TV also made an impression: "They looked so viciously sharp, the world's best dressers... That's how I like my suits to be worn—with a sense of vicious purpose."

John was a denizen of the King's Road. He was known as the kid with dyed-green hair who wore a homemade "I Hate Pink Floyd" T-shirt and second-hand clothes bound with safety pins to keep them from disintegrating. He liked chaos. There was also a sensitive side to him.

Malcolm McLaren was looking for something different to invigorate the rock band he managed. John hadn't sung in a group before, hadn't seriously thought about it, but he did make up lyrics, "ludicrous songs about people killing each other with broken light bulbs." And John had ambition: "I always wanted to be brilliant, excellent, loved and adored right from the start." He flailed about during his audition, which consisted of singing along to Alice Cooper's "I'm Eighteen" as it blasted from the jukebox in McLaren's shop.

In August 1975 when John auditioned, Britain's unemployment was the highest it had been in thirty years. John found London a depressing place, "completely run-down, with trash on the streets." He was angry at Britain's still-influential class system, which denied opportunities in education and employment to members of the working class. He also saw himself as "a person who respected the right of others, and always stood up for the disenfranchised."

Steve Jones renamed Lydon "Johnny Rotten" because of his poor dental hygiene. His teeth were green. Lydon loved Laurence Olivier's portrayal of Richard III—"so utterly vile, it was great"–and revealed that he based his Johnny Rotten character on Olivier's mannerisms in the 1955 film: "nasty, evil, conniving, selfish." With the Sex Pistols' aggressive music, their ripped-up clothes, overall surly manner, and Lydon singing that he's the "Antichrist" in "Anarchy in the UK," one would have expected the group to be violent thugs. But that wasn't the case. As Lydon said in *Rotten*, "The only violence about the Sex Pistols was the anger. We were not violent people."

Although Glen Matlock was a good bass player and songwriter— he's credited with coming up with the music for "Anarchy in the UK" and "Pretty Vacant"—his personality and fondness for The Beatles infuriated Lydon, so as of February 1977, he was out. As the newcomer, John felt that he needed somebody on his side, so the group agreed to his suggestion of Sid Vicious. Sid had an authentic punk image, but he had never played bass before. He had also been involved in incidences of violence. A misguided glass thrown at The Damned during a performance at the 100 Club, shattered, with fragments flying into a girl's eye, had been attributed to him. Sid was incarcerated for that. At a Pistols' performance also at the 100 Club, he assaulted music journalist Nick Kent with a bike chain.

The group's offensive "God Save the Queen," released to coincide with Queen Elizabeth II's Silver Jubilee in June 1977, alienated the group further from British society. As there were few venues that would book them, Malcolm set up a six-date tour of the American South with a concluding concert at Winterland in San Francisco.

With his newfound fame, Sid acquired a new girlfriend, American Nancy Spungen, who introduced him to heroin and initiated his downward spiral. John, concerned for Sid, elected to accompany him and the road crew on the tour bus to keep him away from the drug. As Malcolm, Steve, and Paul were flying to the tour locations, this served to alienate John further from the others. When they got to the final date in San Francisco, John and Sid were considered *persona non gratae*. John was abandoned in San Francisco without a plane ticket, and had to borrow money to fly back to London. Sid scored, overdosed, and then overdosed again on the plane to New York. (Sid died from an overdose on February 2, 1979.)

Although the Sex Pistols elevated awareness of social problems and expressed the frustration of the working class, their primary impact was initiating England's punk rock movement. Give them credit also for later inspiring the punk rock trend in the US, and even later, the grunge sound. Politically they accomplished little. The Conservative government was elected in 1979. A criticism of the American punk groups that followed—none of which was considered a commercial success—was that they were more motivated by the musical trend and the fashion rather than a need to express social discontent.

Interestingly, the gang of punks John hung around with—aside from Sid Vicious whose real name was John Beverley—did well as responsible adults: two teachers, an accountant, and a band leader. And John, who once professed an attraction to chaos and anarchy, expressed a philosophy of passive resistance in the wisdom of middle age, stating, "Gandhi is my life's inspiration." The Sex Pistols were elected into the Rock and Roll Hall of Fame in 2006. In a typical anti-establishment gesture, none of the members attended the induction ceremony.

A MEETING WAS SET up in the dining room at Shutters on the Beach hotel in Santa Monica: John Lydon, Eric Gardner, Stephen Nemeth, my brother-in-law and head of production for Rhino Films, and me. Lydon, shall we say, had filled out from his former undernourished youth. A waitress came over, telling us what a fan of the group she was, not sure who other than John might have been in the Sex Pistols as she looked us over.

During that meeting, and a subsequent lunch, John came across as congenial, goofy. He smiled and gyrated throughout the meal and proved to be a good conversationalist. He cleared his throat of phlegm, and we both discovered that we were allergic to milk (which is different from lactose intolerance). He explained that's how punk fans spitting on their favorite groups started. As he sang, phlegm emerged from his throat and he spat onto the stage. The fans, not understanding his discomfort, imitated the action and the trend developed.

I felt that we needed an English writer, someone familiar with the punk rock scene, the social order, and the colloquialisms. We were contacted by Jeremy Drysdale, who read about our project in the industry trades. He left school at sixteen and got work in advertising, rising to cocreative director of the Visage Company. He worked hard on his writing samples and we told him to fly to Los Angeles—at his own expense—for a lunch meeting at Shutters On the Beach on April 2, 1999. It was the four of us, as before, with Jeremy, who made a favorable impression. He learned later that we were apprehensive that he might be an alcoholic (more on that soon) because he drank four bottles of beer. I was concerned, and it wasn't just because I paid for lunch. The next day Jeremy came down with the flu. For the next three days Stephen left cartons of hot soup outside his hotel room door.

Given our low budget, we considered him the perfect person for the job, even though he'd never written a screenplay before. We paid Jeremy $25,000 for the screenplay. Lydon's option fee and other expenses amounted to an additional $15,000. Jeremy went back to

England, read John's book, made notes, and returned to Los Angeles, this time at our expense, for a story meeting with John. On January 20, 2000, Jeremy took a cab to John's Venice Beach pad—which had once been owned by movie star Mae West—arriving at 11:00 a.m. He pounded on the door, but it took a long time before a grumpy and hung over Lydon answered, addressing Jeremy as "Are you the fucking writer?" Jeremy was asked to sit in the lounge—which was littered with empty bottles—while Lydon "woke up," which included taking a shower.

Upon his return, John was responsive to Jeremy's questions. Jeremy: "I found him to be spiky, intelligent, well-read and quick-witted, and I quite liked him, although he seemed to have a massive chip on his shoulder about the way he had been treated." The two drank beer throughout the session—no food was consumed—and Jeremy had to keep up or John would hurl abuse at him. They worked for eight hours, splitting thirty-six beers.

The next day, Jeremy let it slip that he had a (small) per diem of which John wanted to take advantage by dining at a fancy Marina del Rey restaurant. Unfortunately John was in obnoxious *Rotten* mode and alienated the servers, none of whom seemed to know who he was. They worked for only four-and-a-half hours because John was "very hung over."

One of the problems with the book was that it lacked a narrative flow. John would spray his opinions like a garden hose on high. Interview passages from others on the scene would intrude on John's first-person voice. Had Jeremy been experienced, he might have bridged the book's shortcomings in his first draft.

To John's credit, he was a stickler for accuracy. Most of his comments reflected that concern. In order to make a book or other account workable in a feature film format, liberties have to be taken with the facts. Sometimes numerous characters have to be combined into fewer ones. The same with locations. Time can be an issue, the expanse of years, but in this case the Sex Pistols' duration—a little over two years—was workable. As our projected movie was conceived to accommodate a lower budget— speculatively eight million dollars— the writer has to be aware of the number of locations and extras, among other considerations. As John was also new to scriptwriting, he was bothered when events deviated from how they were conveyed in his book. Sometimes Jeremy had difficulty capturing the voice of a character. John could have helped more here.

Stephen, Eric and I had script notes. John's were the most colorful of all, rendered in a histrionic, near-Ralph Steadman style. I doubt whether anybody else in the movie-making process had experienced comments such as the following: "Doh! Boring! Silly Fuck Off Talk. Middle Class Twat Talk. It reads silly, like a debutante's hissy fit." Sometimes his comments were more pointed: "Either be accurate or deliberately comedic." Jeremy's second draft rectified most of the concerns.

I liked what Guy Ritchie did with *Lock, Stock and Two Smoking Barrels* and thought he would be the perfect director for our film, but he turned it down. Eric suggested Penelope Spheeris because she had directed the *Decline of Western Civilization* series of documentaries, one of which profiled the Los Angeles punk community in 1980. She also showed her comedic sense with *Wayne's World* and *The Beverly Hillbillies*. John met her and liked her. Stephen had Jeremy fly out to meet her and discuss the script. Spheeris, who had written only a fraction of the films she had directed, kept kvetching to Jeremy that she "wrote her own stuff and didn't see why they needed an outside writer."

A number of weeks later, Stephen received a call from John wondering if his character could be played by "a woman, a black child, and an old guy?" It was a bad idea in 2000, and no less in 2007 when six different characters—including a black child—played Bob Dylan in *I'm Not There*. I guess John was ahead of his time.

I was surprised that the project fell apart. I thought John didn't renew the option because he thought he and Penelope could make the movie without us. Or maybe he had now fallen out with Eric Gardner. If he didn't renew with us, he wouldn't have to cut Eric in as a producer. Stephen merely thought that he changed his mind and didn't want to make the film. As of this writing, no movie has been made from Lydon's book.

I had been looking forward to the production. The shortened title of "Rotten" intrigued me. There had never been a feature film with that title. If the movie turned out less than stellar, it would be too easy for dismissive reviewers to say that the movie lived up to its name. It seemed like a very John Lydon thing to do.

MY YARDLEY GIRL

HE MAY NOT HAVE been tall, fashionable, worn much makeup or dressed in mini-skirts, like the models in the cosmetic ads, but she was my Yardley girl, which is to say she looked English: pale skin, crystal blue eyes, and straight blond hair. She even had an English name, Susan Sherbourne. She was a junior, majoring in anthropology. I was a sophomore. I sidled up to her one day in our psychology lecture hall.

She was the first girl I wanted to have a serious relationship with. It was April 1970, the beginning of the spring quarter at UCLA. I was shy, and didn't date much. I had no mentors, no guidance from an older brother or sister, and no help from my middle-aged parents.

Susan was from Sebastopol, a small town fifty miles north of San Francisco. She was smart and reserved. I asked if she knew its most famous resident, Charles Schulz, the creator of the *Peanuts* comic strip. She said she didn't. I gave no thought to how a small town girl related to a large city like Los Angeles.

Our first date wasn't the best. When I picked her up at her apartment in a terraced building on Landfair Avenue, she made it clear that she had a boyfriend who was in the armed services. It didn't deter me. After all, I reasoned, "He isn't here, is he?" Because I felt strongly aligned with the rock culture, being in the armed forces seemed passé, as did belonging to a sorority or fraternity. At the very least you went to college to get a student deferment, especially with the Vietnam War raging. Maybe he wasn't that smart, or had elected not to go to college. Maybe joining the military was part of a small town's culture.

She also said that she had a roommate, who wasn't there when I picked her up. That implied we couldn't go back there to make out, and I wasn't going to take her to the small home I shared with my parents, ten miles away. She also had a puppy, which I thought was odd. How do you care for a dog as a student in an apartment, with no backyard or grassy area?

Our first stop was the Pizza Palace in Westwood Village for dinner. I thought a friend from high school was performing that evening with his jug band. Either I was mistaken, or they weren't scheduled until much later. I ate pizza, but Susan wasn't hungry, which threw me off. We then took in Luchino Visconti's *The Damned* at the Granada Theater on Sunset Boulevard. Sitting through a two-and-a-half-hour movie about Nazism and decadence wasn't the best choice to engender feelings of tenderness on a first date.

It was Saturday, April 25. I'd just come from the Holiday Inn in Beverly Hills, where I'd interviewed the members of Argent, a new British quartet that evolved out of The Zombies, one of my favorite bands. I was in Powell Library, making notes for my article for the UCLA *Daily Bruin*. Nearby on campus the yearly Mardi Gras fundraiser was happening. I wondered where Susan was, and wished I were there with her.

It was a period of unrest on campuses across the US, culminating on May 4, when the National Guard killed four students at Kent State University. The next day protestors rampaged throughout the UCLA campus, breaking windows and doors, and trashing offices. Seventy-four people were arrested; numerous were injured. I felt that people should be able to express their views, but taking over a building or disrupting a university seemed immature to me. I couldn't relate to the behavior, and never participated in a protest march, even though others said it was an easy way to meet girls. At UCLA, similar activities seemed only to deprive the students of the education they would have received had classes not been cancelled, as they intermittently were cancelled, starting on May 5 when Governor Ronald Reagan shut down classes for four days.

One benefit was I got to see Pink Floyd play. On Wednesday afternoon, May 6, the band gave a free concert, performing on the outdoor proscenium of the Women's Gym. At that point in their career, Pink Floyd were a few years away from becoming megastars. As the members of the band were not dynamic performers, they relied on complementary visuals. In the early days it was a liquid light show. In a few years it would be lasers. So, Pink Floyd recreating the meandering music from their most recent album, *Ummagumma*, on a balmy, spring afternoon *sans* the impact of the visual show in a darkened hall and their new 360-degree sound system, didn't cut it for me. Or maybe it's because Susan wasn't there.

On Saturday Susan and I attended a concert at the Long Beach Arena: Sly and the Family Stone with Mountain opening. I was apprehensive as Sly was getting a reputation for showing up late for performances, and sometimes not appearing at all. The evening didn't start well. Mountain, a Cream-like power trio who were mounting the charts with "Mississippi Queen," were too loud. Sly and the Family Stone took the stage late. Sly kept fumbling the lyrics and he experienced problems with his guitar, but the band was solid and played the hits well. It was an exciting show. We stood on our fold-up chairs, launched our arms into the air and joined Sly and the band in shouting "Higher!" We held hands. Susan's fingers were thin, with short nails, and light calluses on the fingertips. I thought it was cool that she was digging for fossils in the La Brea Tar Pits as part of her anthropology studies.

Susan and I saw a lot of each other. After most dates we would make out in my car. We went to a press screening of *Myra Breckinridge* at the Egyptian Theater. Afterward, we sipped drinks in the courtyard.

Susan dressed up that night and wore a stylish hippie dress with a revealing halter-top. She wanted to see the movie *Anne of the Thousand Days*, which was playing at the Loew's Beverly Theater. I wasn't keen on the old English period of Henry VIII and Anne Boleyn, but I was happy in my aisle seat sitting next to her.

A couple of my high school friends were first-year tenants at La Mancha, which offered upscale student housing, even though construction hadn't been completed. We joined them and their girlfriends for a showing of *The Graduate* in the recreation room. (The owners of La Mancha sold out a few years later and the building became a retirement hotel for senior citizens. It changed again, to a regular hotel, the Westwood Marquis, and more recently the chic "W.")

On Friday, May 22, we went to a concert at the Anaheim Convention Center. The Guess Who, a Canadian band riding high on the charts with "American Woman" and "No Sugar Tonight," headlined over Crabby Appleton and funk band Ballin' Jack. I enjoyed hearing the hits. Although "These Eyes," "Laughing," and "Undun" were more like broken love songs, Burton Cummings sang with such a warm voice, they conveyed romance to me that night.

We finally managed to break bread, or at least bagels. I wanted to try the food at the newest restaurant in Westwood Village, the Hip Bagel. Having a hamburger on the harder-than-a-bun bagel didn't work for me.

I half-heartedly asked Susan if she wanted to be my date for the *Daily Bruin* party on Saturday of the following week. I was surprised when she agreed. "Why would she want to go to a party where she didn't know anybody?" I thought, "She must really like me."

The party took place in Jeff Weber's parents' lanai on Sunset Boulevard, near the border of Beverly Hills. I was given "Suzi Q" to sing as a member of the *ad hoc Daily Bruin* band. It was from The Rolling Stones' second album and fit my limited range perfectly. I wanted to spiff up my appearance for the party, so I squeezed into my *bar mitzvah* suit jacket to approach the look of the 1965 Rolling Stones. Unbeknownst to everybody else, I had never sung in public before, and was nervous. Consequently, I failed to fully grasp how much the lyrics expressed how I felt about my Suzi non-Q. I accompanied Jonathan Kellerman on maracas when he sang Ritchie Valens' "Donna," but spent most of the evening sitting next to Susan on a settee.

Driving back to UCLA, she had a strong desire for ice tea, in a can, which was still a new concept. We stopped at Harold's Liquor on Westwood Boulevard. I welcomed Susan back to the car with a kiss, not realizing that she had a mouthful of cigarette smoke.

I met her at her apartment. With her dog in tow, we walked to the last day of our psychology class. When we got there, I was shocked to discover that we had to take the final exam. Because so many classes were cancelled, we were under the impression that a final exam wouldn't be given. The professor qualified it by saying that he wanted to find out what we knew, and that it wasn't going to count that much. Had I known, I would have studied. I got a "C" in the class. During the school break, Susan went home to Sebastopol.

When the summer quarter started, I went to Susan's apartment and was told that she now resided in a fraternity house. During the summer, with far fewer students attending, fraternities rented out their empty rooms. I left a message for Susan, who eventually did get in touch.

There was an appealing double-bill at the Olympic Drive-In, The Beatles' new movie, *Let It Be*, and *The Magic Christian*, which starred Ringo Starr and Peter Sellers. By enticing Susan into the back seat, I was anticipating an evening of more physical intimacy than we'd had in the past, but she soon fell asleep. I was so bored by *Let It Be* I nodded off. This was a harbinger of things to come.

A week or so later, I met her on campus late one day. Sitting on a bench, I expressed how much I liked her, and how I wanted to see more of her. She said that she didn't feel that way about me. That was the end. Later, I thought that if I hadn't expressed myself, I would still be able to see her. It was too painful wanting more, but the writing was on the wall.

That fall quarter, walking to Developmental Sociological Theory in Young Hall, I would pass her walking from her class. The first few times she exchanged my greeting. Subsequently, she made a point of not looking my way. It hurt. She was often accompanied by her now-large dog, and a fellow student. He had a strong jaw, ruddy complexion, and brownish blond hair. He wore kaki shorts and sandals. I could pick him out of a lineup today.

After a time, I emotionally moved on, and didn't think much about Susan. A few years later, United Artists Records gave me money to record "Elementary Dr. Watson," inspired by my relationship with her. Rather than it being about the detective Sherlock Holmes, it was about how clueless I was that there was another suitor. At the time, I asked myself, "How could there be another guy when she was seeing so much of me?" It was the best song I ever wrote. When we made out, her throat emitted a relaxed, two-note "Mmh-uh." I'm not sure when I adopted it, but I noticed doing it at times to release tension.

I remember so much of our time together forty-five years ago. I just can't remember her face.

GRANNY TAKES A TRIP

"One should either be a work of art or wear a work of art"
—From *Oscar Wilde*, inscribed over the shop's door

NIGEL WAYMOUTH HAD RECORDED two albums as a member of Hapshash and the Coloured Coat in the sixties, but I wanted to meet him less as a former musician than as one of the proprietors of the fashionable sixties boutique Granny Takes a Trip, which I thought might make an excellent setting for a sixties rock movie. Although most rock movies focus on a male singer, or male members of a rock band, a Granny Takes a Trip movie, set in a fashion boutique, could have strong female (as well as male) characters in Nigel's partner, the salesgirls, and customers. And, as a movie that takes place primarily in one location, it would suit Rhino Films' usual low budgets.

Having heard that Nigel had come to live in Los Angeles, making his living as a fine art painter, I met him in his loft on Spring Street, in what was once considered the financial district of downtown Los Angeles, in a thirteen-story 1919 structure recognized as a historical landmark. Known as the Barclay Bank Building for its primary business, it had fallen into disrepair. Nigel lived in one large room—a former office space rebranded as "an artist's loft"—with makeshift dividers designating the bedroom and other areas. He was painting a tree on a large canvas. I was impressed with his technique.

Over lunch at a French bistro a couple of blocks away, Nigel recounted having been a passionate R&B and blues fan. While a student at the London School of Economics—from which he graduated in 1964—he had followed The Rolling Stones from gig to gig. His actress girlfriend, Shelia Cohen, had been obsessed with buying vintage clothes at flea markets, favoring unusual and colorful Victorian and Oriental designs. Nigel had suggested they open a store so she could get rid of the stuff—at a profit. Nigel described her: "Bright blue eyes, hair pulled back or cut short, a ringing laugh, and sharp as a tack." Third partner John Pearse apprenticed as a tailor and borrowed the £200 it cost to open the shop from his uncle.

Nigel was familiar with an empty store at the unfashionable end of the King's Road known informally as The World's End, after the pub across the street. The Granny part of the shop's name paid homage to the presumed previous owners of the vintage clothes Shelia had collected, and Trip, to show they were hip, referred to the experience of taking LSD. Earlier, a commercial in which an elderly lady peeled rubber in a Dodge Super Stocker had inspired the Jan and Dean hit "The Little Old Lady from Pasadena," with its "Go, Granny, Go" refrain. But the record hadn't been a hit in Britain, and Nigel & Co.'s whimsical evocation of a grandmother was purely coincidental.

It's odd to think that Britain's hippest boutique was rooted in the arts culture at the dawn of the century, and it wasn't limited to Shelia's clothes. Nigel designed the exterior in an Art Nouveau style. Some described the shop's red and purple interior, with Aubrey Beardsley erotic prints and blowups of vintage risqué French postcards gracing the walls, as evocative of a New Orleans bordello. An ancient gramophone with a large horn speaker was visible inside the entrance, across from an Edwardian peep-show photo machine. (Owing to an exhibit at the Victoria & Albert Museum in 1966, Beardsley became all the rage. Humble Pie featured a Beardsley illustration on the cover of their debut US LP, and Klaus Voormann was inspired by Beardsley's line drawings in designing the Beatles' *Revolver* cover.)

The shop seemed more a place to hang out than an efficient business enterprise. Sam Cooke, Otis Redding, Bo Diddley, and other soul artists were staples of the Wurlitzer jukebox. The Rolling Stones, Bob Dylan, and The Velvet Underground played regularly on the hi-fi. There were only two racks for dresses and jackets, and one display for shirts, with male and female apparel intermixed.

Nigel highlighted the store's eclectic stock in the first few months: "Henley picnic suits, frock coats, band master's coats with frogging, ruffle and lacy shirts, and found dresses from Doucet and Paquin in Paris that were made for Princess Esterhazy in the summer of 1914." Nigel contributed ideas for new apparel. John Pearse was responsible for designing the men's clothes, Shelia the women's. Nigel recalled her most notable designs having included "silver mini dresses, moiré satin blazers with exquisite piping, and delicate silk blouses with ribbon trimmings." Director Michelangelo Antonioni, in pre-production on *Blow Up*, wandered into Grannys and bought the beaded dress that model Veruschka wore in the movie and on the movie's iconic poster. Jane Asher, Julie Driscoll, Anita Pallenberg, Brigitte Bardot, Raquel Welch, and even Barbra Streisand were among Granny's more celebrated female customers.

"The first people to sniff us out were the mixture of Chelsea gays and debutantes," Nigel said. "Then pop stars started coming after them. One morning we were sitting around cross-legged on the floor, passing a joint around and these two blokes came in. They looked around and said, 'This is a nice place isn't it?' We noticed their accents, looked up and it was John and Paul. They were very sweet and impressed with the shop. They came back all the time." The Beatles felt comfortable mixing with Granny's clientele. John Lennon even hawked copies of *International Times*—the underground newspaper the shop sold—to his fellow customers. The Beatles wore Granny's apparel in the photo on the back cover of *Revolver*, as did The Rolling Stones on the front cover of *Between the Buttons*.

The William Morris Company had manufactured colorful, swirling floral patterns for use as wallpaper in the 1890s. In the sixties, the company revived the patterns—re-coloring them in psychedelic hues—this time as furnishing fabrics, for upholstery or curtains. As its initial stock of Victorian hand-me-downs became depleted, the Granny's trio presented a new, more expensive line featuring fabrics from Liberty of London, with William Morris floral patterns. Adding to the cost, Pearse hired the same outworkers who constructed suits for Saville Row tailors. He designed Edwardian-styled jackets that became among Granny's more popular (and lasting) items, worn by members of The Who, The Jimi Hendrix Experience, The Hollies, Small Faces, and The Move. Perhaps the most iconic jacket, bought by George Harrison, was made from a Golden Lily pattern. Thanks to Granny and its imitators, furnishing fabric outsold wallpaper at William Morris for the first time.

Every few months, Nigel redesigned the frontage, later in 1966 with a giant portrait of Native American chiefs Low Dog, followed by one of Kicking Bear. The next year the entire front was painted with a giant pop-art face of Jean Harlow. Sometimes he and his crew worked in the middle of the night, so when people came by the next day it looked like a different place. In 1968 Pearse sacrificed his impaired 1948 Dodge saloon car to create a new exterior. It was cut in half, painted yellow, and bolted to the front to create the illusion that it was driven through the front window.

Eric Burdon and the Animals did a photo session in front of the shop, as too did The Purple Gang who appropriated the name for an April 1967 single. (Producer Joe Boyd recorded it the day after he produced "Arnold Layne" by Pink Floyd, also customers of Granny's.) Their photo session was interrupted when Paul McCartney walked into the boutique.

In 1967 the celebrated novelist Salman Rushdie was a Cambridge University student who occasionally stayed with his university friend Paul Scutt who lived with his mother on the top floor. Because the windows were obscured by the exterior makeover, it was hard to see when one entered. As Rushdie recollected in *The New Yorker:* "You entered through a heavy bead curtain and were instantly blinded." Like others, Rushdie felt intimidated by the ambience. On one occasion, he complained of Shelia dismissing his attempt to be sociable by declaring, "Conversation is dead."

"She was very engaging and full of lively good humor, but she could be indifferent to people she disliked," said Nigel. "It was after hours, and Shelia, fat joint fuming away in her hand, was busy showing John Lennon a new batch of shirts. Salman's untimely interruption with a gauche but cheery, 'Hello, I thought it was time I should introduce myself' did not impress the urbane Shelia, who had suspected that Salman's downstairs' visit was triggered by his desire to meet the famous Beatle (who had arrived in his iconic painted Rolls Royce)."

IN ITS FOURTH YEAR, the partnership began to fray. Shelia, Nigel, and John considered themselves artists, not business entrepreneurs. "We went to a shirt maker to make thirty shirts from our pattern," Nigel remembered. "When we went to pick them up, we saw a whole stack of copies. The maker said that the buyer from Cecil Gee liked our shirt and had him make some for him. We were too naïve, too unbusinesslike to challenge him."

John wanted to remain focused on generating imaginative designs, and bemoaned the emphasis on hippie stock. He and Nigel argued over updating the facade. John wanted to paint a New York skyline behind the refashioned Dodge. Nigel wanted stars. "We were all dysfunctional and too busy enjoying ourselves," said Nigel.

"The shop was never profitable in the sense that we made and kept a lot of money. Famous yes, and quickly. Not long after we opened the shop, *Time* magazine's Swinging London article came out. It should always be understood that it was the name not the clothes that brought most people in. There were other shops selling well-designed hip clothes, like Hung on You and Biba, and our clothes were wonderful, too, but it is the name that makes people, even to this day, sit up and be curious."

Over time, Nigel and Sheila ceased to be lovers. Having "never intended to be in the rag trade," Nigel was easily distracted by such outside interests as designing posters and album covers with Michael English as Hapshash and the Coloured Coat, and playing in a band of the same name with English and others, including members of Spooky Tooth. "It was [producer] Guy Stevens' concept to make a record. He was something of a visionary and a romantic and even though we told him that we didn't know a musical chord between us, he still wanted to turn us into a pop phenomenon. Hapshash had been doing graphic work for him and Island Records and I think Guy loved the idea of being part of my trip."

Nigel may have been a highly influential artist, but is no one's raconteur, and delivered insufficient wonderful anecdotes on which to base a movie. Which isn't to say I didn't enjoy his reminiscences, which added to my understanding of Swinging London. For instance, he told me about the Baghdad House, a restaurant at 142 Fulham Road in Chelsea, where rock stars including The Beatles and The Rolling Stones dined regularly, not so much for the food, but because one could smoke dope freely in the basement, decorated like an Oriental bazaar, with curtained booths—often while cops chowed down upstairs. Nigel said the owner was rumored to have been hired to assassinate Saudi Arabia's King Faisal. His redheaded Scottish girlfriend would belly dance to the accompaniment of oud players.

Granny's three partners eventually sold the shop to their manager, Freddie Hornik, who, with his own partners, was able to revive the business for a few years. Hapshash dissolved around this time and Nigel became a fine art painter. Pearse, after rebranding himself as a film director in the seventies, went back to tailoring, and cultivated a celebrity clientele. Shelia became a spiritualist in Cornwall.

Though well designed, Granny's clothes were made for the moment, often from fabric unsuitable for garments. The shop's velvet trousers often split because they were stitched to accommodate the snug fit of the period. As a result, surviving garments with original Granny Takes a Trip labels are scarce and highly collectible, and go for thousands of dollars. Granny Takes a Trip apparel may be seen in the collections of the Metropolitan Museum of New York and the Victoria and Albert Museum in London. In 2012, Britain's *Royal Mail* reproduced George Harrison's jacket on a postage stamp, crediting Granny Takes a Trip. Clothes designers Tommy Hilfiger and Anna Sui both referenced Granny Takes a Trip as an inspiration for their 2015 summer collections. Hapshash's posters found their way decades later into the Victoria and Albert Museum permanent collections. In October 2000 the museum exhibited Waymouth and English's work as *Cosmic Visions—Psychedelic Posters from the 1960s.* Eight of their posters—as well as a wealth of sixties music—were included in the museum's *You Say You Want a Revolution? Records and Rebels 1966–70,* which closed just prior to the publication of this book.

THE ZOMBIES
RESURRECTED

WITH THE SUCCESS OF The Beatles came countless other English rock groups. Among the best were The Zombies, who can be thought of as the Rodney Dangerfield of the British Invasion. Over five years they released nineteen singles, most of them stellar, but only managed three hits in America and one in Britain. Their acclaimed *Odessey and Oracle* LP even failed to make the charts in the UK. This underrated band, like Rodney Dangerfield's character, clearly "got no respect."

The band was composed of schoolmates from two schools in St. Albans, a suburb twenty miles north of London: Rod Argent, keyboards; Colin Blunstone, lead vocals; Chris White, bass; Paul Atkinson, guitar; Hugh Grundy, drums. Low budget horror movies were the rage with teens in the early sixties, so it was no surprise that original bassist Paul Arnold suggested "The Zombies" when the group became aware of other combos also called the Mustangs. Only decades later can one appreciate how prescient the naming was.

They had been performing in the area—mostly colleges and rugby clubs—for over a year when they realized that they weren't making enough money to sustain an adult lifestyle. In the spring of 1964, with most of the members eyeing college, they were on the verge of breaking up when they were encouraged to enter a newspaper-sponsored battle of the bands, the Herts Beat Music Contest. (Herts was short for Hertfordshire, the county name.) They won, collecting £250, and were offered a recording contract with Decca Records. Chris was twenty-one; the others eighteen and nineteen.

The group was considering recording their version of George Gershwin's "Summertime" (composed in 1934 for *Porgy and Bess*) when producer Ken Jones heard Rod's new composition, "She's Not There," and selected that for their debut. Rod took inspiration from the title of John Lee Hooker's "No One Told Me" and the chord sequence of Brian Hyland's "Sealed With a Kiss." It was only the third song he had written. On "She's Not There," as well as their next few singles, The Zombies presented a distinct sound characterized by Colin's crystalline, breathy vocals, the group's choirboy harmonies, and Rod's jazzy keyboard. Rod's preference for minor chords conveyed an undercurrent of sadness and melancholy, matched by lyrics of missed romantic connections. Some songs evoked a haunting quality, best exemplified on "I Remember When I Loved Her," a B-side recorded in November. Emotionally subdued, Colin sounds like he's singing about a loved one who has died. Rod's organ solo is eerie.

In their early years, the band played rock 'n' roll by Chuck Berry, Little Richard, Jerry Lee Lewis and Gene Vincent, as well as blues and R&B. Somehow, these musical roots that were so apparent with other acts weren't noticeable when The Zombies performed their own compositions. Fortunately, when they focused on Rod's and Chris' compositions, only the influence of The Beatles, by way of harmony vocals and strong melodies, was apparent. The Zombies were too nice. They didn't have the grit to evoke the black experience. As a result, the band developed an appealing English sound.

"She's Not There," recorded on June 12, was released the following month and became a hit on both sides of the Atlantic: number two in the US, twelve in the UK. Academic plans were forgotten. With The Zombies' debut 45 racing up the charts, Decca Records concocted an image for these shy, awkward teenagers. In an effort to distinguish them from the rash of other beat groups, they were presented as brainy high school students "with fifty A & O levels among them." Had Larry Page managed them, in their press photos he might have posed them in lab coats holding smoking beakers. Instead, in their matching suits, much like other bands in 1964, they looked like erudite schoolboys. Two even wore glasses.

As "She's Not There" made its way into America's top five, The Zombies were hastily added to Murray the K's Christmas Show at the Brooklyn Fox Theater. In star fashion, they were met at the airport by two limousines to be whisked to New York. The next day they were dismayed to find out that they were the ones paying even though they hadn't ordered the expensive rides. The other performers included Chuck Jackson, Ben E. King & the Drifters, The Shirelles, Dick and Dee Dee, The Shangri-Las, Patti LaBelle & The Bluebells, The Vibrations, Dionne Warwick, The Nashville Teens, and The Hullabaloos. Most acts performed only a few songs, with shows scheduled five times a day. The Zombies performed "She's Not There" and usually one other song.

The Zombies normally traveled to the Brooklyn Fox by subway, but around the theater they experienced the same fanaticism The Beatles had. In one harrowing episode, girls mobbed Paul, pulled off his shirt and jacket, and pressed him up against a glass door that was about to shatter until police freed him. Other times they were chased by girls bearing scissors determined to cut locks off their hair.

America's reputation as a violent place was confirmed as Hugh and Chris were enjoying a New Year's Day morning stroll in Times Square with members of The Nashville Teens. They were shocked to observe an actual shoot out right before their eyes. A man wearing a stocking mask, who shot a cook at a restaurant moments before, fled into the street as two policemen were dismounting from their horses. He fired at them. They returned fire, striking him in the neck.

A few days later The Zombies played their new single, "Tell Her No," on *Hullabaloo* and *Shindig!*, propelling it to number six. Additional tracks had been recorded in November and December to flesh out an LP, and, with their two American hits, *The Zombies* was released in February. It's hard to imagine now, but The Zombies were a big influence on America's post-Beatles' bands. The Byrds, Left Banke, Love, and Vanilla Fudge all performed Zombies' songs live. Howard Kaylan admitted copying Colin's "soft, innocent" delivery when he sang the verses of "It Ain't Me Babe," The Turtles' first hit.

In the UK, they joined a twelve-date spring tour headlined by Dusty Springfield and The Searchers. The tour booklet described them as "Five educated Zombies with more than 50 G .C. E. [General Certificate of Education] passes between them." They missed two days on the tour to appear in *Bunny Lake Is Missing*, an Otto Preminger directed film starring Laurence Olivier and Carol Lynley. The Zombies had three songs on the soundtrack.

In April they made it back to the States for a grueling Dick Clark Caravan of Stars thirty-three-date tour, joining Del Shannon, Tommy Roe, The Shangri-Las, and ten other acts. There were additional non-Caravan dates, and all the exposure propelled *The Zombies* to number thirty-nine. After which the soaring Zombies took a prolonged commercial dive. While musically they were producing singles that were good enough to make the Top 10, it seemed like their career was managed by one of the hapless zombies in *Dawn of the Dead*. Why weren't they having big hits? Recording albums? And where was the money from their extensive touring? The short-changing became more apparent when The Zombies played the Philippines, where they were even more popular than The Beatles. The Beatles had a harrowing experience when they performed in the Philippines in July 1966. Maybe the news never got to The Zombies.

They arrived at the airport on March 1, 1967. Thousands of screaming fans met them even though it was 2:00 a.m. Their label representative told them they had five records in the Top 10. They played a few shows at the Araneta Coliseum before ten thousand fans a night, but were only paid $300 a show for the whole band. (The group suspected their long-time agent made a side deal to collect more money for himself and soon made a change.) Their promoter confiscated their passports and surrounded them with machine gun-toting bodyguards supposedly for their own safety. Rod referred to it as "real James Bond-type stuff." In order to make real money, later that month they played a few dates for a rival promoter, learning that two of the clubs had mysteriously burned down days following their shows. The Zombies were in fear of their lives until they were able to leave the country.

AROUND THIS TIME THEIR three-year deal with Decca had lapsed. The previous year Derek Everett had moved from EMI to become head of A&R at CBS International. The Zombies convinced him to let them record an album that they would produce themselves. "In 1967 The Zombies, after only three professional years, had already decided to break up," Rod told me in 1987. "Chris White and I, however, wanted to make a parting gesture. We wanted to make a very personal final album, controlling every step of the process from writing to final cut, from production of the music to production of the album cover. We knew the record would be released after the break-up of the group, so we didn't attempt to bow to the pressures of the market place."

"And we did say," added Chris, "that if it was a huge success we would carry on."

The Summer of Love was characterized by good vibes, feelin' groovy, and love was in the air. Even though *Sergeant Pepper's Lonely Hearts Club Band* provided a soundtrack for much of the summer, The Beatles were not in a loving mood. The album was an introspective and somber reflection of the drugs—pot and LSD—they had been taking.

Close friend to The Beatles, Barry Miles, in his memoir *In the Sixties*, observed that quite often The Beatles were stoned during recording sessions although they abstained taking LSD while recording. He said of John, "By the time they started *Sgt. Pepper* he had taken so much acid that he felt burned out." John later told him that during the recordings he was in "a real big depression."

In contrast, The Zombies, who weren't into drugs, entered EMI's Abbey Road studio little more than a month after The Beatles had vacated, and recorded an album that was much more representative of the era. The Zombies made use of EMI's collection of instruments, as well as John Lennon's Mellotron, first used by The Beatles on "Strawberry Fields Forever." The songs, many with romance as a theme, brim with optimism, joy, and celebration. The album was characterized by rich harmonies and warm melodies. If the album wasn't as adventurous as *Sgt. Pepper's*, it was close: "Care of Cell 44" was about a girl soon to come home from prison; "Butchers Tale (Western Front 1914)" about a butcher drafted into World War I who is traumatized at the butchery he sees on the battlefield.

"The songs were inspired by a variety of influences," Rod said, "But they were songs which came from our hearts. They were not the result of a producer or record company imposing their views of what a hit single might be. Some of the songs were romantic. 'Butchers Tale,' 'Brief Candles,' and 'A Rose for Emily' were sparked by literature, the latter by a Faulkner short story. Chris reflected on his experience growing up near Beechwood Park [a girl's boarding school] in his song of that name." Chris pointed out that the events in "Butchers Tale" actually took place in 1916. The song title was transposed incorrectly. It was inspired by Alan Clark's historical novel *The Donkeys*.

The group needed one more song to complete the album, so Rod hastily composed "Time of the Season." The title came from the lyrics of a Miracles song the group used to perform live. Rod misheard the lyric in "Tracks of My Tears" as "It's the close of the season" instead of "if you look closer it's easy (to trace the tracks of my tears)." When he discovered he had been singing the incorrect words, he was abashed, but he liked the phrase and rewrote it as "time of the season." Rod also incorporated a few words he liked from "Summertime." The rhythmic bass line was inspired by Ben E. King's "Stand By Me." Colin didn't like the song, and after numerous takes in trying to get the lead vocal right, he angrily gave up. Refusing to continue, he told Rod that he should sing his own song. Rod was able to convince him, bad mood and all, that he could do it. And he was happy that he did.

The Zombies played great, sang great, and they were so well rehearsed that they were able to bring in the album for $4,000 compared to the $75,000 The Beatles spent. If The Zombies' creativity couldn't quite rival The Beatles, I thought their songs were better.

Interestingly, each album had a song about friendship. Where Ringo's vocal was laid-back on "With a Little Help From My Friends," The Zombies sang with verve on "Friends of Mine." (Paul Atkinson told me that seven of the eight "so in love" couples whose names are chanted in the chorus had split, and that included him—the only Zombie mentioned—and his wife Molly Molloy, a dancer whom he had met on the Murray the K show on which The Zombies appeared.)

Chris and Rod had their flatmate, Terry Quirk, create an illustration for the cover. But neither they, nor anybody else who got an advance look at the painting, noticed that Quirk had misspelled "odyssey" as "odessey."

"Friends of Mine" was released in October, and "Care of Cell 44" the next month. Both were stiffs. The group hadn't had a hit in the UK in three years, and in almost that long in the US. Their successful markets—Japan, the Philippines, Scandinavia—weren't enough to sustain a career. Colin, Paul, and Hugh were also envious of the extra money Rod and Chris made as songwriters. Colin groused that Rod and Chris had cars while he was still taking the Underground. With no momentum and little money coming in—Colin, Paul and Hugh needed to get jobs—it was an easy decision to dissolve the band. The Zombies fulfilled a handful of college dates in December and then broke up. Colin went to work at an insurance company, Hugh sold cars, and Paul trained to program a (mainframe) computer at a bank. Within two years they were all back in music: Colin as a solo artist, Hugh at CBS Records, first in the promotion department and then joining Paul in A&R. Note that ABBA was among Paul's first signings.

Because the singles had flopped, and because he had heard that the band was no more, CBS Records president Clive Davis was inclined to pass on issuing the album for the US market. Al Kooper was a founding member of Blood, Sweat & Tears, but left after the first album. In April 1968, before starting a new job for CBS as an A&R staff producer in New York, he visited London for the first time. When he returned, he listened to the forty LPs he acquired, and thought *Odessey and Oracle*—which he bought at a King's Road record store—"stuck out like a rose in a garden of weeds." He was so knocked out, he convinced Davis to release it. Davis suggested Kooper write an endorsement on the back cover of the US edition.

Issued in June on the Date Records imprint, it was tough going. "This Will Be Our Year" stiffed. So did "Butchers Tale." In January 1969 the label tried "Time of the Season," even though it had failed the previous spring in the UK.

As a young teen, I bought The Zombies' first two singles, but the era was so rich in great pop music that I scarcely wondered why I never heard another of their records on the radio. In March 1969, "Time of the Season" was getting played when I saw *Odessey and Oracle* displayed at Crane's Records in Inglewood. Even though I had only heard that one song, I bought it that day.

"Time of the Season" advanced to number three on *Billboard* by the end of March—eventually selling 1.4 million copies—but *Odessey and Oracle* barely broke into the Top 100. I knew the record was great. Al Kooper knew the record was great. Pete Townshend said it was "great" in *Rolling Stone*. And it did get good reviews, but it wasn't universally considered exceptional. (In 1979, Dave Marsh, coeditor of *The Rolling Stone Record Guide*, slagged it off as "mediocre.") I wondered, where were The Zombies?

IN APRIL THE FOLLOWING year, Rod Argent and Chris White were in Los Angeles promoting their new band, Argent, with a few dates at the Whisky a Go-Go. Rod played keyboards; Russ Ballard, guitar; Jim Rodford, bass; and Robert Henrit, drums. Rod alternated lead vocals with Russ. Chris contributed songs and produced along with Rod. I interviewed them as they lounged around the rooftop pool of the Holiday Inn in Beverly Hills. Although my focus was on their new group, Rod and Chris were happy to answer my questions about The Zombies.

"We were always dissatisfied with the production of our records," Rod said at the interview. "It would come out a lot differently than the sound we had in our heads. So, as an experiment, we wanted to produce an album before we broke up to satisfy ourselves. So we recorded it and then split. It was the first thing we ever produced ourselves and that knocked us out. We were very pleased with it."

In choosing not to reform The Zombies, the members weren't able to take advantage of the vast sums that were dangled before them to perform live. One booking agency reportedly offered $600,000. "I never entertained the possibility," said Rod. "The time spent in trying to reform the group would have resulted in what musical accomplishments I'd achieve going to waste. If you want to make a lot of money, well that's fine. But I have more fun doing what I'm doing now."

A consequence was the proliferation of bogus groups calling themselves "The Zombies" to exploit the group's renewed popularity. Rod: "There are about three American Zombies—two in England—

that we know about. The name was copyrighted, but there's not a damn thing you can do about it."

"You've got to sue them, prove that they're damaging your ability to earn a living," added Chris. "It's difficult because we no longer existed as The Zombies."

"It's not worth the time and the money," continued Rod, "because as soon as we finished suing one, another would spring up." One of the fake Zombies included future ZZ Top members Frank Beard and Dusty Hill.

I liked Argent's first two albums (not the subsequent ones), but questioned Rod's decision not to reform The Zombies when I discovered that they sold only nine thousand each. Rod and Chris spent a lot of time putting Argent together and held to their commitment, bankrolling the group and even subsidizing the early tours that lost money. It helped that Rod was flush with "Time of the Season" money. Chris wasn't too far behind. People, a San Jose group, covered Chris' "I Love You," a Zombies B-side, which became a Top 20 hit in 1968. Success for Argent had to wait until 1972 when "Hold Your Head Up," composed by Rod and Chris, became a top five hit, driving the *All Together Now* album into the Top 30.

I saw Argent again at the Starwood in November 1975. By that time Russ Ballard had left and much of the magic had diminished. I popped backstage and chatted with Rod. (Rod's favorite track on Argent's first album, Ballard's "Liar," didn't do much for the group, but a year later Three Dog Night had a Top 10 hit with it. Ballard was achieving success as a songwriter, and as Argent's sales were declining from album to album, it wasn't hard for him to leave.)

I met Paul Atkinson at a Christmas Eve party at Mike Chapman's house in 1982. He was head of West Coast A&R for RCA Records and invited me to his office for a visit. I played him a cassette tape of The Winos performing "She's Not There" (from 1973), thinking he would get a kick out of hearing Paul Rappaport's guitar arrangement, which was similar to what Carlos Santana played four years later. Paul knew Rappaport from when they both worked for Columbia Records. Through the years, Paul and I became friends, and we worked on a few projects together. The first was The Zombies' *Live On the BBC*.

I got the idea to issue albums by artists who recorded for the various BBC radio programs from *The Beatles Broadcasts*, a superbly produced bootleg album from 1980. As the British musicians union required that the BBC program live music for a certain amount of hours—so union musicians could get paid—there were a number of shows that featured the popular artists of the day. But because these were conceived to only air on that show, the original recording session tapes were not saved. Transcription discs (records) were made and circulated to the BBC's non-UK outlets. Not all of the recording sessions survived, but those that did were on discs.

It was difficult to deal with the BBC. They thought of these sessions as providing content for radio. Even though most had not been played since their original airing, they had difficulty understanding why anyone—meaning Rhino—would want to make them commercially available. It took three years for me to make a deal with the BBC and The Zombies and to produce the album.

When I heard the songs on the cassette tape the BBC mailed me, I was surprised at how many were covers of soul hits, as The Zombies' records revealed no great interest in this genre. Paul explained that the band performed songs they liked, and as they weren't having hits, they included these more familiar songs in their set. I chose the songs, with Paul and Rod's input, from the better of their covers: "This Old Heart of Mine" (Isley Brothers), "It's Alright," "You Must Believe Me" (Impressions), "When the Lovelight Starts Shining Through His Eyes" (Supremes), among others. I thought fans would enjoy hearing these songs the group never released on their own records.

We had presented a quality package with previously unseen photos. Over the next two years The Zombies received royalties, so they felt comfortable enough with Rhino for the company to reissue *Odessey and Oracle* in 1987. I brought back the original album cover color separations in my suitcase so we could copy the original UK release rather than the American one. I was happy to make the album available again, on vinyl, and compact disc for the first time. It sold thirty-five thousand copies for us.

THE ZOMBIES TOURED IN 2015. That was nothing new. Since 2001, Rod and Colin along with Rod's cousin Jim Rodford (after eighteen years with The Kinks) played intermittently as The Zombies. This time around, Chris and Hugh joined them—now four-fifths of the original band—to perform *Odessey and Oracle* in its entirety for the second set. In the group's professional guise, it's almost as if they were real zombies resurrected. To think, these seventy-year-olds reunited to recreate an album they originally recorded but never had the satisfaction of performing on tour.

The seeds of this reunion were planted when *Rolling Stone* published "The 500 Greatest Albums of All Time." In the magazine's 2003 poll, *Odessey and Oracle* placed at eighty. In June 2009, the four surviving members reassembled for the Mojo Honours List dinner to collect the magazine's Best Classic Album Award for *Odessey and Oracle*. In 2011 the Foo Fighters covered "This Will Be Our Year" and in 2013 Eminem sampled "Time of the Season" in "Rhyme or Reason." The members were bemused at getting all of this recognition forty years later. They knew they'd made a great album, but, in their words, "Nobody was interested at the time." It was never a hit, and never even charted in their native England.

"It was a wonderful surprise and it's helped to validate what we did and to take a bit of the edge off the sadness of the band having to split," Colin told the *Guardian*. "It made us feel like we were on the right line with what we were doing because at the time I'm not sure we felt that we were."

I saw the show a week before Halloween at the Saban Theatre in Beverly Hills. Rod, Colin, Chris, and Hugh were dedicated, hitting all the right notes, and they seemed to be enjoying themselves. Although their voices weren't as supple as when they were younger, it hardly diminished the magnificent performance. Even though Paul Atkinson was not part of the reunion (having perished from liver and kidney disease in 2004), guitarist Tom Toomey reproduced his parts in a way that gave me a new appreciation for his contribution to the album.

I have never before been part of an audience that was so astute, so loving. Bob Lefsetz writing in his newsletter referred to it as a "religious experience." I was glowing for days.

The Zombies proved that good music is timeless. Their music, originally made by teenagers for teenagers, resonates fifty years later, and it's not just with people who experienced it when it was first played on the radio. In the audience there were many in their forties, and more than a few in their twenties. The Zombies and the other artists of the British Invasion made great music, and we're all the better for it.

PLAYLISTS

THE MOST IMPORTANT THING about writing about the music is the music itself. I think the best way to experience music is sitting in front of a good stereo system. I'm also aware that many people prefer the convenience of listening through their computers or mobile devices. One advantage of the Internet is that music is accessible, and this includes many obscure recordings that can be found on YouTube and other sites.

What follows are suggested playlists to accompany some of the artist focused chapters that I feel are among those artists' best recordings.

THE DAVE CLARK FIVE

1. Glad All Over
2. Bits and Pieces
3. Do You Love Me
4. Zip-A-Dee-Doo-Dah
5. Can't You See That She's Mine
6. On Broadway
7. Because
8. Everybody Knows (I Still Love You)
9. Come Home
10. Reelin' and Rockin'
11. I Like It Like That
12. Catch Us If You Can
13. Over and Over
14. At the Scene
15. Anyway You Want It
16. Try Too Hard
17. Look Before You Leap
18. You Got What It Takes
19. The Red Balloon
20. Julia

HERMAN'S HERMITS

1. I'm Into Something Good
2. Can't You Hear My Heartbeat
3. Silhouettes
4. Mrs. Brown, You've Got a Lovely Daughter
5. Wonderful World
6. I'm Henry VIII, I Am
7. Just a Little Bit Better
8. A Must to Avoid
9. Listen People
10. Leaning on the Lamp Post
11. Hold On!
12. This Door Swings Both Ways
13. Dandy
14. No Milk Today
15. East West
16. Jezebel
17. There's a Kind of Hush
18. Don't Go Out Into the Rain
19. I Can Take or Leave Your Loving
20. Here Comes the Star

PETER NOONE

1. Oh You Pretty Thing

THE HOLLIES

1. I'm Alive
2. Look Through Any Window
3. I Can't Let Go
4. Bus Stop
5. Stop Stop Stop
6. Pay You Back With Interest
7. On a Carousel
8. King Midas In Reverse
9. Dear Eloise
10. Wings
11. Step Inside
12. Do the Best You Can
13. Listen to Me
14. Sorry Suzanne
15. He Ain't Heavy, He's My Brother
16. The Baby
17. Long Cool Woman (In a Black Dress)
18. The Air That I Breathe
19. Sandy
20. There's Always Goodbye

THE KINKS

1. You Really Got Me
2. All Day and All of the Night
3. Tired of Waiting for You
4. Who'll Be the Next In Line
5. Set Me Free
6. Till the End of the Day
7. Where Have All the Good Times Gone
8. A Well Respected Man
9. Dedicated Follower of Fashion
10. Sunny Afternoon
11. I'm Not Like Everybody Else
12. Dead End Street
13. Big Black Smoke
14. Waterloo Sunset
15. David Watts
16. Death of a Clown (Dave Davies solo single)
17. Autumn Almanac
18. Days
19. Lola
20. This Time Tomorrow

MANFRED MANN

1. Do Wah Diddy Diddy
2. 5-4-3-2-1
3. Sha La La
4. Come Tomorrow
5. Oh No Not My Baby
6. With God On Our Side
7. If You Gotta Go, Go Now
8. You Gave Me Somebody to Love
9. Pretty Flamingo
10. I Put a Spell On You
11. Just Like a Woman
12. Semi-Detached Suburban Mr. James
13. Each and Every Day (Day Time Night-Time)
14. Ha! Ha! Said the Clown
15. The Mighty Quinn (Quinn the Eskimo)
16. Everyday Another Hair Turns Grey
17. Up the Junction
18. My Name Is Jack
19. Fox On the Run
20. Ragamuffin Man

PAUL JONES

1. I've Been a Bad Bad Boy
2. Privilege
3. Free Me

THE YARDBIRDS

1. For Your Love
2. A Certain Girl
3. I Ain't Got You
4. Smokestack Lightning
5. Heart Full of Soul
6. I'm A Man
7. Still I'm Sad
8. Train Kept A-Rollin'
9. Evil Hearted You
10. Shapes of Things
11. You're a Better Man Than I
12. Jeff's Boogie
13. Over Under Sideways Down
14. The Nazz are Blue
15. Happenings Ten Years Time Ago
16. Psycho Daisies
17. Little Games
18. White Summer
19. Goodnight Sweet Josephine
20. Think About It

JEFF BECK

1. Hi-Ho Silver Lining
2. Beck's Bolero

THE SPENCER DAVIS GROUP

1. Keep On Running
2. When I Come Home
3. Somebody Help Me
4. Every Little Bit Hurts
5. I Can't Stand It
6. Strong Love
7. Searchin'
8. It Hurts Me So
9. The Hammer Song
10. Georgia On My Mind
11. Gimme Some Lovin'
12. Midnight Special
13. Back Into My Life Again
14. I'm a Man
15. I Can't Get Enough of It
16. Look Away
17. On the Green Light
18. Looking Back
19. Time Seller
20. Balkan Blues (Spencer Davis and Peter Jameson)

THE TROGGS

1. Wild Thing
2. From Home
3. With a Girl Like You
4. Our Love Will Still Be There
5. Lost Girl
6. I Want You
7. I Can't Control Myself
8. Any Way That You Want Me
9. Give It To Me
10. I Can Only Give You Everything
11. Night of the Long Grass
12. Love Is All Around
13. Cousin Jane
14. You Can Cry If You Want to
15. Lover
16. Come Now
17. Everything's Funny
18. Feels Like a Woman
19. I'm On Fire
20. Strange Movies

THE ZOMBIES

1. She's Not There
2. You Make Me Feel So Good
3. Tell Her No
4. Leave Me Be
5. She's Coming Home
6. Whenever You're Ready
7. I Love You
8. Kind of Girl
9. I Remember When I Loved Her
10. I Can't Make Up My Mind
11. Just Out of Reach
12. I Must Move
13. I'll Call You Mine
14. Indication
15. Gotta Get a Hold of Myself
16. Care of Cell 44
17. Butchers Tale (Western Front 1914)
18. Time of the Season
19. Friends of Mine
20. Imagine the Swan

GLAM ROCK

1.	DAVID BOWIE	Suffragette City
2.	SWEET	Blockbuster
3.	T. REX	Bang a Gong (Get It On)
4.	SUZI QUATRO	48 Crash
5.	WIZZARD	See My Baby Jive
6.	T. REX	Jeepster
7.	DAVID BOWIE	Prettiest Star
8.	SLADE	Mama Weer All Crazee Now
9.	SWEET	Ballroom Blitz
10.	GARY GLITTER	Do You Wanna Touch
11.	MUD	Dyna-mite
12.	SWEET	The Six Teens
13.	SPARKS	This Town Ain't Big Enough for the Both of Us
14.	DAVID BOWIE	Rebel Rebel
15.	SLADE	Cum On Feel the Noise
16.	T. REX	
17.	STEVE HARLEY & COCKNEY REBEL	Make Me Smile
18.	VULCAN	Much Too Young
19.	T. REX	Telegram Sam
20.	SWEET	Fox On the Run

BONUS TRACK:

"Let Me Tell Ya" by U. K. Jones, released in February 1969, sounds like the first record in a style that would later be referred to as Glam.

PIRATE RADIO OBSCURITIES

1. MAL RYDER & THE SPIRITS — Lonely Room
2. THE IVY LEAGUE — That's Why I'm Crying
3. THE SORROWS — Take a Heart
4. THE ACTION — I'll Keep Holding On
5. JIMMY POWELL & THE DIMENSIONS — I Can Go Down
6. STEVE DARBISHIRE — Yum Yum
7. THE THOUGHTS — All Night Stand
8. FINDERS KEEPERS — Light
9. THE RENEGADES — Thirteen Women
10. THE IVY LEAGUE — My World Fell Down
11. A WILD UNCERTAINTY — Man With Money
12. THE CREATION — Painter Man
13. TWICE AS MUCH — True Story
14. ALLEN POUND'S GET RICH — Searchin' in the Wilderness
15. THE BATS — Listen to My Heart
16. THE MERSEYS — The Cat
17. THE FLIES — House of Love
18. DOUBLE FEATURE — Baby Get Your Head Screwed On
19. VINCE EDWARDS — I Can't Turn Back Time
20. UNIT FOUR PLUS TWO — Too Fast, Too Slow

INDEX

Symbols

A

B

Y

Z

In the 1970s in the backroom of a record store, Harold Bronson and Richard Foos were making history— and so, Rhino Records was born. Harold Bronson's *The Rhino Records Story* tells the tale of how a little record shop became a multimillion dollar corporation. This behind-the-scenes look at a company considered by many to be the industry's best, reveals the secrets to their success. Written from the perspective of cofounder Harold Bronson, *The Rhino Records Story* divulges a unique business approach which made Rhino what it was at the height of its success. In a mix of hard work and good humor, the story of Rhino Records takes shape. Struggling against corporate interests, the demands of rock star personalities, and a perpetual underdog reputation, Bronson provides an exclusive insight into how Rhino excelled. By the fans, for the fans, Rhino Records is the story of rock history, evolving pop culture, and a unique understanding of the music that mattered